THE

REDWOOD COUNTRY

A. W. ERICSON

THE
REDWOOD COUNTRY

HISTORY · LANGUAGE · FOLKLORE

Lynwood Carranco

The Redwoods

The most prominent and interesting physical feature of the Redwood Country lies in her forests of redwood. Aside from their consideration as objects or factors in the commercial and industrial world, these forests hold a weird fascination for every beholder, and the visitor who views them in their primeval majesty for the first time gazes upon the gigantic trunks and towering spires in speechless wonderment and admiration.

These immense trees now stand as the most remarkable monuments of vegetable growth in the world—gigantic in size, symmetrical and straight as an arrow, firmly planted and rooted. They appear as the unmoved, unchanged sentinels of the passing centuries, except that they grow larger, taller, more grandly majestic as the centuries fly by like shadows into the past.

KENDALL/HUNT PUBLISHING COMPANY
DUBUQUE, IOWA

Contents

PART I: HISTORY

1. California Redwood Empire Place Names by
   Lynwood Carranco and Andrew Genzoli 3
2. A Study in Prejudice: The Chinese and Humboldt
   County, California by *Lynwood Carranco* 23
3. Redick McKee and the Humboldt Bay Region,
   1851-1852 by *Chad L. Hoopes* 53
4. Bret Harte in Union (1857-1860) by *Lynwood Carranco* . . 75
5. Two Men and a Mill by *H. Brett Melendy* 91
6. California's First Railroad: The Union Plank Walk, Rail
   Track and Wharf Company Railroad by
   Lynwood Carranco and Mrs. Eugene Fountain 105
7. The Samoa Peninsula by *Lynwood Carranco* 121
8. Seth Kinman by *Chad L. Hoopes* 151
9. The Northern California Vendetta by
   Lynwood Carranco and Estle Beard 159
10. Anza's Bones in Arizpe by *Lynwood Carranco* 167

PART II: LANGUAGE

11. The Boonville Language of Northern California by
    Lynwood Carranco and Wilma Rawles Simmons 183
12. "Boontling"—Esoteric Speech of Boonville, California by
    Myrtle Read Rawles 195
13. Logging Railroad Language in the Redwood Country by
    Lynwood Carranco 209
14. Americanisms in the Redwood Country by
    Lynwood Carranco 221

PART III: FOLKLORE

15. Three Legends of Northwestern California by
    Lynwood Carranco 231
16. A Miscellany of Folk Beliefs from the Redwood
    Country by *Lynwood Carranco* 239

v

Del Norte County

Humboldt County

Mendocino County

The
Redwood Country
of
California

Preface

This book is a collection of articles on the Redwood Country that have appeared in professional journals in the last fifteen years. As a member of the Humboldt County Historical Society and the Mendocino County Historical Society, I have enjoyed researching the history of both counties. Fellow members, specifically Mrs. Martha Roscoe, the late Lawton Bussman, and Wallace Martin from the Humboldt group, have always been willing to help as have Estle Beard, George Ward, and John Keller from the Mendocino group. Mrs. Frances Purser, who worked beyond the call of duty to develop the local history collection at Humboldt State University, has always been more than helpful in supplying historical materials. Floyd Bettiga, Art teacher at College of the Redwoods, suggested the cover picture and drew the map of California.

My interest in local history began when I found an old copy of Bledsoe's *Indian Wars of the Northwest* in the Samoa dump when I was in the sixth grade. Later at the Eureka Junior High School I discovered Coy's *Humboldt Bay Region, 1850-1875.* After World War II, I wrote a term paper called "A Brief History of the Peninsula" for a freshman English class at Humboldt State College. In 1956, while teaching at the Arcata High School, I revised the paper and submitted it to *The Humboldt Times.* Mr. Andrew Genzoli published the article in its entirety, calling it "Samoa's Story." I have revised and included the article because of the numerous requests for it by local students and teachers. The justification for the Anza publication in this anthology is that Anza, among others, had a hand in founding the city of San Francisco, the cosmopolitan southern gateway to the Redwood Empire.

This anthology is affectionately dedicated to friend and collaborator Andrew "Andy" Genzoli, historian for the Eureka *Times—Standard.* His popular column and his many historical articles have stimulated many people to enjoy and to research local history through the years. He has published many pamphlets on local history; he was President of the Humboldt County Historical Society, the largest in the state, for two terms; he taught local history successfully for many years in the Eureka Adult Educational Program; he conducted a historical program over one of the local television stations; and he is presently teaching local history at the College of the Redwoods.

Mr. Genzoli has served for ten years in state historical advisory capacities. He served under Governor Edmund Brown, Sr. for two years on the old California History Month Commission, and Governor Ronald Reagan appointed him to two terms on the present Commission on California State Landmarks, which in 1970 established locally two new state historical landmarks: the Arcata and Mad River Railroad at Blue Lake and Tsurai, the Yurok Indian village at Trinidad. In June, 1975, the Commission approved two more historical landmarks: the designation of the Humboldt Harbor Historical District site in the Hal Larsen Vista Point at Spruce Point, overlooking Humboldt Bay and Bar, and an application for a Ferndale Historical District, submitted by the Ferndale Historical Committee sponsored by the Chamber of Commerce.

I hope that students, history buffs, oldtimers, and new people in the Redwood Country will enjoy the articles in this book.

Lynwood Carranco
College of the Redwoods
Eureka, California

Acknowledgments

Permission from Columbia University Press to reprint "Logging Railroad Language in the Redwood Country" from *American Speech* (May, 1962) and "The Boonville Language of Northern California" from *American Speech* (December, 1964).

Permission from Lorrin L. Morrison and Carroll Spear Morrison, Editors and Publishers, to reprint "California's First Railroad: The Union Plank Walk, Rail Track, and Wharf Company Railroad" from *Journal of the West* (April, 1964); "California Redwood Empire Place Names" from *Journal of the West* (July, 1968); "Anza's Bones in Arizpe" from *Journal of the West* (October, 1969); "A Study in Prejudice: The Chinese and Humboldt County, California" from *Journal of the West;* and "The Northern California Vendetta" from *Journal of the West.*

Permission from the University of California Press to reprint "Three Legends of Northwestern California" from *Western Folklore* (July, 1963); "Americanisms in the Redwood Country" from *Western Folklore* (October, 1963); "A Miscellany of Folk Beliefs from the Redwood Country" from *Western Folklore* (July, 1967); and permission from Myrtle Read Rawles and the University of California Press to reprint "Boontling"—Esoteric Speech of Boonville, California" from *Western Folklore* (April, 1966).

Permission from Professor H. Brett Melendy and the California Historical Society to reprint "Two Men and a Mill" from the *California Historical Society Quarterly* (March, 1959); "Bret Harte in Union (1857-1860)" from the *California Historical Society Quarterly* (March, 1959); permission from Chad Hoopes and the California Historical Society to reprint "Redick McKee and the Humboldt Bay Region, 1851-1852" from the *California Historical Society Quarterly* (September, 1970).

Permission from Chad Hoopes and Leroy R. Hafen, ed., *The Mountain Men and the Fur Trade* (Glendale, California, 1965) to reprint "Seth Kinman."

PART
I

HISTORY

California Redwood Empire Place Names

Lynwood Carranco *and* **Andrew Genzoli**

California place names exhibit three characteristics. First from fifty to sixty percent of the toponyms are of English or American derivation. Second, Spanish or Mexican names compose twenty to thirty percent of the total places. Third, California Indian, European, or other names of unknown origin make up only ten to fifteen percent of the State's toponyms.[1]

In the Redwood country—the Humboldt Bay area—over ninety percent of the place names are of English or American bases. Spanish or Mexican toponyms are practically non-existent, amounting to less than one percent of the total. Indian place names are also less than the standard, with only four percent. Regional dominance of nature over man can be deduced from the place names, natural features in the North Coast abounding in comparison with those of other portions of California.[2]

The names throughout the region tell that the area was the home of Indian tribes of high culture, with mature geographical and universal concepts. Indian names are plentiful at river mouths and in river valleys, for example, Weitchpec means "flowing together of two streams."[3] The tribal names, Mattole, Klamath, and Hoopa, became place names of the territories that these tribes occupied. Arcata and Loleta are examples of Indian place names, incorrectly interpreted and applied by the early settlers.

Events and personalities of the first American explorers became the raw materials for numerous toponyms. Examples of pioneer inhabitants who gave their names to settlements which developed with their guidance are Garberville, Rohnerville, Blocksburg, and Gasquet.

The elements of nature, the landforms, the vegetation, the hydrographic features, and the distinctive fauna served as bases for many place names. The distinctive flora lend their names to places, such as Willow Creek, Ferndale, Kneeland Prairie, and Dows Prairie.

The distinctive and abundant animal life was acknowledged in the following toponyms: Bear, Eel, Elk, and Salmon River. An example of a place name of ethnic or geographic origin of a certain segment of the population is Scotia, named after many of the lumbering families who came from Nova Scotia.

The early history of the Humboldt Bay region revolves about a series of efforts to find a harbor along the Pacific Coast. The Spaniards came in 1775, landing at Trinidad Bay and exploring the immediate area, thereby extending the rights of Spain north to the forty-second parallel which was subsequently fixed as the northern boundary of California. About twenty-five years later, the Russian-American Company extended its field of operations along the coast southward. Subsequently, in 1806, Jonathan Winship sailed from Sitka to Humboldt Bay. He explored the bay, and soon departed for San Francisco. Later, the Hudson's Bay Company took over this territory as its exclusive trading and hunting ground. The first Hudson's Bay exploring and trapping party descended the Klamath River and penetrated into the country as far as Weitchpec in 1827, and later controlled the entire country north of San Francisco.

Meanwhile the Missouri traders and trappers appeared. Jedediah Strong Smith went through the country in 1828, and Ewing Young traveled in Mendocino County and up the Sacramento Valley in 1833. The American fur traders were anxious to find a harbor in Northern California which they could make the center of their fur trade, and to which they hoped to bring a world-wide trade in peltry which was then centered in St. Louis. Both Smith and Young failed in search for a harbor, and the country about Humboldt Bay was a wilderness until the Gregg party found the bay in 1849—and the history of the county began as a settled part of California.

In contrast to many parts of the State, the Humboldt Bay region was not greatly affected by the Spanish and Mexican influence. The Spaniards Hezeta and Bodega entered a bay on June 9, 1775. On June 11, the Spaniards took possession of the land, naming the port "La Santisima Trinidad," because possession was taken on the feast day of the Holy Trinity.[4]

The Spaniards usually used two different methods in naming places. The padres almost invariably chose names of a religious significance, often the name of a saint upon whose day the party happened to arrive at a given location. The soldiers were usually influenced by some striking circumstance, usually trivial or humorous, but often picturesque. A good example is the naming of the present-day Little River below Trinidad. From the top of Trinidad promontory the Spaniards saw a river "which empties into the sea from between two mountains . . . at a distance of three-fourths of a league to the south." While investigating the river they saw many turtle doves, and they named the river "Rio de las Tortolas."[5] Although Padre Francisco Palou, in HISTORICAL MEMOIRS OF NEW CALIFORNIA (edited by Herbert E. Bolton, 1926) says that this river was named "El Principio," the river is named both "Little River" and "Rio de las Tortolas" on the United States Coast and Geodetic Survey map of 1851.

Other than "Trinidad," used for the Town of Trinidad and Trinidad Bay, "Mendocino," "Punta Gorda," and "Punta Delgada," all coastal promontories, are the only Spanish names that have survived through the years. The name of the northwesternmost county, Del Norte, is evidently Spanish, but is pronounced "Del Nort" by the local people. Del Norte County, north of Humboldt County, was created during the eighth session of the California Legislature in 1857. In 1856 the county seat of Klamath County was changed from Crescent City to Orleans Bar. Because of this the people of Crescent City clamored for the creation of a new county. In 1857 a bill was introduced that provided for the creation of a new county to be known as "Buchanan" for the newly-elected President of the United States. In this form it passed the assembly, but in the senate the name was amended to read "Del Norte." This bill was vetoed by the governor because of the many errors, but he later approved a corrected bill which became a statute.[6] The name was applied to the new county because of its extreme northern position. Other names that were suggested were "Alta," "Altissima," and "Rincon."[7]

The origin and discovery of "Cabo Mendocino" cannot be satisfactorily explained. Its first recorded use is in the report of the voyage of Francisco Gali in 1584, but there is no indication that he was responsible for the name other than given the first record of its use. The name was probably given to some point on the northwest coast in the neighborhood of 42° by a returning Philippine galleon sometime between September, 1581, and December, 1584, and named in honor of Lorenzo Suarez de Mendoza, conde de Coruna, viceroy of New Spain from October 4, 1580, to June 19, 1583.[8] "Cabo Mendocino" appeared on the maps of Ortelius in 1587.[9]

The cape might also have been named for Don Antonio de Mendoza. Padre Don Antonio de la Ascension, who was on the Vizcaino Expedition in 1602-1603, said that when Don Antonio de Mendoza was viceroy of New Spain in 1542, he sent out two ships to the Philippines. The first land that the men saw on the return trip was Cabo Mendocino, and they gave the name "Mendocino" in honor of the viceroy.[10]

The cape was not specifically identified with the cape at latitude 40°27' until 1791 when Malespina, from a calculation at sea, located the cape at 40° 29'. Dudley's map of June, 1579, of the coast line of Sir Francis Drake's Reconnaissance shows Cape Mendocino. The most westerly point in the United States (except points in Alaska and Hawaii) is also shown on the map showing Vizcaino's exploration, dated January, 1603.[11]

In 1775, while Hezeta was in Trinidad Bay, he saw a bold headland to the south (probably "Table Bluff") and named it "Punta Gorda."[12] The name appeared on the early Spanish maps before 1793 north of "Cabo Mendocino." In 1851 the protruding headland was mentioned as False Cape Mendocino. In 1854 George Davidson, who was a member of the first party sent by the United States Coast Survey to chart the Pacific Coast, labeled the old Spanish name to the present Punta Gorda south of Cape Mendocino and renamed False Cape, "Cape Fortunas," a name originally given to Point Arena by Ferrer in 1543.[13]

In 1865 A.J. Doolittle published the first official township map of Humboldt County, which was carefully compiled from the United States Land and Coast Surveys, with personal observations. This important map is *not* listed in the Glossary and Bibliography of CALIFORNIA PLACE NAMES by Professor Erwin G. Gudde.

The protruding headland above Cape Mendocino is named Cape Fortunas or False Cape on the Doolittle map, and Point Gorda is given to a protruding point south of the Mattole River and at the mouth of Cooskie Creek. At the present time Punta Gorda is recorded on all maps for this point. In 1940 the Geographical Board officially established the name False Cape, dropping Cape Fortunas.

Bodega is given credit for applying "Punta Delgada" (thin) to Point Arena in 1775 on his voyage down the coast. The name was in common use in the latter part of the eighteenth century.[14] Charles Wilkes was the commander of the first United States expedition to explore the interior of California in 1841. He applied "Punta Delgada" to the point just above Shelter Cove—even if the point was not narrow—and the name remains today.[15]

Jonathan Winship is given credit for first discovering and entering the waters of Humboldt Bay in June, 1806. Sitka's Governor Baranof offered Winship a contract to hunt sea otter along the California Coast, and he also furnished Winship with one hundred Aleuts. Arriving at Trinidad, the expedition spent twelve days hunting and trading with the Indians for furs, and it was at this time that a group of Aleuts discovered the bay. Winship later found the entrance and sailed the *O'Cain* into the bay. He named the entrance "Rezanov" in honor of Alexander Rezanov, the Russian Imperial Chamberlain, and called the bay the "Bay of Indians."[16] No documentary evidence exists to show that anyone else visited the bay, other than visits to the area between 1806 to 1812 by the Russian-American Company. In 1809 Winship made another voyage to the "Bay of Indians."[17]

The Americans began to develop an interest in Northern California when California became a permanent possession of the United States, February 2, 1848, by the Treaty of Guadalupe Hidalgo. Although interest temporarily waned with the discovery of gold at Sutter's Mill, January 24, 1848, a renewed interest developed with the discovery of gold in the Trinity River country. A discovery of rich gold deposits by Major Pierson B. Reading caused a scramble of miners into the Trinity country. In 1845 he had discovered a large stream while trapping beaver and otter. In 1849 he explored down the river, naming it "Trinity" because he supposed that it emptied into Trinidad Bay. This discovery encouraged a search for the mouth of the Trinity River by land and by sea, since it was difficult to obtain supplies for the mining camps from the Sacramento Valley.

By the winter of 1849, the population in the mining camps had increased out of proportion to the supplies brought in overland from Sacramento. The rainy season forced the mines to suspend operations and forced the supply route to close. A possible solution to the miners' predicament was to find and develop a trail to a "large and beautiful bay surrounded by fine and extensive prairie lands," which according to the Indians, was an eight-day journey to the west.

Dr. Josiah Gregg, a well-known trapper and explorer through his book, COMMERCE OF THE PRAIRIES, and supposedly employed by the United States Government to search for the lost harbor of Trinidad,[18] was the leader of an expedition to head west not only by the choice of his fellow-adventurers, but also because he alone had a specific place to reach. The party consisted of eight men: Dr. Josiah Gregg, Thomas Seabring, David A. Buck, J.B. Truesdell, James Van Duzen, Charles C. Southard, Isaac Wilson, and L.K. Wood.[19]

On November 5, 1849, the Gregg party began the journey from Rich Bar on the Trinity. After many hardships over the rugged mountain ranges and through the almost impenetrable redwood forest, the party emerged near the mouth of Little River—nearly as possible to the point of north latitude that the old Spanish charts gave for the location of this elusive harbor of Trinidad.

The men believed that the mythical bay was to the north, and they followed the coast line about twelve miles until a large lagoon stopped them. They retraced their steps and examined Trinidad Head, which they named "Gregg's Point." After discovering the bay, which they named "Trinity Bay" because they believed it to be the bay shown on the Spanish maps, they headed south.

At the Eel River the Gregg party split. Gregg, Truesdale, Van Duzen and Charles Southard decided to follow the coast down to San Francisco. The other four proceeded up the Eel River, then south to the nearest settlement. On February 25, 1850, Gregg, while riding towards the Sacramento Valley with his three companions, fell from his horse near Clear Lake and died in a few hours without speaking, supposedly of starvation.[20]

The circumstances of Dr. Gregg's death have remained a mystery to the present time. The question of whether Gregg died at the hands of a member of his party was brought out by H.T. Dimick in 1947[21] and by Professor Hyman Palais in 1963.[22] There is no story by an eyewitness of the death of Gregg. Mr. L.K. Wood who told the story was not present and he received his information from Charles Southard, who had no knowledge of medicine. The survivors of the trip never made any statement for publication regarding Gregg's death. The *Alta California* of March 7, 1850, stated the following facts:

We learn from a member of the Trinidad Expedition recently returned (Southard), that Captain Josiah Gregg of Missouri, author of the *Commerce of the Prairies*, etc., died in the vicinity of Clear Lake on the 25th. He joined the company of Trinidad adventurers in November last, and encountered with them the hardships and perils of their fatiguing travel. So incessant and severe were the trials of the journey that his physical powers sunk under them, and an absence of medical attendance, added to general debility, caused his death as above. Captain Gregg was intimately known to a great number of our citizens and his writings have given his name popularity abroad.

Gregg's family could never discover the complete details of his death nor could they recover his valuable notebooks or personal effects. Gregg died near Clear Lake and was buried in a shallow grave dug with sticks. The site was unmarked and has never been discovered. Were his notebooks and personal effects buried with him? Many people have wondered at the scarcity of information concerning the death of the well-known figure. There had been continuous dissension on the trip to find the lost harbor of Trinidad. If Gregg had been working for the United States Government, then the disappearance of his notebooks is a great loss.

Local historians have tended to minimize the importance of

Gregg. The Gregg Party has become the Wood-Gregg Party and even the L.K. Wood Party. Louis K. Wood, who later lived in Arcata and who became the first county clerk, published the story of the discovery of Humboldt Bay in *The Humboldt Times* of April 26, 1856.[23] Gregg's COMMERCE OF THE PRAIRIES made him an authority on western America. He explored unknown areas and laid out new routes over which to carry on trade, and he was a well-known man. It is strange indeed that the other seven members did not know of Gregg's fame as an author or of his experience as an explorer—or even wondered why he carried surveying equipment with him!

While Gregg's party headed west, another party left the Trinity mines for San Francisco, seeking Trinidad Bay by means of the ocean route. The San Francisco papers gave space to accounts of the various proposed expeditions to Trinidad, and many vessels sailed north in February and March of 1850.[24]

The members of the Laura Virginia expedition, sailing in the schooner *Laura Virginia*, have an important place in the history of the Redwood region. The schooner, under the command of Lieutenant Douglas Ottinger, was chartered by San Francisco adventurers to establish a depot for distribution of merchandise to the Trinity Mines.[25] Sailing up the coast they saw from the masthead a "large bay," but were unable to find the entrance.[26] The ship sailed north of Trinidad to Point St. George. Again arriving at Trinidad on April 4, a land party under Elias H. Howard, who later became district attorney of Humboldt County, was sent south along the coast to find the supposed bay seen on the way north. The party, which consisted of Howard, H.W. Havens, S.B. Tucker, Robert La Mott, S.W. Shaw, and a Mr. Peebles, discovered the bay and on April 9, four days later, the *Laura Virginia* returned to Trinidad Bay and received the Howard party.

That afternoon the ship was opposite the entrance, and H.H. Buhne, the second officer, was ordered to attempt the first entry in a small boat and to make soundings on the bar. He was successful and he repeated the act in the afternoon with boats, loaded with passengers, tents, and provisions, landing on the north peninsula. The next day, Buhne's party moved across the bay to a red bluff (Buhne's Point), where the future settlement of the short-lived Humboldt City was established.[27] Three days later on April 14, 1850,[28] Buhne guided the schooner into the bay and the ship was anchored near the point where the camp had been established. Once ashore, the members of the association took possession of the land.

On May 20, 1850, Charles H. Gilman, a member of the Laura

Virginia expedition when he was only nineteen years of age, wrote a
letter to his sister Ellen G. Perler in Baltimore. The slightly damaged
letter, written from "Humboldt Harbour," gives a descriptive view of
the harbor:

> Where is Humboldt Harbour? I hear you say. That you do not know is
> certain. . . . On the 20th of last March I set out from San Francisco in the Schr.
> Laura Virginia for . . . coast called Trinidad Bay into which Trinity river was said
> to empty—on which river much gold . . . still more is expected. After sailing for
> 6 days and . . . one continued rain storm, and S.W. Gale we anchored in Trinidad
> Bay and found that sure enough Trinity river did not empty into it. So we up
> anchor and put out. It would take more time then I have now to enter into a
> detail of all the cruising that we did during the next month. We explored the
> coast from San Francisco nearly to the mouth of the Columbia River and of the
> 23rd of April entered a large bay which we discovered about 25 miles south of
> Trinidad Bay and christened it Humboldt Harbour. It is an immense lagoon
> having but one entrance that about 3/4 of a mile wide between breakers, its
> length is about 20 miles averaging in width about 2 miles. The land is the most
> beautiful I ever saw—large hills sloping down to the water, and beautiful plat-
> teaus. The red wood, cedar, spruce, Hemlock, oak, and alder abound. Fruits such
> as raspberries, strawberries, currants, Heazels, cherries, etc. are abundant. Many
> fine roots are also found, but what exceeds all I ever saw is the quantity of game
> and fish. Elk, deer, black and grizzly bear, beaver, otter. Geese, ducks, curlews,
> snipe, robin, partridge are without number. In this Bay so bountifully supplied
> by nature we have made a location . . . rich mines are within two days . . . have
> every prospect of succeeding in accomplishing the object of our enterprise—by
> location of suitable land for a township in the neighborhood of the coast mines.
>
> The Indians are numerous and most of them . . . though we have several
> chiefs on our side . . . yesterday we undertook to recover some rigging . . . had
> stolen from the Schr. Eclipse which went . . . a few days ago. It resulted in a
> fight and the death of 3 indians and several wounded. We set fire to and . . . their
> houses. We are warned by several chiefs to . . . an attack soon, but if they should
> attack as I have no fear of the result for there are over 50 of us here and we
> could easily whip a thousand indians. We go armed all the time. [29]

Probably the biggest mystery in the area through the years has
been the namer of Humboldt Bay. There have been many stories and
many versions on the naming of the Bay. Gudde (CALIFORNIA
PLACE NAMES, 1965) mentions that "Buhne and Douglas Ottinger,
commander of the expedition, are responsible for the present name
which honors Alexander von Humboldt, who was then at the height
of his fame." In Europe the name of Alexander von Humboldt, the
German scientist and explorer, was only eclipsed by Napoleon. From
1799 until 1804, he traveled extensively in South America, Mexico,
and the United States. On this expedition Humboldt laid the founda-
tion in their larger bearings on the sciences of physical geography and
meteorology. His services to geology were based on his study of
volcanoes of the new world. He added knowledge to every known

field of science—meteorology, botany, zoology, and archaeology. In North America he was honored by having counties, rivers, and cities named after him. Darwin called him "the greatest scientific traveler that ever lived." [30]

>Humboldt never reached the northwest coast of California. While in Cuba in 1804 to pick up his plant collections, he received an invitation from President Thomas Jefferson to visit the United States. Six weeks were spent in this country, mostly with Jefferson at Monticello. Alexander von Humboldt died in 1859. [31]

In 1886, the editor of a local newspaper, making an effort to honor the specific person who named the bay, printed a letter that Elias H. Howard, a member of the Laura Virginia expedition, received from Captain Douglas Ottinger, who was in command when the bay was discovered. Ottinger's answer was as follows:

> Regarding the name of Humboldt being given out of discovery, I have to say that it was proposed and objection made to name the bay Ottinger harbor. I declined to have it so named, and mentioned the probability that Baron von Humboldt had seen it as a lake and as he traveled in California before our discovery, I suggested the name of Humboldt and it was adopted. Being an officer in the service of the United States and under the secretary of Treasury, I made a report to him of our discovery and informed him of its discovery and of the forests of timber . . . and sent my report, open to Col. Collier, then collector of customs at San Francisco to extract any portion then transmit it to the treasury department, which he did . . . find this letter of transmission in the files at Washington, but the report itself cannot be found on the file, nor anywhere in the department where it ought to be. I think the sacredness of the archives has been desecrated. [32]

Professor George Davidson, who worked for the United States Coast Survey, was also puzzled about the name of the bay. On March 29, 1890, he spoke to Captain Buhne, who was then sixty-nine years of age. Buhne said that the Laura Virginia party, after a discussion whether the bay should be called Humboldt Bay or Buhne Bay, decided to name the bay after Humboldt. [33]

Wallace Elliott in his history has the following to say about the naming of the bay:

> At a meeting held April 17th on Humboldt Point, of which Captain Ottinger was Chairman, and E.H. Howard, Secretary, it was thought to be time to fix on some name for the bay. Various names were proposed. Among others, "Ottinger," "Folsom," "Laura Virginia," but all were voted down. The Secretary then presented the name of "Humboldt," in honor to the great philosopher and traveler, whose visit to the Central and South American States on the Pacific had enlarged and enriched the field of enthnological and physical science, but as yet had not been recognized by any local appellation bearing his name. It was adopted without opposition. [34]

In the introduction Wallace Elliott gives Elias H. Howard credit for contributing information to the history, published in 1881, yet it was Howard who was interested in the namer of the bay and who wrote to Captain Ottinger in 1886!

Stephen W. Shaw, a San Francisco artist, has also been given credit for naming the bay, and most of the evidence certainly makes him the most logical choice. S.W. Shaw was at one time the best known artist in California. He was born in Vermont in 1817. After spending eight years in the South, painting portraits of well-known people, he came to California from New Orleans by way of the Isthmus route, making the Pacific voyage in the *Humboldt.* He arrived in San Francisco in August, 1849. He followed the prospectors to the mines and returned to San Francisco. The following was taken from a local history of the San Francisco Bay area:

> Being a member of the expedition that discovered Humboldt bay, he was of the first party which entered the bay in an open boat just as the sun was setting, April 5, 1850. Some of the party wished to name it for him and for other members of the company, but he objected and insisted that it should be called Humboldt. He made a sketch of the bay and surroundings and named the islands; was there several years, and during that time painted a number of portraits among them being one of the old chief. Returning from that expedition, he located permanently in San Francisco.[35]

The overlooked Doolittle map of 1865 has a historical account of the early discoveries of the bay in fine print. Many of the well-known local citizens were given credit for information. Doolittle said the following:

> S.W. Shaw, the prize artist of 423 Montgomery St., after making a reconnaissance and map of the Bay, from admiration of the great explorer, renowned scholar, and author of *Cosmos,* Baron A. von Humboldt, applied the name (by lettering it in) to the Bay, as did Frémont to the Humboldt River, Nevada; the illustrious Humboldt probably never having heard of either. He also well named Table Bluff, Salt River, and Pacific Township.

An account of the discovery of Humboldt Bay, which included a sketch of the bay by S.W. Shaw, appeared in a San Francisco journal in 1850, but the unknown author does not specifically refer to the namer of the bay:

> We continued our explorations by land and sea with energy, and our efforts were rewarded by the discovery of one of the most beautiful and extensive harbors on the Pacific Coast, a sketch of which was made by S.W. Shaw, a well-known artist and a member of the company. In honor of the first explorer of this coast, whose name is identified with enterprise and science, we christened the same in due form, "HUMBOLDT HARBOR."[36]

Edwin A. Sherman wrote a biography of S.W. Shaw which appeared in a book published by the Masons in 1893, and he stated that "Shaw mapped the bay and wrote 'Humboldt bay' across its face."[37]

Later in life, Robert La Mott, one of the six members of the Laura Virginia expedition who walked from Trinidad Bay to the entrance of Humboldt Bay, made the following statement:

> ... In the meantime, the party of six came down the coast and camped that night under a tree on the peninsula, at a point near where the lighthouse was subsequently erected. While the party was gathered about the campfire that night the members decided to name the magnificent body of water which lay spread out before them Humboldt Bay, in honor of the distinguished naturalist, Baron von Humboldt. S.W. Shaw, who was an artist, made a sketch of the bay during the afternoon.[38]

Another story is that the Laura Virginia expedition gave the name because the land formation resembled a "Humboldt," which in geology supposedly referred to land which rises sharply from the sea to rising timbered mountains.

The discovery and settlement of Humboldt Bay early in 1850 led to the rapid development of the western or coastal part of Trinity County, and to a decided political rivalry between this western district and the mining region on the Trinity River. During the spring of 1852, the legislature had been petitioned to divide Trinity County, but without result.[39] A renewal of the agitation the next year led to the creation of Humboldt County in 1853. The name was taken from Humboldt Bay, which had been so named in 1850 in honor of the scientist Alexander von Humboldt.[40]

The supposed Indian name "Qual-a-wa-loo" for Humboldt Bay is another puzzle. Local historians have never questioned this name. The editors of THE QUEST FOR QUAL-A-WA-LOO give no documentation for the Indian word. A.J. Doolittle said that Qual-a-wa-loo was the Indian name for the bay. George Davidson, who was on Humboldt Bay in 1851 as a member of the first party to survey the coast, was probably the first to use the term. In 1891 he said, "In 1851, 1853, and 1854, I was in the Bay, and it was in one of these years that I obtained from the Indians their name of the Bay as "Qual-a-wa-loo."[41]

George Gibbs, who wrote the Journal of the McKee expedition through northwestern California in 1851, would certainly be a more reliable source, since he mingled freely with the Indians, dividing his time between map-making and language study. He used the word "Walla-walloo":

I obtained a partial vocabulary of their language (Mad River Indians), which resembles substantially that used round the bay, and at Eel river. Beyond the Mad river a different one prevails. The Bay Indians call themselves as we were informed, Wish-osk; and those of the hills, Te-ok-a-wilk; but the tribes to the northward denominate both those of the Bay and Eel rivers, We-yot, or Walla-Walloo.[42]

Even though anthropologists from the University of California have made intensive studies of local Indian place names and the Wiyot language, no evidence could be found of either word. "Wala 'wal" meant "rather early" in the Wiyot language.[43] Wiyot was the name for the Eel River delta, but writers have applied the name to all Indians who spoke this language, whether living on Eel River, Humboldt Bay, or Mad River. The Wiyot name for Humboldt Bay was Wike. No Yurok name (Indians of lower Klamath and north of Humboldt Bay) could be found for the bay.

Humboldt Bay was also named "Mendocino Bay" by the Brannan Party about April 5 or April 6, 1850, about seven or eight days before the *Laura Virginia* entered the bay. Sam Brannan was in command of the *General Morgan*, which anchored at the mouth of Eel River April 4. The next day Brannan and his brother John crossed the bar in two small boats and traveled up the river. They could not recross the bar because of heavy seas. The party then moved north, carrying their boats around Table Bluff and discovered the bay. They later rejoined their ship at Trinidad.[44]

Humboldt Bay was discovered to afford a shorter route to the northern mines, and the establishment of towns followed the discovery of favorable sites. Trinidad was the first settlement to be established, on April 8, 1850, by the Captain Robert A. Parker party from the *James R. Whiting*, and another party under Captain Warner of the *Isabel*. The town was first called Warnerville on April 10, after Captain R.B. Warner (not mentioned in CALIFORNIA PLACE NAMES).[45]

The towns on Humboldt Bay were laid out by well-organized companies: the Laura Virginia Association, the Union Company, and the Mendocino Exploring Company.[46] The Union Company was composed entirely of men who had come overland from Sonoma with the returning members of the Gregg expedition.[47] This group arrived on the scene in the middle of April after the Laura Virginia Association had established its settlement at Humboldt Point (Buhne's Point).

The Josiah Gregg party had spent Christmas Day, December 25, 1849, camped on a plateau overlooking the bay on the north. This location was the first place that the Union Company returned on April 21, 1850, to lay out a town called "Union Town." The Union Company included Eureka among its claims. Eureka, which was later to become the county's metropolis, was the last of the early towns to be founded.

In May, 1850, the members of the Mendocino Exploring Company arrived at the bay and located at Eureka. On May 13, 1850, the representatives of the Union and the Mendocino Companies signed an agreement whereby the Mendocino Company was to be permitted to share in the establishment of the new town, which was to be called "Eureka." The leading figure in the Mendocino Company was James Ryan, under whose direction the town was surveyed.[48] Ryan was assisted by W.D. Davis and Captain Wasgatt. James Ryan was chosen the first *alcalde* or mayor, and the first board of trustees consisted of J. Ryan, H.P. Osgood, and W.H. Blanchard. The site was covered with heavy timber, which extended to the waterfront. Twenty-three persons were included in the new town.[49]

Another mystery of the area is the meaning of the place name "Arcata." Union Town was shortened to "Union" by usage. The following appeared in a Eureka paper in 1855:

> We would call the attention of our representative in the Legislature to the necessity of an act incorporating the towns of Union and Eureka. All of our property holders, whom we have consulted are unanimous in recommending and urging the passage of such an act. . . . The permanent and ultimate advantages to be derived from it are incalculable. If such a bill passes, we suggest that the Indian name of this place—Arcata—be substituted for that of "Union."[50]

On March 15, 1856, the Humboldt County Court entered the order incorporating Union under the name and style of "Union," omitting the suffix, "town," but in May, 1856, the court declared the act of incorporation for Union invalid. On March 20, 1860, Union was changed to "Arcata" by an act of the legislature.[51]

There is no reference to the meaning of the name in *The Northern Californian*, published at that time in Arcata. In the issue for March 28, 1860, there is merely the statement that "the town of Union was now changed to Arcata to avoid confusion with another town of the same name."

Although the editor of *The Humboldt Times* was against the changing of the name, he did attempt to give a definition for the name:

> UNION DISSOLVED—Among the various humbugs which enter into the heads of people now-a-days we know of none of a recent date more glaring than that which prompted the people of Union and vicinity to sign a petition to the

Legislature to have the name of their quiet and otherwise unassuming little village changed from "Union" to "Arcata." The bill passed on the 13th inst., and is now a law. We are truly sorry that this attempt to change the name of Union has been made. We regard it as an overdrawn effort to bring the town into notice, and we are only surprised that those ambitious denizens who interested themselves in the matter did not ask to have it dubbed New York . . . or something else rather than the senseless and unmeaning digger name, "Arcata." . . . Some romantic people about here ran away with the idea that "Arcata" is a legitimate digger word, and means "Union." This is not correct. It means a certain place in town where the diggers were once in the habit of congregating, which in our language would be about the same as "down thar" or "over yonder."[52]

Many oldtimers still insist that Arcata means "a bright and sunny spot." Irvine, in his history, quotes a letter that was written by Mrs. R.F. Herrick on November 29, 1859:

When we crossed the bay and viewed our surroundings, we thought Arcata was the most beautiful place we had ever seen in California. The Plaza looked like green velvet, and the dark background of great redwood trees was the most beautiful I had ever seen. When I saw Arcata first, the sun was shining over it. I then thought that the Indian name, which means a bright or sunny spot, was very appropriate.[53]

Another legend is that some Indians came to the camp of some explorers and made them understand that they were looking for, or going to, Ar-ka-ta. The white men thought that the word meant an Indian maiden whose name was Katie and that the Indians were looking for "Our Katie."[54]

Another story is that the name was derived from a tribe of Indians who were the survivors of a terrific upheaval of the past. The Indians supposedly had a wigwam where the plaza is now. After the great upheaval the "big walking water" (ocean) came carrying away the huge trees and many of the Indians. The "still water" (bay) remained. The surviving Indians made a camping ground where the plaza now is and called it "A-Ka—E-Ta," meaning "Sit-Down-Eat." [55] Another meaning for the place name is a "shallow, peaceful water or lagoon," which referred to Humboldt Bay.

The late Jerry Jim of Eureka told the following story that was told to him by his father, who was called "Ho-dar-ros-samish." His father was the Indian guide who volunteered to take the Gregg party around the bay. The party camped at "Goad-la-nah" which is where Arcata is now located. The name meant "a land a little above the water or bench land."[56]

For several years the Eureka Chamber of Commerce carried on an investigation concerning the origin of the names of the towns in *arcata*

Humboldt County. Their final decision was that Arcata was an Indian name meaning "where the boats landed." In the early days the bay came up to the lower part of town.

Gudde says that the name of the Indian village at the site was "Kori," mentioned in the Indian Report, September 21, 1851. This is an error. Gibbs mentioned that "the Indians of Trinidad are called by them (Wiyot) Chori." "Tsurai" or "Chori" was the Yurok name for Trinidad, meaning "mountain."

A scholarly guess as to the meaning of Arcata would be the following. Little River was the frontier between the two tribes, the Yurok (Trinidad and lower Klamath areas) and the Wiyot (lower Mad River, Humboldt Bay, and lower Eel River areas), and intermarriage between the tribes, especially near the tribal frontier, was common. In the Yurok language an element, "O-," prefixed to stems, made what is substantially a locative in Latin, for example, "O-Lke 'loL," "on the ground."[57]

The Yurok "Keto" meant flat or level and was applied to either land or water. "O-ke'to" was a place name for Big Lagoon which meant "where the water is flat or calm."[58] The evidence shows that Arcata could be a corruption of "O-ke'to"—"where it (land) is flat." The Gregg party arrived December 24, 1849 "on a beautiful plateau near the high land and redwoods at the northeast end of the bay.... This plateau is the present site of the town of Union, now Arcata."[59] And this "flat land" or plateau was one of the first places to be selected for a town site.

Eureka, the county seat of Humboldt County, is the metropolitan center of Northwestern California. How did Eureka—"The City on the California State Seal"—receive its name? The name and namer is another local mystery that has never been solved. Gudde quotes the late Thomas B. Doyle of San Francisco, who collected an extensive file on California Place names: "The settlement was established by the Union and Mendocino companies, headed by C.S. Ricks and J.T. Ryan of San Francisco, and named on May 13, 1850."

The term "Eureka," the Greek expression for "I have found it," became very popular after the California Constitutional Convention of 1849 approved the great seal of the State, with the inscription "Eureka." The name is a common one throughout the United States. The most popular story on the naming of Eureka is the following. When the first settlements were founded, a United States Land Office was established in this area. Deeds were sent to Washington, D.C. A clerk could not find any record for the new town, but he finally found a record for Humboldt City, and he cried, "I've found

it!" Another clerk then said, "Then name the new town 'Eureka.' "
In the 1930's the Eureka Chamber of Commerce tried to verify this
story so that Ripley could use it for his "Believe It or Not" column.

William S. Clark, son of Dr. Jonathan Clark, one of the earliest
pioneers and a nephew of James Ryan, is given credit for the following story. In 1852 a group of men, headed by Ryan, bought an old
side-wheel steamer, the *Santa Clara*, in San Francisco, loaded it with
mill machinery, and headed for Humboldt Bay to build a lumber
mill. The steamer was almost lost at the entrance of Humboldt Bay,
but once inside, Ryan, who was an excellent machinist, began looking for a location for the mill, which was to be improvised from the
old ship. He anchored the boat near the foot of D Street, opposite
the location where the Monte Carlo Hotel used to stand. Ryan said,
"This is a good location for the mill; 'Eureka, I have found it.' " And
so the name of the town was uttered by James Ryan.

This popular story cannot be correct since Eureka was mentioned as early as May 27, 1850, in the *San Francisco Alta California*.
George Gibbs, in September, 1851, with the McKee expedition, mentioned that, "We did not visit Eureka, our trail running too far inland."[60]

The late Thomas P. Brown, well-known San Francisco author
and historian, compiled a booklet for Wells Fargo Bank, in which he
stated that Eureka, the city, was named shortly after the word
Eureka had been adopted (1849) as California's state motto and
included in the design of the state seal.

Probably the most plausible story is the following. When Ryan
and the party were in the bay, they divided into groups to find a site
for the town. Ryan came back and said, "Eureka, I have found a
site." He had found a prairie of solid land from the present A Street
to F Streets and from Third Street to the bay. Much of the surrounding area at that time was marsh land. Before night set in, a town of
tents had sprung up on the prairie.[61]

James T. Ryan, the leading figure in the Mendocino Company,
is given credit for naming the town in many of the stories, but the
mystery of the name or namer has never been definitely established
and probably never will.

Fortuna, the third largest city and situated in the beautiful Eel
River Valley, has had three names: Slide, Springville, and Fortuna.
Gudde says the following:

> The place was opened for settlement in the late 1870's by a minister
> named Gardner, who owned the land. He named it Fortune because he believed
> it was an ideal place in which to live. Later, for the sake of euphony, he changed
> its appellation to Fortuna.

On March 20, 1888, Gardner's addition of fifty-two lots were added to the town, already comprised of eighty-eight lots, but no documentation was found that mentioned that Gardner was responsible for naming the town "Fortuna."

The town was first recognized by the United States Government when a post office was established in 1874 under the name of Slide. This popular name was derived from the hill just north of town called Slide Hill. On October 12, 1874, Henry Rohner, Alexander Masson, M.N. Weber, and G.F. Gushaw organized the Springville Mill Company, which helped to establish a permanent community. This name was used because of the many springs in the surrounding hills. On May 5, 1875, the town of Springville was filed with sixteen lots. Although the town was called Springville, the post-office continued to be known as Slide. On April 5, 1880, Postmaster W.J. Swortzel tried to have the post office changed from Slide to Springville, but was refused because there was another Springville in Ventura County. On July 3, 1888, the post office was changed to Fortuna (fortune), and the name was also adopted for the town.[62]

A popular story on the naming of Fortuna concerns a certain Jack Hosier. In the early days there were two Odd Fellow Lodges in Eureka called Humboldt Lodge, No. 77, and the Fortuna Lodge, No. 221. Jack Hosier, an active worker in the Fortuna Lodge, moved from Eureka to Springville. As Springville increased in population, a movement was started to give the town a different name. Jack Hosier, who was very popular, suggested the name of "Fortuna." Fortuna was selected from many names either because of Hosier's popularity or because of the attractiveness of the name.[63]

An intensive study of place names and folklore has never been done in the Redwood country, and the authors of this paper hope that this additional research will add substance and new facts concerning the origin and meaning of local place names and will further round out the picture of California place names.

REFERENCES

1. Eder Herbert, "The Geographical Uniqueness of California Northwest Counties: Humboldt and Del Norte Counties" (unpublished Ph.D. dissertation, Dept. of Geography, University of California, Los Angeles, 1963), p. 162.
2. *Ibid.*, p. 163.
3. T.T. Waterman, YUROK GEOGRAPHY (Berkeley: University of California Publications in American Archaeology and Ethnology, 1920), p. 257.
4. "Journal of Don Juan Francisco de la Bodega y Quadra, Captain of the Schooner *Sonora*, at Trinidad Bay, June 9-19, 1775," translated in Robert Heizer and John Mills, THE FOUR AGES OF TSURAI (Berkeley: University of California Press, 1952), p. 22.

5. *Ibid.*, p. 28.
6. Owen C. Coy, CALIFORNIA COUNTY BOUNDARIES (Berkeley: California Historical Survey Commission, 1923), pp. 18-19.
7. *Assembly Journal*, 8th Session (1857), pp. 167, 212, 291, 437, 438, 448. *Statutes*, 1857: p. 34.
8. Henry R. Wagner, THE CARTOGRAPHY OF THE NORTHWEST COAST OF THE NORTHWEST OF AMERICA TO THE YEAR 1800 (Berkeley: The University of California Press, 1937), Vol. II, pp. 396-397.
9. *Ibid.*
10. Henry R. Wagner, "Spanish Voyages to the Northwest Coast," *California Historical Society Quarterly*, Vol. VII (December, 1928), p. 366.
11. George Davidson, THE DISCOVERY OF HUMBOLDT BAY (San Francisco: Geographical Society of the Pacific Publication, 1891), p. 18.
12. "Journal of Don Bruno de Hezeta, Commander of the Expedition and Captain of the Santiago, at Trinidad Bay, June 9-19, 1775," translated in Robert Heizer and John Mills, THE FOUR AGES OF TSURAI (Berkeley: University of California Press, 1952), p. 35.
13. Wagner, *Cartography*, p. 446.
14. *Ibid.*
15. Charles Wilkes, NARRATIVE OF THE U.S. EXPLORING EXPEDITION (Philadelphia: 1845), Vol. V, Chapters v, vi.
16. Owen C. Coy, THE HUMBOLDT BAY REGION 1850-1875 (Los Angeles: The California State Historical Association, 1929), p. 29.
17. Chad L. Hoopes, *Fort Humboldt, Explorations of the Humboldt Bay Region* and *The Founding of the Military Fort.* Published by California State Division of Beaches and Parks, 1963.
18. Clearence E. Pearsall, *et. al.*, THE QUEST FOR QUAL-A-WA-LOO (San Francisco, 1943), p. 113.
19. *Ibid.*, p. 116.
20. *Ibid.*, p. 158.
21. H.T. Dimick, "Reconsideration of the Death of Josiah Gregg," *New Mexico Historical Review*, Vol. XXII (July, 1947), pp. 274-285.
22. *The Humboldt Times*, December 21, 1963.
23. The narrative appeared again in *The Humboldt Times*, February 7, 1863. The story can also be found in the *West Coast Signal* (Eureka, California) for March 20, 1873, *Quarterly of the Society of California Pioneers*, Vol. IX, No. I (April, 1932), p. 43, and Irvine's HISTORY OF HUMBOLDT COUNTY (San Francisco, 1915), pp. 28-44.
24. Coy, *Humboldt Bay Region*, p. 29.
25. Hoopes, p. 32.
26. Coy, p. 45.
27. The Laura Virginia Association voted to give Baron von Humboldt a choice lot in the city of his name, and a deed was sent to him with a full account of the adventures of the company. Later, von Humboldt sent the association a letter thanking the men for their kindness.
28. There are various dates concerned with entering the bay. Ottinger gives April 14.
29. Courtesy Chad Hoopes, history instructor, College of the Redwoods, and The Society of California Pioneers.
30. Alexander von Humboldt, THE ENCYCLOPEDIA AMERICANA, 1948 ed., Vol. 14.
31. *Ibid.*
32. *The Humboldt Times*, November 6, 1886.
33. Davidson, p. 16.
34. HISTORY OF HUMBOLDT COUNTY (San Francisco: Wallace Elliott & Company, publishers, 1881), p. 170.

35. HISTORY OF SAN FRANCISCO BAY (San Francisco, 1892), p. 256.
36. *Journal of Commerce,* San Francisco, April, 1850. Reprinted in *The Humboldt Times,* May 29, 1886.
37. FIFTY YEARS OF MASONRY IN CALIFORNIA (San Francisco: George Spaulding & Company, 1893), p. 123.
38. Robert LaMatt, *Statement (MS.* in Bancroft Library). Also published in *Humboldt County Souvenir* (Eureka: Times Publishing Company, 1904), pp. 8-9.
39. *Senate Journal,* 3rd Session (1852), 58.
40. *Statutes,* 1853:161.
41. Davidson, p. 13.
42. George Gibbs, *Journal of the Expedition of Colonel Redick McKee, United States Indian Agent, Through North-Western California, Performed in the Summer and Fall of 1851.* In Henry R. Schoolcraft, HISTORY, CONDITIONS AND PROSPECTS OF THE INDIAN TRIBES OF THE UNITED STATES (Philadelphia: Lippincott, Grambo & Company, 1853), Vol. III, p. 133.
43. Gladys A. Reichard, WIYOT GRAMMAR AND TEXTS (Berkeley: University of California Publications in American Archaeology and Ethnology, 1925), p. 139.
44. Dr. Poett, "A Report of the Progress and Discoveries of the *General Morgan* Exploring Party to Mendocino Bay," *Alta California,* April 24, 1850.
45. A.J. Bledsoe, INDIAN WARS OF THE NORTHWEST (San Francisco: Bacon & Company, 1885), p. 130. Also in Elliott, p. 101.
46. Coy, *Humboldt Bay Region,* p. 52.
47. L.K. Wood in Elliott, p. 95.
48. Coy, p. 58.
49. *Humboldt County Souvenir,* p. 10.
50. *The Humboldt Times,* January 20, 1855.
51. *Statutes of California,* 1860:109.
52. *The Humboldt Times,* March 24, 1860.
53. *History of Humboldt County,* p. 62.
54. Mrs. Eugene Fountain, *Blue Lake Advocate,* October 7, 1965.
55. *Ibid.*
56. Pearsall, p. 138.
57. Waterman, p. 198.
58. *Ibid.*
59. L.K. Wood narrative in QUEST FOR QUAL-A-WA-LOO, pp. 138-139.
60. Gibbs, p. 132.
61. Interview with Martha Roscoe who interviewed William Clark, nephew of James T. Ryan, in the early 1930's.
62. Andrew Genzoli, *Fortuna,* 1953. A pamphlet prepared for Fortuna's Diamond Jubilee, 1878-1953.
63. W.H. Jewett, *Humboldt County Historical Society News Letter,* March-April, 1964.

FIGURE 1-1. Eureka in 1854. Courtesy Humboldt County Historical Society.

A Study in Prejudice: The Chinese and Humboldt County, California

Lynwood Carranco

On Sunday, May 4, 1969, a Golden Spike celebration was held in San Francisco to commemorate the centennial of the transcontinental railroad. Mrs. Chinn Lee Shee Wing, ninety-eight years of age and daughter of a Chinese '49er, unveiled a plaque to pay tribute to the 12,000 Chinese who helped build the Central Pacific. A week later a crowd of twenty thousand people turned out for the big centennial celebration fifty-six miles from Ogden, Utah, on the northern fringe of the Great Salt Lake. The occasion was the reenactment of completion of the "impossible railroad"—the meeting of the Union Pacific and the Central (now Southern) Pacific, 100 years ago.

And along with the thousands of railroad buffs and devotees of Western Americana, had come the politicians: four U.S. Senators, seven Congressmen, the Governor of Utah—and Federal Transportation Secretary John Volpe, the principal speaker, who succeeded in infuriating the Chinese delegation from San Francisco by virtually ignoring the 12,000 Chinese who helped to build the Central Pacific over the Sierra mountains to Promontory, Utah. "Who else but Americans could drill ten tunnels in mountains thirty feet deep in snow and who else but Americans could chisel through miles of solid granite?" asked Volpe. Who else indeed—but the 12,000 Chinese![1]

Dr. March Fong, a California assemblywoman, promptly demanded a public apology from Volpe for ignoring the thousands of Chinese who labored on the transcontinental railroad. "As you must know," Dr. Fong said in a telegram to Volpe, "many of these workers performed their labor under virtual servitude and to slight them now 100 years later must be termed either an oversight or an insult."[2] Oversight or insult—this was another incident in the history of the long-suffering Chinese in California.

The historian Hubert Howe Bancroft says that "Ship-loads of paper and printer's ink had been spoiled and breath enough wasted to sail those ships in reiterating the proposition . . . that the Chinese must go," even though some authorities claim that the western shore of the continent was theirs by the right of discovery.[3] Since 1571 the Chinese have not only visited Mexico, but have also become residents, being employed in shipbuilding and other trades.[4]

In 1848 Charles V. Gillespie, who proposed to introduce Chinese immigration into California, brought the first Chinese—two men and one woman—from Hong Kong in the clipper bark *Eagle.*[5] By August, 1852, there were approximately 18,000 men and 14 women, and people were beginning to be concerned over the desirableness of such a vast immigration of the Chinese.[6]

The Chinese were first treated as "fellow-citizens" by the Californians, and were given a prominent place in the celebration of the Admission of California as a State in the Union. Governor John McDougal, in his message to the legislature on January 7, 1852, referred to the Chinese as "one of the most worthy citizens of our newly adopted citizens" and expressed a desire for their further immigration and settlement.[7] As late as May 12, 1852, the *Daily Alta California* mentioned the following:

Quite a large number of the Celestials have arrived among us of late, enticed thither by the golden romance that has filled the world. Scarcely a ship arrives that does not bring an increase to this worthy integer of our population. The Chinese boys will yet vote at the same polls, study at the same schools and bow at the same altar as our own country-men.

Many Chinese came to make their fortunes in a rich new country. But the great mass of Chinese immigrants came not of their own initiative but under a system of contract, which paid their passage in turn for a stated term of labor at certain rates of wages, which were high for the Chinese, but very low for the Californians. This contract system was administered by the Chinese Companies in accordance with Chinese laws.[8] These organizations, known as the "Six Companies," became very wealthy and powerful. By 1876 the Companies had imported 141,300 Chinese laborers. A slave syndicate also was responsible for importing about 6,000 Chinese women to the United States for the purpose of prostitution.[9]

Although the Six Companies attempted to pass themselves off as benevolent organizations, interested only in the welfare of the Chinese under contract, the early Californians accused them of importing large numbers of coolies and prostitutes under contract, as well as illegal extortion and evasion of the law. These Companies controlled and governed all the Chinese in the country with an iron hand, becoming a substitute for their native village and patriarchal associations. They had their own laws, which if broken, were carried out swiftly without regard to the laws of the United States.

In order to control their people, the Companies had a secret organization, whose members were called "highbinders" or "hatchet-men." These men not only policed the Chinese, but ruthlessly avenged any infraction of the rules of the Companies. Only rarely did the state convict any Chinese man for murdering one of his own countrymen in the Chinese quarter.[10]

It is controversial whether the Six Companies did or did not exist to help their fellow countrymen, but the belief spread among Americans that the typical "coolie" was not a free and independent laborer, but that he was ruthlessly exploited by shrewd speculators. This belief was well-circulated to intensify the feeling of hostility toward all Chinese in California.[11]

The early Californians welcomed the Chinese immigrants because there was a shortage of dependable laborers, and the Chinese were good and faithful workers. Although the Chinese were employed in many occupations, they also flocked to the mines from the beginning. The first Chinese came to Humboldt County in northwestern California in 1850 on their way to the gold fields on the Trinity River.[12]

Because of their un-American ways, the Chinese grouped together and never interfered with the white miners. As a rule they only worked the claims that the whites abandoned or passed by. A white man usually worked for $16 to $20 a day, while a Chinese man was satisfied with $5 or $8 a day.[13] When the whites failed to mine their daily quota, they often attacked the Chinese. The first recorded friction between the two races seems to have occurred in Humboldt County in June of 1856 when a group of whites attacked some Chinese who had discovered gold. The sheriff finally settled the issue by driving the whites away.[14] Lawless whites would at times have target practice by firing their guns at the Chinese while they were working.[15]

The white miners appealed to the state legislature for relief against the Chinese because they worked for less wages and because they sent their money back to China instead of investing it in the state. In 1850 the state legislature passed a law requiring a foreign miner's license. This license became prohibitive to the Chinese and drove them from the mines and into the towns and cities, where they were employed in truck gardening, farm labor, household duties, fishing, common labor, and in anything that the white man would not do.[16]

The Chinese, as previously noted, had settled in all parts of Humboldt County in the early days of gold mining on the Trinity and Klamath rivers, and in 1854 the local paper mentioned that "The Chinese are still pouring in!—heading for the gold fields."[17] The Humboldt County *Census* of 1860 lists thirty-eight Chinese, most of them living in the Eel River area.

Gradually, because of the scarcity of gold and the foreign miner's license, the Chinese began to settle near and in the towns. A news item of March 14, 1868, stated that two Chinese men were brought into court in Eureka and charged with robbery and assault, indicating they were within the jurisdiction of the city's courts.[18] Another item in the local *Humboldt Times* of 1868 stated that "the Chinese are coming, oh dear! No they are not, they are right here." By 1874 a "Chinatown" had been established in Eureka, and the Chinese were also living in Arcata at this date.[19]

Most of Eureka's Chinese, over two hundred including twenty women, lived in the heart of what is now Eureka's business district, the block bounded by Fifth, F, Fourth, and E Streets. There were a few families, but most of the Chinese included men and prostitutes. Most of the buildings were poor shacks. The land and property belonged to white citizens who had a profitable investment, renting to the Chinese for six or eight dollars each month. The ground on which these shacks were located was low and swampy, and a creek followed a gulch which ran through the block from northeast to southeast and emptied into a slough below the present Fourth and E Streets. The slough had been filled at Fourth Street to improve the street, and thus cutting off the creek and leaving Chinatown without drainage. Into this area a stagnant pool of water developed, and the refuse from kitchens of seventeen houses and outhouses was dumped. The Chinese were always personally clean, but the newspapers complained of the nauseating odors caused by this filth.[20]

In spite of their miserable environment, some of the Chinese became clever business men, and some of their children were enrolled in the local public schools.[21] Their truck farms around Eighth and K Streets supplied Eureka with most of its vegetables. They had wash houses at the foot of F Street where they did all the laundering. Many Chinese worked as house servants, janitors, and cooks in local households, logging camps, and ranches. The Chinese worked in the woods as swampers and fire tenders.[22] As early as 1875 they were brought to the county to construct roads and railroads. The fishing industry also attracted the Chinese, and they became excellent cannery workers.[23]

As a rule the majority of the Chinese were well treated, but there were the usual bigoted feelings of an ignorant or frustrated majority who bullied and made the Chinese the butt of practical jokes. The Chinese were excellent blackberry pickers, but in the woods they were abused by men and boys. A newspaper editorial of June 23, 1877, complained of this ill-treatment, stating the following:

A Chinese man was almost killed in the woods by a white man, and that there are some Chinese if attacked will defend themselves. The best way to do is to let them alone. They will mind their own business and if others would do the same there would be no trouble.

The system of contract labor was an influence in bringing the Chinese to Humboldt County. As early as 1875, Charles J. Barber, in an agreement with Sum Chung, an agent for the Six Companies, brought fifty Chinese to the county.[24] In 1883 the Chinese worked in the construction of the Eel River and Eureka Railroad.[25] The Chinese coolies built the mountainous Wildcat Ridge road from Ferndale to Petrolia. The evidence comes from oldtimers who remember when their parents used to speak of the coolies. Chinese coins have also been found along the thirty miles of winding roads.[26] The Chinese also built the Old Coast road from Bear Creek Valley to Shelter Cove in southwestern Humboldt County.[27]

Gradually the tension between the whites and the Chinese increased. But to be objective one must remember the anti-Chinese feeling that had swept throughout California. Strong prejudice was directed against all foreigners, but the Chinese, especially, were singled out because of their strange un-American ways. The Eureka newspapers reported this feeling, and the expulsion of the Chinese from Eureka was another incident in this general movement.

The year 1876 marked a definite turning point in the history of anti-Chinese agitation in California. Up to this point, most of the barbarous and obnoxious anti-Chinese legislation adopted in California had been declared unconstitutional as being in violation of treaty provisions, the Fourteenth Amendment, or the federal civil rights statutes. The federal courts, as a matter of fact, were constantly preoccupied with California's race legislation in the period from 1860 to 1876. The Chinese in California had wisely decided to defend their rights along strictly legal and constitutional lines. It was the "coolies" from Asia, not the Indians or Negroes, who made the first great tests of the Civil War amendments and the legislation which came with these amendments.[28]

The campaign shifted from state to the national level, from Sacramento to Washington. In 1882 a measure suspending Chinese immigration for ten years was finally forced through Congress.[29]

The three Eureka newspapers all began active campaigns against Chinese immigration and Chinese suffrage. But on the whole the *Northern Independent* seemed to have an objective attitude toward the Chinese problem. Their editorials reflected an honest concern over the thousands of Chinese entering California each month.

The competition of Chinese labor was a crucial one in California. In San Francisco the Chinese owned most of the boat and shoe factories, and they controlled cigar making, the laundries, and the clothing trade. Because of this the wages were reduced for the white workers. But this competition with the Chinese or the reduction of wages did not occur in Humboldt County. Once a year, according to the *Weekly Times-Telephone* of May 3, 1884, there was a local scare on the subject of labor and wages. The newspapers took up the cry of "Too many laborers—starvation wages!" At this time wages for all kinds of labor, skilled and unskilled, were higher in Humboldt County than everywhere else in the state.[30]

The Chinese culture, in contrast to the American culture, also influenced anti-Chinese feeling. The Chinese were aliens in every sense. The color of their skins, their features, their smallness of stature, their foreign language, their different customs, their religion—all of these contrasted strongly with their Caucasian counterpart, and increased the feeling of revulsion toward them.[31]

But the real source of conflict occurred in the early 1800's with the arrival of a different class of Chinese in Eureka. In the new element were two factions belonging to different Companies, and they were members of rival Tongs. These Chinese were armed with bulldog pistols, knives, iron bars and other weapons. Some of these Chinese men were "highbinders," and they were very dangerous.[32]

The new element established brothels, gambling dens, and opium dens, and in general took advantage of their countrymen. The Reverend Charles Andrew Huntington came to Eureka in 1883 to head the Congregational Church, and he remained in this area during the 1880's and 1890's. In his *Memoir of the Life of C.A. Huntington* (Yale University Library), he mentioned that these vices were the major source of conflict:

Chinatown was said to endanger the public morals by reason of their use of opium; their habit of gambling, and their heathenish disregard of Christian morality, and they were the objects of universal hatred because they were a menace to the public morals.[33]

As early as 1878, the citizens of Eureka became agitated with these vice dens, since white men and women and even boys visited them. On January 6, 1878, two white women visited an opium den and became insensible from the effects of the opium. The editor of the local *Humboldt Times* stressed this concern in 1881:

Opium smoking is becoming one of the fixed vices of this country. . . . In this city there is no ordinance to prohibit its use. . . . It is the Chinese quarters of this city are utilized for that abominable purpose. The patrons of the dens are generally said to be young men, and sometimes women . . . that they have been seen to enter and leave China houses in the night.[34]

The local citizens also protested the houses of prostitution in Chinatown even though these brothels were operating in the white section. As early as 1869 the newspapers claimed that these places were a danger to the morality and safety of the city, "and that these places destroyed the morals of the youth and children of the city." Thus the living habits and conditions of Chinatown, along with the opium dens, gambling houses, and whore houses, were the cause of much anti-Chinese feeling.[35]

The Chinese were also regarded as a menace to the democratic institutions, since they practiced a sort of quasi-government among themselves. They showed no desire to become citizens of the United States. The local newspapers began an active campaign against Chinese immigration on these grounds. The Chinese were compared with other immigrant groups who came with their families to make a permanent residence and to become part of California, politically and socially.[36]

This campaign by local and state newspapers continued for many years. On the whole the Californians thought that the Chinese were slaves who established a quasi-government which acted in defiance of state law. Gradually most citizens began to stereotype the Chinese as uncivilized heathens without respect for law and order.

Although the Chinese did not become troublesome until about 1883 with the coming of the rival Tongs, they apparently liked to shoot their guns. In 1868 the Grand Jury indicted two Chinese men, Tin Quy and Pou Yong, for assault with intent to kill and to commit robbery.[37] On two different occasions in 1881, the Chinese fired their guns in defiance of an ordinance which prohibited such actions.[38]

At times the Chinese openly defied the law, and there was little hope of convicting any of them unless there was white testimony. The Chinese blocked the police and superior courts in Eureka because they would not testify against one another. They did not re-

spect the oath, and they would lie in court, even if there was extreme
hatred involved:

They have prevarication reduced to a dead line, and perjury to a fine art. If 20 of
them swore over a pile of burning paper that Ah Gee did the shooting, 25 more
would swear over the blood of a decapitated rooster's head that Ah Sam was the
guilty man.[39]

The citizens were soon convinced that Chinese trials were useless
since it was impossible to get any satisfactory justice through legal
proceedings.

At a meeting held on March 9, 1882, the citizens of Eureka
voiced their attitude, to adopt resolutions urging Congress to restrict
the immigration of the Chinese:

We have anxiously watched the hordes of Mongolian paupers, criminals and
prostitutes flooding our shores; we have seen our civilization almost subverted
and our children driven from all avenues of honorable labor by aliens, foreign to
our tongue, religion, customs, laws, and social relations. . . .[40]

About 1883 the two rival Tongs in Chinatown posed a serious
problem because they had imported professional gun and hatchet
men from San Francisco. These men were "highbinders of the most
dangerous sort," and soon riots, murders, and assaults became com-
monplace.[41]

Many disturbances occurred in the year 1884. On Sunday,
August 24, a shooting match occurred between the two Tongs. Officers Vansant, McGarrighan, and Deputy Sheriff Cutler arrested
seven of the Chinese, but were released by Judge Denver Sevir at the
Eureka Police Court.[42] On August 26, the *Daily Times-Telephone*
issued the following warning: "A genuine riot may be looked for in
the Chinese quarter at almost anytime. . ." On the same day another
shooting took place with bullets flying across Fourth Street. Again
several Chinese men were arrested with no results.

After a riot on September 23, the *Daily Times-Telephone*
stressed the attitude of the citizens of Eureka:

One thing was apprised of, however, and that is that the Chinese are becoming
an intolerable nuisance to our people, and if some means cannot be devised to
make them behave, they should be made to leave.[43]

Another shooting occurred in Chinatown on December 20,
which caused more excitement in Eureka. A bullet crossed Fourth
Street and passed through the wall of a house owned by D.R. Jones.
The following comment was printed in a local paper: "These heathens have been hailing their pistols a little too loosely of late and
steps should be taken to check them before some innocent party is

hurt."[44]   But the Chinese "highbinders" continued to have their "pistol practice," and they continued to ignore the law.

On Sunday morning, February 1, 1885, more serious violence broke out at Fourth and F Streets, across the street from the *Humboldt Times* building. The front page of the newspaper reports the news:

Just as we were going to press last night a serious riot broke out in the Chinese quarters just opposite our office. Some ten or twelve shots were fired. . . . We do not know the extent of damage, but saw one Chinaman laid out with a bullet through his lung. Dr. Davis took the ball out of his back. He is a gone Chinaman. We saw another fellow with a wound in his hand. The Officers captured about a half dozen pistols, and locked up as many Chinamen. Since the above was in type it has been learned that another one was shot in the abdomen and will die.[45]

The *Daily Times-Telephone* published an editorial entitled "Wipe Out the Plague-Spots," which called for the removal of Eureka's Chinatown by the board of health:

Under the present condition of things there is not only danger from a moral point of view, but continual danger to life and property. It will not do for our citizens to longer permit such life-taking demonstrations as the one witnessed in the Chinese quarter, and one of the principal streets of the city, last Saturday night. It was only a wonder . . . that some innocent pedestrian was not made to bite the dust. Such a result is liable to come at any time, as long as the representatives of two conflicting Chinese companies are allowed to live in such close proximity. If ever such an event does occur—if ever an offending white man is thus offered up on the altar of paganism, we fear it will be goodbye to Chinatown.[46]

The very next evening, Friday, February 6, 1885, at 6:05 p.m., the climax came. Two Chinese men on the north side of Fourth Street below Rick's stable began shooting at one another. City Councilman David C. Kendall lived at the corner of Fifth and E Streets, just outside the Chinese section. Leaving his home after dinner, he walked down E Street, heading toward his downtown office. The Chinese men fired about nine or ten shots in quick succession as Kendall was crossing Fourth Street. A bullet hit him, and he fell on his face. M.F. LaGrange was first on the scene, and Kendall's wife, who had come out when she heard the shooting, was also soon at his side. Kendall was carried to his home where he spoke a few words to Dr. Gross and W.H. Wyman before he died.[47]

At the same shooting, Louis Baldschmidt, a youth who was working at the Pratt Furniture Store, was also shot in the foot while going home to his supper.[48]

The news spread rapidly, and Eureka was soon ablaze with

excitement. Hundreds of idle men—loggers, miners, mill workers, sailors, and drifters—soon gathered at the corner of Fourth and E Streets, clamoring for action and shouting "Burn Chinatown" and "hang all the Chinamen."[49] Police officers captured a Chinese man who was supposed to have killed Kendall, and with considerable difficulty the captive was taken to jail.[50] Before the evening was over, twenty Chinese men had been arrested for the shooting of Kendall, and Sheriff T.M. Brown was afraid that the men would take over the jail. This was the first time in the history of the county that a law enforcement agency had called upon the National Guard. But before the situation could get out of hand, some of Eureka's leaders called for a meeting at Centennial Hall on Fourth Street between F and G Streets.[51]

In less than twenty minutes after Kendall's death, some six hundred men met to discuss the recent development. Mayor Walsh was named Chairman of the meeting and H.H. Buhne was appointed secretary. A.J. Bledsoe, Frank McGowan, and James Brown spoke on the evils of Chinatown and its menace to the community. T.M. Brown and George W. Hunter, who spoke next, sympathized with the angry crowd but counseled moderation.[52]

The men in the hall were very excited and a resolution was actually proposed to go into Chinatown and massacre every Chinese man. When this was frowned on, the next proposition was to loot Chinatown, to tear down the buildings, and to drive the Chinese beyond the city limits.[53]

The crowd was almost at the rioting point. If any clue had been known as to the identity of the killer, they would have lynched him immediately. No such clue was known, however, and Hunter moved that a committee of fifteen men be appointed to go to Chinatown and notify the Chinese to pack up and leave within twenty-four hours. The committee members were H.H. Buhne, chairman, C.G. Taylor, Frank McGowan, W.S. Riddle, E.B. Murphy, W.L. Mercer, W.J. Sweasy, A.J. Bledsoe, N.A. Libbey, Dan Murphy, James Simpson, James Brown, W.J. McNamara, H. Libbey, and F.P. Thompson.[54]

Some respected citizens of Eureka objected to the resolution forcing the Chinese to leave Eureka. Reverend Huntington, for example, spoke against the resolution:

We all deplore the death of our fellow citizen, Mr. Kendall. But no Chinaman had any design on his life. His death was entirely accidental. The Chinaman who fired the shot is guilty . . . but the rank and file of the people in Chinatown are as innocent of the death of Mr. Kendall as I am. . . . You have no right to drive them from their homes than you have to drive me from my home.[55]

The authorities were powerless to control such a mob. If the mayor and some of the aldermen and other citizens had not called the meeting to order, and by reason and argument succeeded in diverting the energies of the multitude into peaceful channels, much blood would have been shed and much property would have been destroyed. The mob did not riot and Captain Keleher's Guard retired before morning.[56]

The committee met and sent for three leaders from each rival Tong. The Chinese were told that they had to leave Humboldt County within twenty-four hours. Representatives of the committee visited every part of the city and surrounding area and told the Chinese the decision of the committee. By 8:00 p.m. of the 6th, every Chinese man in Eureka was packing his personal goods to prepare for departure the next day.[57]

There was no violence during the night of February 6. The local *Daily Times-Telephone* mentioned that "We trust that wise counsels will prevail today . . . the life of the lamented Kendall could not be atoned for by the stretching of one hundred of their worthless necks."[58]

On the morning of Saturday, February 7, there was much activity on Fourth Street. Piles of household belongings, clothing, and merchandise were heaped onto the street and loaded into wagons and all types of transportation available. Before noon twenty-three loads were piled on the Humboldt Bay docks to be placed aboard two steamships which were in the harbor at the time, the *City of Chester* and the *Humboldt*.[59] On the 7th the committee also brought Chinese from the nearby ranches and cookhouses, and they were housed in warehouses near the bay.[60] In 1880 a gang of Chinese men had extended the Arcata and Mad River Railroad three and one half miles to Isaac Minor's Warren Creek Mill. At this time the Chinese were working on branch railroads at Warren Creek, and these men were herded together and taken to Eureka.[62] Seeing they had no alternative, they offered no resistance. A few Chinese had tried to escape by way of Arcata and Eel River, but they were captured and taken to Eureka.[62]

During the night of February 6, some persons built a scaffold with a hangman's noose dangling from it on Fourth Street between E and F Streets. A sign on the gallows read: "Any Chinaman seen on the street after three o'clock today will be hung to this gallows."[63]

Despite criticism and ridicule, many Eureka citizens defended the Chinese, who had to leave their jobs and businesses.[64] Some did not wish to part with their Chinese servants, but were finally forced

to give them up. Intolerance and bigotry were more in evidence. The
Reverend Huntington was hanged in effigy in front of Centennial
Hall because some men found a Chinese servant hiding in his home.
Charley Way Lum, a Chinese boy, was on his way to the warehouses
on the bay as ordered, but a crowd of hoodlums dragged him to the
gallows and put the noose around his neck in the presence of hun-
dreds of people. No one, not even the police, interfered until the
Reverend Rich ordered the crowd to release the boy.[65]

The streets were crowded with people who watched the movements of the Chinese with close interest. The crowd was orderly, and
the Chinese were not molested. The committee separated the rival
Tongs: one hundred and thirty-five Chinese and fifty tons of merchandise were put on board the *Humboldt,* and one hundred and
seventy-five Chinese and one hundred tons of merchandise on board
the *City of Chester.* Four of the passengers were merchants who had
resided in Eureka from ten to fourteen years.[66]

Although rough seas prevented the steamers from departing
until the next morning at 6:00 a.m., February 7, 1885, marks the
date of the expulsion of the Chinese. The delay in departure caused a
few demonstrations, but on the whole the crowds were orderly.[67]

The steamers arrived in San Francisco on Monday, February 9,
1885. The Chinese quickly scattered throughout the lanes and alleys
of San Francisco's Chinatown. Mr. Lindsay, the Eureka City
Marshall, accompanied the Chinese to San Francisco to assist the
Harbor Police in identifying the "highbinders" who were among the
Chinese. Again there were no arrests because of no positive proof.[68]

At a meeting of the Ong Cong Gong So organization in San
Francisco, the law-abiding Chinese stated that a large delegation of
the "worst highbinders in the state" had arrived from Eureka. An
example was the notorious "Adam Quinn" who had just completed
an eight-year sentence at San Quentin for blackmailing and robbery.
He had gone to Eureka the previous week to "practice his trade."[69]

A reporter of the *San Francisco Call* interviewed Colonel F.A.
Bee of the Chinese consulate about the expulsion:

We intend to wait quietly until the excitement dies down and then seek redress
in the courts. The whole trouble in Eureka has been caused by a few highbinders—law breakers. There is a sheriff and other officers of the law in Eureka,
and they ought to have arrested all law breakers. All the Chinese expelled are not
criminals. Many of them are peaceable merchants, whose businesses have been
broken up by their expulsion. Somebody will have to pay for the injury done
them.[70]

The men who ran the Chinese out of the city were very fortunate that their plans did not backfire. First, the Chinese did not own any real estate. Most of the miserable shacks in which they lived were rented to them by C.F. Ricks and other citizens of Eureka. If they had owned property, the United States government would have stepped in, even though the government of China was weak and could not properly support the rights of her citizens in the United States. Second, it was also unusual at that time of year for two vessels to be in port so that most of the Chinese could leave at once. The two steamers arrived in San Francisco when business was quiet, and no ships were expected to arrive. Few people were at the docks. Recent storms had disrupted communication, and the authorities in San Francisco had no knowledge of the Chinese incident in the isolated town of Eureka. If the officers had known they probably would have met the steamers and made the captains return the Chinese. The Chinese immediately scattered, and it was impossible to collect them for reshipment. [71]

The popular fable states that the mysterious country of China was determined to live in isolation from the world and so built an enormous wall to protect its empire from invaders. The Great Wall had its counterpart, not only in the vast hemispheric wall built by the Occidental world which was comprised of legal statutes, but in a specific "invisible wall" built around Humboldt County.

A large crowd assembled at Centennial Hall on Saturday, February 7, in the afternoon at 1:00 p.m. to hear the report of the citizens' committee. This was Humboldt County's "unwritten law" against the Chinese and other orientals—which was to be enforced for the next sixty years! The following resolutions were adopted:

1. That all Chinamen be expelled from the city and that none be allowed to return.
2. That a committee be appointed to act for one year, whose duty shall be to warn all Chinamen who may attempt to come to this place to live, and to use all reasonable means to prevent their remaining.
3. That a notice be issued to all property owners through the daily papers, requesting them not to lease or rent property to Chinese. [72]

The Eureka Common Council met that same Saturday night in their regular session. Mayor Thomas Walsh presided and the following councilmen were present: A. Cottrell, T. Baird, D. Murphy, T. Cutler, and W.H. Wyman who took over the duties of the clerk who was absent. The mayor briefly and "with feeling" announced the death of Councilman David Kendall. Councilman Murphy made a motion, and it was ordered that the Council hear the report of the committee from the citizens' meeting and that no further business be transacted until Wednesday evening, February 11.[73]

W.S. Riddell, secretary of the citizens' committee then read the resolutions passed at the afternoon meeting, and A.J. Bledsoe, also of the committee, spoke in regard to the subject matter. A petition signed by many citizens and taxpayers was received, "praying that the Chinese quarters be removed." The Council then passed a resolution "declaring the Chinese quarters in the city a nuisance and that steps be taken to remove the same outside of the city limits." The following was included in the minutes:

Resolved: that the citizens committee appointed by this meeting go before the common council of the City of Eureka who meet tonight and demand that the common council take immediate action towards declaring the Chinese quarters in the city quarters in the City of Eureka a nuisance and removing same from the city limits. Per order of the committee.[74]

The anti-Chinese fever also spread to the City of Arcata. On February 7, 1885, George W.B. Yocum called a meeting. The crowd appointed a committee and issued an ultimatum to the Chinese to leave by February 11, 1885. The Chinese obeyed the order and all moved out of the city limits of the town.[75]

During the same week, a group of citizens also held an anti-Chinese parade in Crescent City, and the citizens demanded that "The Chinese Must Go." But they permitted only one Chinese man to remain in Del Norte County. The Chinese were not totally expelled until April, 1886.[76]

About three months after the expulsion, two former Chinese residents tried to get railroad contracts in Eureka, but were denied by the committee of fifteen.[77] On May 2, 1885, Lemon, the contractor for the Eel River and Eureka Railroad Company, made preliminary arrangements to use Chinese labor. The people objected, and Lemon hired white workers.[78]

Later throughout the year of 1885, many of the Chinese returned to the area. Chinese peddlers began to sell their wares in Eureka,[79] and Chinese leaders tried to establish a town near Eureka in order to carry on their business as they had done before the expulsion. On January 7, 1886, a Chinese man named Charley Mock tried to negotiate the purchase of property on Second Street with the aid of a white citizen. Upon being informed of the deal, the newspapers urged property owners to be on their guard in matters of selling and leasing land to the Chinese, because if they gained possession of real estate, the law could interfere on their behalf. Mr. Charley Mock soon left town at the "advice" of several citizens.[80]

The Eureka papers of January, 1886, announced the coming anniversary of the tragic death of city councilman Dave Kendall and asked the citizens to renew their pledge. The dramatic incident of the preceding year was printed again:

The death of one of Eureka's most highly esteemed citizens at the hands of a Mongolian highbinder resulted in the expulsion of the Chinese from the city limits, and so far as we are aware no Chinaman has lived within them for twenty-four hours since that date. It was the duty of a committee of fifteen citizens to see that none of the Mongols be allowed to return, and that from the 7th day of February, 1885, no new ones coming over should be allowed to locate within the limits of Eureka. Eureka was the first point in the United States to take this step and was a fact heralded to the remotest corner of the nation.[81]

The committee of fifteen held a meeting on January 12, 1886, to make arrangements for a mass meeting to be held on February 6 in honor of Kendall. A.J. Bledsoe called for the citizens of Arcata, Ferndale, Springville (Fortuna), Rohnerville, Hydesville, and Salmon Creek to attend and to decide on some lawful means to expel all the Chinese in Humboldt County.[82]

A week before the anniversary of the Chinese exodus was observed in Eureka, the citizens of Arcata held an anti-Chinese meeting in Richert's Hall. Mr. Chandler, of the Blue Lake Mill Company, Mr. Falk, of the Falk, Hawly and Company, and Isaac Minor all spoke against the Chinese and said that the Chinese should leave immediately. James Beith, E.S. Deming, R.M. Fernald, G.W.B. Yocum, and R. Burns were chosen as a committee of five to attend the meeting in Eureka.[83]

The anniversary meeting was the largest ever held in Eureka up to that time. Three hundred persons came from Arcata. There was much discussion at the meeting. The Honorable J.P. Haynes said that "the cry in the past had been 'The Chinese Must Go,' but now it is 'The Chinese Must Never Return.' " The suit against the City of Eureka by a Chinese man named Wing Hing for $132,820 was announced. In honor of the event Eureka offered aid to the people of the neighboring towns to get rid of their Chinese. C.S. Ricks explained that he was the loser to the extent of $300 each month by the expulsion of the Chinese. He said that he had been accused of being a "Chinophile," but that he had only hired white laborers.[83] Then the people adopted the following resolutions:

Resolved that it is the sense of this meeting that we regard with disgust and unqualified disapprobation the action of any person in selling or leasing real estate to the Chinese, that in our estimation such a person is a traitor to his race and a fit subject for the censure of all citizens.

Resolved that we now pledge our honors that we will not either directly or indirectly patronize any person who in anywise deals or trades in goods, wares or merchandise manufactured by Chinese.[84]

The citizens of other towns soon followed the suggestions of the committee of fifteen of total expulsion. By January 26, 1886, Rohnerville ordered its Chinese to leave.[85] In Ferndale the Chinese had to sell their laundries. A certain Sam Que was quoted that he was satisfied but "he no likee leevee Ferndale."[86] The citizens of Crescent City held meetings the first week of March, 1886, to "remove all Mongolians from our midst." Hobbs, Wall and Company and J. Wenger and Company, the principal mill owners, signed a pledge to "discharge all Chinese labor on or before the 13th day of April 1886."[87]

A week after the Eureka meeting, the citizens of Arcata met at the Excelsior Hall in Arcata to draw up the following resolutions:

1. We, the citizens of Arcata and vicinity, wish the total expulsion of the Chinese from our midst.
2. We endorse the efforts of Eureka to exclude all Chinese settlements in the city and environs.[88]

The Chinese who were expelled brought a law suit against the City of Eureka. A Chinese man named Wing Hing brought suit in the United States Circuit Court against the City of Eureka to recover $132,820. This represented the claims of fifty-two Chinese men who had assigned their claims to Hing. The complaint charged

... that a mob of disorderly persons assembled together and without authority of law, broke into the premises of plaintiff and fifty-five other Chinese persons and firms, and carried away and destroyed goods belonging to them of the value of $75,245, by reason of which carrying away and destruction Hing and other Chinese suffered damages to themselves and business to the amount of $57,670.[89]

B.J. Akerman, Deputy U.S. Marshall, filed the complaint in the Humboldt County Clerk's Office and served the papers on Mayor Walsh.[90]

The suit caused much excitement in Eureka, since the damages claimed were many times greater than the entire Chinese population of Eureka had ever claimed on the assessment rolls, which was only $2,800.[91] When the Chinese suit against the City of Eureka—*Wing Hing vs. Eureka*—was finally called, S.M Buck, the city attorney, went to San Francisco to represent the city. The case was summarized in a local paper:

The suit of Wing Hing vs. the City of Eureka is ended. Mr. Buck of Humboldt appeared for the defendant city and moved to strike from the complaint all damages claimed for driving the Chinese away, and for loss of business. Judge Sawyer granted this motion and ordered all claims stricken out except those for injury to property. As no property was molested or injured, this action of the Court virtually disposes of this important case in favor of the city of Eureka.[92]

About twenty Chinese men still remained in the Humboldt Bay area. This group, living near Arcata, began to leave, and on April 30, 1886, the last of the county's Chinese left aboard the *Humboldt*.[93]

Myths and legends develop over any cataclysmic event, and the Chinese expulsion was no exception. The popular story that still exists today is that Charley Moon was the only Chinese man who was allowed to stay in Humboldt County. He was working on the Charley Bair ranch in the Redwood Creek area, and he was not molested. Charley, who was well-liked and respected, married an Indian woman and raised a large family. When a group of citizens came from Eureka to get Charley Moon, Mr. Bair threatened them with a gun, and the men returned to Eureka empty-handed.[94]

But there is evidence that others lived back in the isolated mountainous area of the county. Mrs. Brenda Catanich, who formerly taught school on the Klamath River from 1904 to 1907, said that she knew three elderly Chinese men who had married Indian women. Billy Bow, a Mr. Fong, and John Cook were good citizens who worked as farmers and miners. They sent their children to the white man's schools. At the time of the Chinese expulsion, the three-day journey on horseback over the mountains to the isolated Klamath River was too great an undertaking, so the Chinese were left undisturbed. The Chinese never journeyed far from the river, and Chinese relatives visited them from Siskiyou County. And there were probably others who lived in this isolated country.[95]

In October of 1886, excitement again reached a high pitch in Eureka. The Cutting Packing Company, which operated a fish cannery on the Eel River, decided to import a crew of fifty Chinese. The citizens of Eureka held a mass meeting on October 13 to name a committee. The committee, composed of W.J. McNamara, J.F. Coonan, W.F. Mercer, F. McGowan, and A.C. Spear, proposed resolutions that declared "the members of the Packing Company to be traitors to the white race" and urged the citizens of Humboldt County and Ferndale to drive the Chinese out.[96]

A delegation from Eureka went to Ferndale, demanding a mass meeting to fight the return of the Chinese. At the meeting, which was held in the Old Roberts Hall, speakers from Eureka harangued the crowd and read anti-Chinese letters. But when a rising vote was taken, it was found that the valley citizens were against the anti-Chinese proposition, and some even spoke of the mistreatment of the Chinese.[97]

The people of Ferndale finally decided to allow the Chinese to remain until after the fishing season.[98] They left in December aboard the *City of Chester*, and the Cutting Company agreed not to bring the Chinese to the county again. But later the company, which had spent about $36,000 in the area, threatened not to reopen without Chinese labor. They were allowed to use Chinese labor in 1887 and again in 1889. The Chinese left at the close of each season.[99]

All was quiet on the Chinese front until September 1906 when Eureka again seethed with excitement. The Starbuck-Tallant Canning Company of Port Kenyon near Ferndale imported twenty-three Chinese and four Japanese from Astoria, Oregon, to work at the cannery.[100] The local steamship agent even tried to get the Santa Fe Railroad to furnish a boxcar which could be pushed to the wharf so that the people of Eureka would not get excited when the Chinese landed.[101]

There was much excitement in the local papers. The glaring headlines of the *Humboldt Times* stated: " 'THE CHINESE MUST GO!'—Such Was the Unanimous Sentiment at the Mass Meeting Last Night."[102] Once again the citizens were indignant that the unwritten law of Humboldt County had been violated by the business men of Ferndale and the Port Kenyon Cannery. A meeting was held at the Labor Hall on Second Street and those present called for immediate expulsion. Dr. W.E. Cook and E.P. Hawkins, President of the Longshoreman's Federation, and others condemned the Chinese. Those at the meeting even thought about sending a petition to the Board of Supervisors to close the Eel River to fishing if the Tallant Company did not come to terms.[103]

The next day representatives of the Building Trade Council of Eureka and members of the Fortuna Board of Trade went to Ferndale to learn why Ferndale had ignored the unwritten law of the county and "contaminated the air of the county with the filthy Chinese whom the fathers of the present generation were forced to resort to strenuous means to eject."[104] According to the local papers there were a thousand or more woodsmen ready to flock to Fortuna if the Chinese were not asked to leave.[105]

Other meetings were held again in Eureka and Fortuna on October 3, and the citizens passed resolutions to reject the offer of the cannery to use Chinese. The people of Ferndale finally made the decision to send the Chinese back and to attempt to operate with white labor. The Japanese were not asked to leave.[106] On October 4, the twenty-three Chinese men were placed in a boxcar at Port Kenyon and shipped back to the railroad wharf in Eureka, and then transferred to Gunther Island. The Chinese were housed in an old cookhouse, and a deputy sheriff was placed in charge so that the Chinese would not be molested. No one else was allowed on the island.[107]

The committee in charge of expelling the Chinese requested donations to feed the Chinese for a few days and to pay their passage back to Astoria. They also published a list of "anti-Chinese contributors" in the local papers " . . . so that posterity may run back over them and see who is instrumental in ejecting the Chinese from the county in 1906."[108]

The *Roanoke* arrived in Humboldt Bay Monday, October 8, and eighteen of the twenty-three Chinese men sailed for Astoria. The other five were given permission to sail on another steamer for San Francisco. One newspaper stated: "On the steamer *Roanoke* they will shake the Humboldt dust from their sandals, satisfied the county is a fine place, but no place for a Chinaman, and such is the report they will carry to their friends."[109]

The editors of the local newspapers gave credit to District Attorney Gregory and Sheriff Lindsay for this peaceful expulsion, since they personally persuaded the officials of the cannery to send the Chinese away before the local people could decide to take the law in their own hands. The Ferndale merchants paid the Chinese half of their contract price. Lee Eso, the Chinese boss, said "Good for Chinamen—money, no work—bad for boss Chinaman."[110] After this incident the *Daily Humboldt Standard* summarized the Chinese situation:

It can truthfully be said that the county stands as a unit on the Chinese exclusion and there is no doubt but that our people will work harmoniously together in their stand to prevent them becoming residents of this county.[111]

In the first week of November of 1909 the Japanese Tsuchiya brothers established a Japanese art goods store in the Brett building on Fifth Street near E Street in Eureka. On early Sunday morning November 5, about 2:45 a.m., an explosion rocked the city: some unknown persons had dynamited the Japanese store. A stick of dynamite was placed in the recessed doorway of the store and set off by means of a long fuse. A reward of $1050 was offered to anyone who could offer any information leading to the arrest of the bombers.

The City of Eureka offered $500, and private parties offered the rest of the money. Mr. F. Tameguchi, a Japanese interpreter, arrived from San Francisco to investigate the incident, and he said that he was pleased at the efforts to find the bombers. No arrests were ever made, the store was never reopened, and the two Japanese men were never heard from again.[112]

On August 2, 1913, a Japanese junk was discovered on the Pacific beach, four miles north of Samoa on the Peninsula. Deputy Immigration Inspector W.J. Nichols arrested three Japanese, who were part of a crew of nine Japanese who had crossed the Pacific from Japan to the Humboldt coast in a crude junk! The other members, who were weak from lack of food, were captured a short distance beyond Big Lagoon. Captain Ozaki, who had deserted the others to evade capture, was later caught. One of the crew members, Sahey Inouye confessed to some kind of an attempted smuggling plot, but the details were never revealed. On August 13, the nine Japanese were taken to San Francisco in the custody of immigration authorities, to be later deported back to Japan.[113]

In the winter of 1926 the original Hartsook Inn, in southern Humboldt County, burned down. The San Francisco owners, in order to get the popular inn rebuilt for the summer trade, sent up a group of oriental workers to clean up the ruins. They were on the job for just a short time when a group of laborers, accompanied by the sheriff, came down and literally ran them out of the county. About the same time some orientals were sent to Shelter Cove to help set up a canning unit. But in order to avoid trouble, the sheriff arrived first on the scene, and the orientals left.[114]

An extremely bigoted incident occurred in 1930 which is difficult to understand. The Japanese Ambassador, who arrived in San Francisco on his way to Washington D.C., decided to travel through the Redwood Country by private car and then by train from Portland to the Capital. Whether he wanted to see the famous redwoods or whether he wanted to test the notoriety of the unwritten law of the county is not known. A group of citizens from Eureka met him just south of Garberville, and they escorted him through the county to the Del Norte County line, without allowing him to stop. He was told to keep going.[115]

When the Americans took over Japan at the end of World War II, they recovered official documents whose contents were revealed in many newspaper and magazine articles. One article listed the various reasons why the Japanese had attacked Pearl Harbor. One of the reasons was the unwritten law of Humboldt County against the orientals, and special notice was given to the humiliating incident of the Ambassador.[116]

In 1941 the minister of the Presbyterian Church of Eureka scheduled a Chinese minister from China to speak at an evening service as a guest speaker. This event was publicized by the news media which informed the public that the service would be broadcast by remote control by radio station KIEM. But a few minutes before the broadcast the remote control lines "mysteriously" went dead, and the service was cancelled.[117]

In July of 1944, during World War II, twenty-seven Nisei were brought from a relocation camp near Redding to be tried in a United States District Court in Eureka for draft evasion. They were acquitted and sent back to the camp.[118] A letter to the editor showed that there was concern and that attitudes were beginning to change:

Many of us who are native Humboldters and whose parents arrived when Eureka centered itself in and around First, Second and F Streets held our breaths when we learned that 27 Japanese were to be brought here and tried in our midst. We sincerely hoped that the dogs of race prejudice would not succeed in getting out of hand. The trial of these 27 Japanese is without parallel in the U.S.

These defendants were treated courteously. These people reached our city, one that is known the length and breadth of the Orient as being definitely anti-Oriental. They were protected by a quiet dignified sheriff's office. In transport between jail and court there were no demonstrations. They arrived without counsel, and two young American attorneys, both natives of Humboldt, took over their cases. A fair right-minded American judge, Louis Goodman, saw to it that they were given a fair trial, and in the end rendered an outstanding decision. I wonder if some of us "native Humboldters" were to find ourselves in a similar position in Japan, if we would be afforded the same justice and fair play that we have afforded these American-born Japanese. I sincerely hope that, when it is again possible for these men to write to their relations in Japan, they will be so kind as to write about Humboldt County and the City of Eureka and the real American folk they found there.[119]

Local people tell many stories about their confrontation with the Chinese and other orientals in other areas of California and the Orient. Most of the stories center on San Francisco's Chinatown, the largest in the United States. Humboldters, while eating at the many Chinese restaurants, have been treated graciously. But once the Chinese knew that their guests were from Humboldt County, the gracious treatment immediately changed to indifference or even hostility. Even in far-off China local travelers have had the same experiences with the Chinese.

This writer was raised in the company town of Samoa on the peninsula, the former headquarters for the huge Hammond Lumber

Company. When an oriental ship came in to load lumber, the young and old of the community would come to the wharves to observe the orientals—usually Japanese. The orientals were a curiosity as they wandered through the town or bought goods at the company store. But as a rule they were not allowed to leave their ships when they docked at Eureka across the bay.

Anti-Chinese sentiment continued virulent long after 1885. Racial discrimination has persisted; indeed, well into the twentieth century a tendency to glory in the anti-Chinese attitude was much in evidence. Books, editorials, and pamphlets since that date have boasted that no "heathen Chinee" has dared to settle in the county. A business directory of Humboldt County was published by one of the local newspapers in November of 1890. It contained the following:

In the matter of Chinese competition, a question of such paramount importance all over the coast, not alone to the wage worker but to many of the trades and business enterprises, Humboldt is above any county in the State of California blessed. There is not a Chinaman in Humboldt County, except in the mines on the Klamath River. . . . To those who have experienced the misery of having this degraded and debasing element in their midst, and realize the futility of redress at the hands of the U.S. Courts . . . this simple fact of itself is no small recommendation where seeking a home as far removed from vicious example as possible. Nature's benefactions to Humboldt County have been many, but we pride ourselves on having, by our own efforts, eradicated a festering, putrescent sore from our vitals.[120]

A book put out by the Humboldt Chamber of Commerce in 1893 contained the following lines:

One fact makes Humboldt unique among the counties of California, and indeed, on the Pacific Coast—we have no Chinese. Our workingmen are not compelled to come into competition with the degraded coolies of the Orient. There was a time when the Chinee had quite a colony here, but in one of their "Tong" wars a stray bullet from the pistol of a highbinder struck and killed a prominent citizen of Eureka. . . . The community rose as a man and drove every Chinese out of the county. That was in 1885, and since then Humboldt has had no Chinese. Even in far-off China, the coolies know that they are not permitted to come here, and none ever attempt it.[121]

In 1901, a pamphlet, entitled *Survey No. 83 of Fieldbrook*, was published and contained "Ten Reasons Why Humboldt County is the Best County on the Pacific Coast for Business and Residence." Reason number nine was "Because it has no Chinese and none need apply."

As late as 1937 the *Humboldt Times* published a souvenir edition on its 85th anniversary. An article entitled "No Oriental Colonies Have Thrived Here Since the Year 1885" boasted:

Humboldt County has the unique distinction of being the only community in which there are no oriental colonies. . . Although 52 years have passed since the Chinese were driven from the county, none have ever returned. On one or two occasions off-shore vessels with Chinamen crews have stopped at this port, but the Chinamen as a rule stayed aboard their vessels, choosing not to take a chance on being ordered out. Chinese everywhere have always looked upon this section of the state as "bad medicine" for the Chinaman.

The following section appeared on page 65 and on the 1941 *Charter and Revised Ordinances* of the City of Eureka, published by order of the mayor and council:

Sec. 190. No Chinese shall ever be employed, either directly or indirectly, on any work of the city, or in the performance of any contract or sub-contract of the city, except in punishment for a crime. Nor shall any provisions, supplies, materials, or articles of Chinese manufacture or production ever be used or purchased by or furnished to the city.

In 1959 a Council-Manager form of City Government was introduced by the City of Eureka, and a new charter was drawn up. The new charter automatically repealed many of the old sections, and Section 190 was eliminated. But the section would have been invalid because in December of 1943 the Chinese exclusion acts were repealed and made resident Chinese aliens eligible for citizenship, and in 1950 the District Court of Appeals in California, following the lead of the United States Supreme Court, held the Alien Land Act of 1913 and 1920 unconstitutional.[122]

The first Chinese came to Eureka to settle in the early 1950's. One of the first was Mr. Ben Chin who opened up the Canton restaurant. Later Mr. James Chin and his family arrived from Portland to lease the Red Robin Cafe in Arcata. Although they had been warned about Eureka, they stopped in the city on their way south. They liked the area so much that they decided to stay.[123]

Their son, Dan Chin, who came to Arcata at the age of ten, says that he only encountered racial prejudice once when he was in the fifth grade when some "young brats" made some derogatory remarks about his race. Dan Chin, who was co-valedictorian of the 1969 graduating class at Eureka High School and who maintained a 4.0 grade point average while in high school, was awarded a scholarship to Stanford University where he will major in pre-medicine.[124]

In 1958 Jack and Fumiko Kanbara, of Japanese descent, came to Arcata when he joined the staff at the Humboldt State College library. Fumiko, after some initial problems, was hired as an elementary school teacher in Eureka. She said that at first she had some qualms about the local people, who gave her "surprised glances," but that she was accepted by all she met. Even in the early 1960's when she went shopping in Eureka and Arcata with her two small girls, people would stop to stare, and children would whisper "Chinese."[125]

At the present time there are only six Chinese families and some other Chinese individuals in Humboldt County, numbering less than forty in a total population of over 106,000. Most of them are associated with the four Chinese restaurants in the area.[126] In the 1950's oriental students from California and the Orient began to enroll at Humboldt State College in Arcata, helping to lower the bars of prejudice and to condition the local people to orientals.

Broad-minded, intelligent citizens have many times discussed the attitudes indigenous to the area. But one must first try to understand the thinking and actions of a people in an isolated area. The Humboldt Bay Country of northern California had to wait for more than sixty years for a railway communication with the outside world, the ocean furnishing the only highway for commerce. It was not until 1914 that the north and south sections of railroads were joined so that products could be shipped by rail to any part of the country. The many rugged mountains between Humboldt Bay and other settled sections of California caused this isolation. In a region so detached, independence in thought and action developed to such a degree as to affect the ideals and political opinions of the people. Before World War II the local self-consciousness of the Humboldt Bay people was an interesting characteristic of the region, and even today it is still noticeable in the older people who have never lived long outside the area. The anti-Chinese sentiment was to prevail for a long time, for the expulsion was the result of a deeply held attitude which developed into a sense of pride and even to one of boasting that no oriental dared to enter Humboldt County.

When I discussed the thinking and attitudes of the local people through the years with the late Mrs. Emily Jones, former Eureka mayor, and who was born in 1885, the year of the Chinese expulsion, she mentioned the following which was in agreement with other oldtimers with whom I have talked. Many of the first lumbermen were from Nova Scotia: they were very clannish and narrow-minded; they controlled local business to an extent; and they tried to keep others from getting a foothold. This trend has continued through the years. And this is why the City of Eureka and Humboldt County have lagged behind the rest of the State. The lumber companies have always been very powerful, since timber has always been over seventy percent of the basic industry. Those in power have always cooperated with the timber men. Each generation "has developed a herd of sacred cows, and if new ideas, activities, or projects did not prove profitable to this herd, they would be dropped. The sacred cows have had to have the best of everything."[127] In other words, a few men have controlled all from behind the scenes. And if they could not make money, they have never helped a new cause.

Recently when the few local Chinese were asked if they had encountered racial discrimination, they answered in the negative. So there is hope. Times are beginning to change in regards to oriental discrimination—even in the Redwood Country—after eighty years.

REFERENCES

1. *San Francisco Sunday Examiner & Chronicle*, May 18, 1969.
2. *Ibid.*
3. Hubert Howe Bancroft, *The Works of Hubert Howe Bancroft—History of California, 1860-1890* (39 Vols., San Francisco, History Company, 1890), Vol. VII, p. 335.
4. *Ibid.*
5. Zoeth Skinner Eldredge, *History of California* (4 Vols., New York Century History Company, n.d.), Vol. IV, p. 307.
6. Bancroft, *Works*, p. 336.
7. Rockwell D. Hunt, ed., *California and Californians* (San Francisco, Lewis Publishing Company, 1926), Vol. II, p. 360.
8. Eldredge, *History*, p. 309.
9. Bancroft, *Works*, p. 336.
10. *Ibid.*, p. 344.
11. Hunt, *Californians*, p. 362.
12. Issac Cox, *The Annals of Trinity County* (Eugene, Oregon, 1940), p. 37.
13. Bancroft, *Works*, p. 337.
14. Doris Chase, *They Pushed Back the Forest* (Sacramento, California, 1959), p. 53.
15. Charles Yuill, "The Chinese Before 1885," Speech (Humboldt County Historical Society), January, 1954.
16. Bancroft, *Works*, p. 377.
17. *Humboldt Times*, October 14, 1854.
18. *Ibid.*, March 14, 1868.
19. Personal interview with Peter Rutledge, October, 1953.
20. Charles Andrew Huntington, *Memoir of the Life of C.A. Huntington* (Yale University Library, Coe Collection, No. 96, 1899), p. 220. Also, D.L. Thornbury, *California's Redwood Wonderland: Humboldt County* (San Francisco, Sunset Press, 1923), p. 65.
21. Huntington, *Memoir*, p. 222.
22. Personal interview with Peter Rutledge, February, 1956.
23. *Daily Times-Telephone*, December 23, 1884.
24. Humboldt County, *Records*, p. 221.
25. *Weekly Times-Telephone*, February 24, 1883.
26. Personal interview with Dr. Hyman Palais, May, 1961.
27. Personal interview with Martha Roscoe, May, 1961.
28. Carey McWilliams, *Brothers Under the Skin* (Little, Brown & Company, Boston, 1951), pp. 91-92.
29. *Ibid.*, p. 92.
30. *Weekly Times-Telephone*, May 3, 1884.

31. Bancroft, *Works*, p. 355.
32. *Daily Times-Telephone*, February 7, 1885.
33. Huntington, *Memoir*, p. 221.
34. *Humboldt Times*, January 29, 1881.
35. *Daily Times-Telephone*, February 5, 1885.
36. *Northern Independent*, August 19, 1869.
37. *Weekly Humboldt Times*, March 14, 1863.
38. *Ibid.*, January 29, 1881.
39. *Daily Times-Telephone*, February 14, 1885.
40. *Weekly Humboldt Times*, March 11, 1882.
41. *Daily Times-Telephone*, February 7, 1885.
42. *Ibid.*, August 27, 1884.
43. *Ibid.*, September 24, 1884.
44. *Ibid.*, December 24, 1884.
45. *Humboldt Times*, February 1, 1885.
46. *Daily Times-Telephone*, February 5, 1885.
47. *Ibid.*, February 7, 1885.
48. *Ibid.*
49. *Ibid.*
50. *Weekly Times-Telephone*, February 14, 1885.
51. *Daily Humboldt Standard*, February 9, 1885.
52. *Weekly Times-Telephone*, February 14, 1885.
53. Huntington, *Memoir*, p. 224.
54. *Weekly Times-Telephone*, February 14, 1885.
55. *Memoir*, p. 225.
56. *Daily Humboldt Standard*, February 9, 1885.
57. *Ibid.*
58. *Daily Times-Telephone*, February 9, 1885.
59. *Ibid.*, February 8, 1885.
60. *Daily Humboldt Standard*, February 9, 1885.
61. *Blue Lake Advocate*, February 21, 1957.
62. *Daily Times-Telephone*, February 7, 1885.
63. Huntington, *Memoir*, p. 226.
64. *Ibid.*
65. *Ibid.*, p. 227.
66. *Weekly Times-Telephone*, February 14, 1885.
67. *Ibid.*
68. San Francisco *Daily Report*, as quoted by *Weekly Times-Telephone*, February 14, 1885.
69. *San Francisco Call*, as quoted by *Weekly Times-Telephone*, February 14, 1885.
70. *Ibid.*, February 14, 1885.
71. Thornbury, *Humboldt County*, p. 67.
72. *Weekly Times-Telephone*, February 14, 1885.
73. Minutes of the Eureka Common Council, February 7, 1885.
74. *Ibid.*
75. *Daily Times-Telephone*, February 12, 1885.
76. Chase, *The Forest*, p. 55.
77. *Weekly Times-Telephone*, April 4, 1885.
78. *Ibid.*, May 16, 1885.
79. *Ibid.*, January 16, 1886.
80. *Ibid.*
81. *Ibid.*
82. *Ibid.*
83. *Ibid.*, February 13, 1886.
84. *Ibid.*

85. *Daily Times-Telephone,* January 26, 1886.
86. *Weekly Times-Telephone,* February 27, 1886.
87. *Ibid.,* March 4, 1886.
88. *Ibid.,* February 20, 1886.
89. *Ibid.,* January 30, 1886. The transcript of the trial is on file at the Humboldt County Clerk's Office.
90. *Ibid.*
91. *Ibid.*
92. *San Francisco Chronicle,* March 31, 1886, as quoted by the *Weekly Times-Telephone,* April 3, 1886.
93. *Ibid.,* May 1, 1886.
94. *Blue Lake Advocate,* June 21, 1956.
95. *Eureka Independent,* February 29, 1956.
96. *Weekly Times-Telephone,* October 14, 1886.
97. *Ferndale Enterprise,* October 15, 1886.
98. *Ibid.,* December 17, 1886.
99. *Ibid.,* October 21, 1887; December 13, 1889.
100. *Humboldt Times,* October 2, 1906.
101. *Daily Humboldt Standard,* September 29, 1906.
102. *Humboldt Times,* October 2, 1906.
103. *Daily Humboldt Standard,* October 2, 1906.
104. *Humboldt Times,* October 2, 1906.
105. *Ibid.,* October 3, 1906.
106. *Ibid.,* October 4, 1906.
107. *Ibid.*
108. *Ibid.,* October 6, 1906.
109. *Ibid.,* October 6, 1906.
110. *Ibid.,* October 9, 1906.
111. *Ibid.,* October 5, 1906.
112. *Humboldt Times,* November 6, 1909.
113. *Humboldt Times,* August 2, 1913.
114. Personal interview with Andrew Genzoli, Historian for the Eureka *Times-Standard,* August, 1969.
115. *Ibid.*
116. *Ibid.*
117. Jean Neilson, *Times-Standard,* December 11, 1969.
118. Personal interview with Wally Lee, veteran newspaperman of the Eureka *Times-Standard,* August, 1969.
119. Emily Jones, "Open Letter to Editor," *Humboldt Standard,* July 25, 1944.
120. *The History and Business Directory of Humboldt County* (Eureka *Daily Humboldt Standard,* 1890), p. 91.
121. J.M. Eddy, *In the Redwood Realm* (Eureka, 1893), p. 23.
122. Personal interview with Melvin Johnson, City Attorney for Eureka, California, August, 1969.
123. Personal interview with Daniel Chin, August, 1969.
124. *Ibid.*
125. Personal interview with Fumiko Kanbara, August, 1969.
126. Personal interview with Daniel Chin, August, 1969.
127. Personal interview with the late Mrs. Emily Jones, September, 1969.

FIGURE 2-1. An early photograph of Eureka's Chinatown. A Chinese man and Chinese signs appear at the present northeast corner of 5th and E Streets. Courtesy Humboldt County Historical Society.

FIGURE 2-2. Eureka's Chinatown just after the expulsion of the Chinese. The shacks to the right and across the street were inhabited by the Chinese. City Councilman David C. Kendall was killed in the immediate foreground. Courtesy Humboldt County Historical Society.

FIGURE 2-3. The legendary Charley Moon who was supposed to be the only Chinese man allowed to stay in Humboldt County after the expulsion of the Chinese. Courtesy Humboldt State College Library.

FIGURE 2-4. Twenty-three Chinese men being taken to Eureka from Gunther Island to be shipped out of the County in 1906. Courtesy Humboldt County Historical Society.

3

Redick McKee and the Humboldt Bay Region, 1851-1852

Chad L. Hoopes

The white settlement of the Humboldt Bay Region precluded the bloody conflicts between the new settlers and Indians, which in time forced the federal government to employ Redick McKee to find a solution to the California Indian problem. Before settlers arrived in the Humboldt region, however, the United States military authorities realized the importance of good Indian and white relations in California and assigned agents to three areas. On April 7, 1847, General S.W. Kearny appointed John A. Sutter agent for the area along the Sacramento and San Joaquin rivers; M.G. Vallejo agent for the area north of San Francisco Bay; and J.D. Hunter agent for the area south of San Francisco Bay. The office of Indian Affairs, under the jurisdiction of the War Department, asked these men "to maintain peace, to distribute presents, and to reclaim ex-neophytes."

In 1849, when Indian affairs were placed under the guidance of the Interior Department, it appointed Adam Johnston agent to manage the Indian situation.[1] The impossibility of the task is obvious and by the end of 1850 there were hostile movements of Indians in most areas of California. Governor Peter Burnett saw the problem in this perspective:

The Indians saw their lands, for which the General Government showed no interest to treat, passing out of their possession to a people that had no sympathy for them, crowding into their choice places, diseases were thinning their tribes. They accepted the notion that they were a doomed race. Discouraged and moody, the Government failing to provide for their wants, the Indians saw the prospect of starvation following. To avert it came thefts from the settlers. The whites were not slow to punish the thieves, nor the Indians to avenge their wrongs with murder. Volunteer companies organized expeditions to quell the disturbance; they failing, the militia were called out, and then there was a pretty bill of expenses on the Indian War Account.[2]

Indian hostilities by 1850 served to impress upon Congress the necessity for some arrangement to appease the Indians and the whites. Accordingly, President Millard Fillmore authorized three Indian Commissioners for California, who brought with them a philosophy that to feed the Indians for a year would be cheaper than to fight them for a week and that to locate the California Indians on their own reservations would be fundamental for peace. Redick McKee, George Barbour, and O.M. Wozencraft received commissions from the Department of Interior designating them Indian Agents in California, effective October 10, 1850.[3]

These commissions and an appropriation of $25,000 had been authorized September 30 by Congress to "enable the President to hold treaties with the various Indian Tribes in the State of California."[4] The agents accepted their appointments, but their investigation of the salary schedule disclosed that no appropriation had been made for their salaries and expenses. Therefore, on October 15, 1850, their functions as Agents were suspended before they had begun. Since $25,000 had been appropriated in the act for negotiating treaties with the Indians, the Agents were then, by a new act, appointed commissioners for that purpose. The act provided wages of eight dollars for each day actually employed and ten cents per mile for travel. After arriving in California, they were to hire a secretary for clerical work and interpreters when needed, at the lowest compensation. Retrenchment in expenditures was necessary with such a small appropriation, when compared to the great object the commissioners expected to attain—peace between Indians and whites.

The Interior Department possessed little knowledge respecting the character of the Indians in California. The determination to obtain information concerning the Indians' manners, habits, customs, and the extent of their civilization became the primary concern and object of the department. In conjunction with this study, the Department authorized the commissioners to make treaties and compacts with the Indians, to sustain the peace, and, if needed, to recommend the building of future military installations within areas of conflict.[5] In other words, the commissioners would initiate a new system making the Indians wards of the federal government.

Redick McKee bonded himself, "with security satisfactory to the Attorney General," to care for the finances; the appropriation of $25,000 given to McKee for disbursement would cover $6,500 for Indian presents and supplies, $2,000 to each of the commissioners for support of their families, $2,500 for traveling expenses and freight, and $14,000 for a contingency fund for operations in California. McKee, however, expected operational costs to be two or three times greater, and $14,000 would never suffice. He suggested to the Department of Interior before leaving Washington for San Francisco, that an appropriation of $150,000 be made for their proposed operations on the coast. Congress ignored McKee's plea, and, in 1851, allotted only $25,000.[6]

The first leg of Redick McKee's journey to California took him across the Isthmus of Panama. He left New York on November 5 and arrived at Panama on December 4. Four days later he sailed for San Francisco on the *Northern.*[7] As the steamer made its way north along the Pacific Coast, McKee remarked that he gave much thought to his newly acquired responsibility—that of preventing the destruction and extermination of the California Indians. In the absence of direct, positive instructions with little or no counsel and advice, McKee realized that he must develop his own program for the Indians, based on "his honest desire to promote at once the best good for the Indians."[8]

He reached San Francisco on January 13, 1851. Here the three commissioners met and organized, electing John McKee, the son of Redick McKee, secretary of the commission. The commissioners made an appointment to see Governor John McDougal and members of the legislature in session at the Capitol in San Jose. From them McKee expected to learn the facts connected with the recent Indian disturbances throughout the state. But McDougal spoke very bluntly to McKee, expressing to him his belligerent feelings toward the Indians. The governor had ordered the formation of armed volunteers to "chastise" the Indians. Finding that chastisement had been expensive, McDougal now wanted him from the federal government, and this session of the legislature had passed a joint resolution requesting Washington to establish forts on the California borders to protect the settlers.[9]

As signed by the governor, the resolution read:

Whereas, a large portion of our State is unprotected from the different tribes of Indians that live upon our borders, and that these tribes are frequently engaged, and are now at war, with the citizens of this state; and in consequence of our present unprotected conditions, there is no security for either life or of property; and this State not having the means of extending that protection to its citizens which their present necessities require; *and whereas,* it is the duty of the Federal Government to protect its citizens from the incursions of either internal or external enemies, therefore it is *Resolved,* the Senate concuring, that our Senators be instructed and our Representatives be requested, to use their best efforts to have a portion of the United States troops established on our borders, and also to have a line of forts erected along the same for the purpose of protecting our citizens. *Resolved,* that the Governor be requested to forward a copy of the foregoing Preamble and Resolutions to each of our Senators and Representatives in Congress.[10]

The legislature sent the resolution to Senator William M. Gwin in Washington. The arguments contained within the document were persuasive and were effectually presented to Congress by the Senator. Later, as a consequence of this resolution and of the work of Redick McKee and Edward F. Beale, the War Department sent the Fourth Regiment, United States Infantry, to the Pacific Division in the summer of 1852. Two companies of this military unit, under the command of Robert Buchanan, established Fort Humboldt in February 1853.[11]

The governor's austere dealings with the Indians convinced McKee and his colleagues that it was not safe for them to visit the tribes without a military escort. Many direct injuries had been inflicted upon these tribes by the volunteers; and many promises of restitution and redress had been made to them that remained unfulfilled. Thus, the Indians had lost confidence in the white man, and they were now desperately fighting for their lives and property. To stave off starvation, the Indians slipped into the valleys at night to steal cattle and food from the settlers. These depredations brought on the cry of the white man to "kill off the whole damn race." Somewhat dismayed, the commissioners could see a two-fold problem facing them—appease the whites and save the Indians.

During the early spring of 1851, accompanied by a military escort from Benicia, the commissioners succeeded in making treaties with several tribes along the Stanislaus, Tuolumne, and Merced rivers. These treaties were the first attempt to segregate Indians on a reservation in "what was primarily a white man's country."[12] In the wake of this success, McKee sent an estimate to the Department of Indian Affairs for a $75,000 appropriation that he needed to continue to achieve favorable results with the Indians. Congress, however, did not acknowledge McKee's estimate for the second time and appropriated $25,000 in 1851 to settle the California Indian problem, making the total to date $50,000. McKee viewed the decision of Congress a blunder and a mistake: he believed total war would erupt unless the Indians were appeased and their dissatisfactions stopped.[13] In this Deficiency Act, a section abrogated and annulled the commissioners' functions as commissioners and appointed them agents to negotiate with the Indians of California, "as the President of the United States may designate for that purpose; and no officer or agent so employed shall receive any additional compensation for such service."[14]

The agents desired to divide the state into three districts so their policies could be more justly realized and accomplished. Several additional possibilities, however, existed for this action: e.g., diminishing jealousies between the agents as evidenced in their individual correspondences to Washington; improving coverage of the areas of trouble within the state; and ameliorating the demands from the settlers to end the Indians' depredations.

Upon notification, the Interior Department did not approve of the agents' plan of division. Nonetheless, on May 1, the agents met at Camp Barbour on the San Joaquin River to carve out a temporary three district division.[15] The agents drew lots for their district: McKee gained the Northern District, Wozencraft the Middle District, and Barbour the Southern District. The agents notified the department of their decision:

We, as a joint body commissioners, have for the time being with a view of proceeding to the three districts of Country simultaneously. We wish to impress on the Department the great necessity of quieting and pacifying the Indians in this country before they become accustomed to the usages of war, before they learn and gain that dangerous experience. It is our opinion, if they should gain that knowledge, we will have the most formidable of all the aborigines of the continent to contend with, and a protracted war, terminating only by their extermination and at a fearful cost of life and treasure.[16]

These were wise words, and the officials in the department were cognizant that the agents were aware of the true situation and were acquainted with the necessity of devising better coverage and control of the Indian tribes. The department approved their decision on the grounds that the agents could best serve the public interest because of their proximity to the problem.

In view of the vast extent of country to be traversed by the agents in carrying out their duties, the move to cease functioning as a commission and to work individually suggested an advance in the right direction. More important, however, were the pressing demands of the settlers to have something done about the Indian depredations in specific settlements, not in each district as a whole. This was the basic factor that forced the agents to make the division. And, regardless of what the future held, the agents devised the policy to pacify the Indians—"it is, in the end, cheaper to feed the whole flock for a year than to fight them for a week."[17] This policy, although very realistic, was unsubstantial because by June, 1851, McKee, the disbursing agent for the three divisions, had no funds to institute the policy and to make treaties with the tribes. He complained, "I have not been advised even of the means of realizing the $25,000 appropriated for 1851 by the last Congress; and if I was able to do so, the whole amount would be required to meet the liabilities already incurred by us in the discharge of the trust confided in us." [18]

McKee supposed the appropriation had been sent, but it had not arrived. Agent Barbour, on Kings River, received McKee's letter telling of the "pitiful" grant of money by Congress. The agent wanted to know how the department expected them to keep the Indians in good humor by such a liberal allowance. "How this is to be done," wrote McKee, "is beyond my arithmetic." [19] But his arithmetic managed to put the federal government in debt $716,294.79 by 1852, when only $50,000 had been appropriated by Congress.

The Northern District had fallen to Redick McKee, and, regardless of the lack of funds, he planned to go to Humboldt Bay to hold councils with the Indians and to arrange for them to buy cattle at seven cents a pound. The source of McKee's misinformation regarding excessive cattle in the Humboldt Bay country is unknown. During this period the settlers needed their few cattle for draft animals and for reproduction. There was not enough beef to feed Indians accustomed to a diet of roots, sea food, and game.

The June voyage to Humboldt Bay did not materialize. McKee was very anxious to go north, but, as he wrote:

I was embarrassed in arranging for the journey by the want of money in the chest, as well as the lack of reliable information as to the numbers and locations of the Indian tribes inhabiting those wilds. From all the information yet collected from traders, miners, and travelers, who had visited the coast and penetrated the interior of the still lately unexplored district, the Indians were quite numerous, and by far the most warlike of their race in the state. Their principal settlements were said to be on the Russian, Eel, Trinity, Scott, and Klamath Rivers. [20]

While McKee waited for funds and made preparations for his journey to Humboldt Bay, a committee of citizens from Trinidad Bay arrived in San Francisco the middle of June. It demanded that McKee protect the settlers from the marauding Indians by making treaties with the "savages." If he did not, the former were going to call on the governor for volunteers to exterminate the "belligerents." McKee remarked:

I explained to the gentlemen my readiness, and, indeed, my great anxiety to visit their country and do all in my power to redress their grievances and *promised* that, if at all possible, I would set out with an escort of United States Troops immediately after the arrival of the steamer due in San Francisco 4th of July, 1851. [21]

McKee would not begin his laborious and expensive journey to the wilds of the north country because he anticipated that the

Interior Department would soon remit the appropriation needed to finance the expedition. If the department did not, however, McKee would ask T. Butler King, Collector of the United States Customhouse, to cash a draft for $15,000 to pay pressing liabilities and to pay for the expedition. If he was unsuccessful in this bid, the expedition would be postponed still longer. McKee's detention in San Francisco for several weeks would cause him anxiety, for his journey to Humboldt Bay was paramount. The citizens committee returned north with some satisfaction that McKee would honor his promise.

The steamer arrived on schedule, but without the appropriation. Nevertheless, a dispatch from the department arrived, stating that Congress had appropriated $42,000 for general purposes and salaries: $25,000 for holding treaties, $6,750 for salaries, $9,000 for agents' salaries, and $1,500 for interpreters.[22] On July 10 assuming that Congress would release this appropriation, McKee obtained an advance of $5,000 from King, but only part of the $15,000 requested. King declined to loan McKee $15,000 without authorization from the Treasury Department.[23] McKee used $3,000 to pay against his debts and used the remainder to cover the expenses of his expedition to Humboldt County.

Of the $42,000 appropriation, only $27,500 was ever remitted to McKee to pay his debts. The disposition of the remaining $14,500 is unknown. The money due King, the sums due merchants for supplies, and the salaries due employees were debts which McKee could not postpone. Trusting that Congress would soon pay his vouchers, McKee borrowed $5,000 from the Banking House of Sather and Church to pay his most pressing liabilities. And for the remaining debts, he issued "Certificates of Indebtedness payable upon receiving funds from Washington." Of McKee's total expenditures, $716,394.79, arising from contracts to supply the Indians, Congress only satisfied claims amounting to $287,000.[24]

Congress did not honor Redick McKee's bank note for several years. In order to obtain an extension of time from the bank while he presented his case to Congress, McKee mortgaged his homestead property. For five years he was forced to pay $125 a month interest on the loan which amounted to $7,500. Not obtaining relief from the federal government and not able to continue the interest payments, McKee lost his property, valued at $30,000. McKee wrote to Congress:

If I had not confidence in the disposition of Congress to redress real grievances when satisfied of their existence, I should have lost all faith in human nature. My experience will, I hope, prove a warning to future disbursing agents, not, under any circumstances, to advance one dime for Uncle Sam, unless prepared, as I was not, to make the old gentleman a donation of the amount.[25]

In 1870, McKee received $9,659.16 in reparation payments against his claim of $48,880. Congress acknowledged that McKee had been honest in his dealings with the Indians and in his capacity as disbursing agent. But he had borrowed money without permission, and he had failed to allow the Department of Interior to judge the expediency of needed measures. McKee was an idealist; and, when the Department of Interior neglected to furnish McKee specific orders, he could only allow his conscience to guide him.[26]

After McKee received the $5,000 from King, he moved north to Sonoma. On August 9, 1851, he was notified that an escort of thirty-six dragoons, under the command of Major W.W. Wessells, would join his expedition. Wessells had arrived at Sonoma from Benicia the previous day, but because arrangements were not completed, the expedition's first move north was deferred until August 11.[27] Redick McKee employed Thomas Seabring to guide the expedition to Humboldt Bay over the Sonoma Trail,[28] and George Gibbs for his Indian interpreter.[29]

The first seventy miles of the Sonoma Trail followed the valleys of Sonoma Creek and Russian River. Leaving the Russian River at its source, the trail crossed a divide, a series of mountains between the Russian and Eel rivers. This rough and dangerous crossing consists of nearly one hundred miles of heavy timber, brushy hills, mountains, gulches, and gorges. The trail then continues along the South Fork of the Eel to where it joins the main fork, which empties into the Pacific Ocean. Fortunately no member of the expedition lost his life, but two horses, four mules, and eight cattle perished.[30]

General J.M. Estill of Vallejo, commander of the 2nd Division of California Militia, overtook the advancing column about five miles north of Sonoma on August 14. He reported to McKee that he and his men were under orders from the governor to "furnish him protection to Clear Lake." Estill also sold a herd of 300 cattle to McKee to feed to the Indians—at a cost of $3,000.[31] The expedition of 70 men, 140 horses and mules, progressed north, passing through the settlements and on into Indian country.

Meetings were held with the various tribal chiefs along McKee's route. At these meetings, the agent spoke through his interpreter, George Gibbs, and his comments to the chiefs basically followed this speech:

I come from the Great Father, the President, at Washington, the most powerful and the richest chief in this continent, and anything I may do in his name will be final and binding upon you, if he approves. That Great Father, my Chief, has conquered this country, and you are his children now, and subjects in all things to him. Brothers, we know you were the original owners of these broad lands, and the Spaniards, Mexicans, and Californians have been in turn your conquerors and masters, until finally the President, My Great Chief, has conquered and owns this country. The President has learned that his red children in California are at war with the whites and among themselves, are poor and ignorant, and he has now sent me among them to inquire into their condition.[32]

The chiefs were usually awed by McKee, by his kind words, and wanted to know who this Great Father, the President, was. They wanted to know where he lived, and if he was a good chief. McKee answered their questions, and the chiefs gave their approval of this Great Father and were happy to become his subjects.

The first of McKee's six treaties was made at Camp Lupiyuma, west of Clear Lake Valley on August 20, 1851. McKee gave all of Clear Lake Valley proper to eight tribes upon the condition that the tribes would live peaceably and would agree that all other tribes the President might send to the reservation would be received as brothers. Before reaching Humboldt Bay, another treaty was signed with Fernando Feliz on August 22.

After much hardship, the McKee party reached the vicinity of Humboldt Bay on September 10. The party camped at the "Big Bend of the Eel River," about twelve miles from Humboldt City, expecting to remain in the area several days. McKee planned to resolve the problem between the Indians and the settlers of the Eel River Valley by establishing a reservation there.

The new settlers in the valley had taken the extremely fertile soil of the bottom lands along the river for farming, and twelve new farms had been established near present day Fortuna, Ferndale, and Loleta.[33] McKee, while visiting with these settlers, learned that many Indians made their homes in the bottom lands and that they could possibly be assembled for a meeting. McKee requested Charles W. Robinson to induce these Eel River Indians to visit his camp. (Robinson had married an Indian woman for reasons of peaceful cohabitation with the Indians while he developed his farm.) He and the other settlers had lived only a few months among the natives of this valley, making it impossible for them to establish a means of communicating verbally with the Indians. But through rigorous motions and expository remarks, Gibbs communicated with several Indians who left McKee's camp, with food and presents, to inform their brethren of McKee's invitation to sign a peace treaty. While waiting for the Indians to return, McKee visited Humboldt City. He met with the residents to obtain their opinion of what course he should follow toward settling the Indian-white problem in this area. They agreed with McKee that a government supervised reservation was indeed necessary. The agent returned to his camp the following day to learn from Robinson that the Indians were fearful of accepting his invitation to council. The Indians believed "that some design was meditated for their destruction, or that some injury would be inflicted upon them."[34] Thus, no Indians came to McKee's camp and no treaty was signed with the Eel River Indians.

Several men from Humboldt City returned McKee's visit. Their purpose was to further discuss the present Indian-white problem. One of these men, a Mr. Dupern, formerly of Norfolk, Virginia, and a merchant in Humboldt City, agreed to descend the Eel River to its mouth, in the company of Charles Robinson and George Gibbs, to explore the country and to approximate boundaries for an Indian Reservation. Also, they would make a last attempt to induce the Indians to visit McKee's camp. The explorers spent one night with the Indians, but failed to gain the natives' acceptance of their proposition to make a treaty.[35]

The idea of a reservation was utmost in McKee's mind. The exploring party returned and declared to him that the lands south of the Eel River were found to be suitable for a reservation and would "interfere as little as possible with the whites already settled." McKee was thoroughly convinced that a reservation was in order and planned a reservation plot. The agent, finding it impossible to meet with the Indians, moved his camp to Humboldt City. There, with the citizens, he discussed his chosen site for the Indian lands.

The local residents agreed with McKee that the southlands were a logical location and should be selected at once because the white settlers would soon take the choice sections, leaving the Indians the uncultivable lands. Future conflicts would no doubt result if this took place. McKee plotted the following area for the Eel River Reservation:

That the portion of country lying between Eel River and the Mendocino mountains, described as follows, shall be reserved: commencing at a point upon the south side of the Eel River, opposite the small creek where on the agent and escort were encamped; thence running in a southwesterly direction parallel to the general trend of the coast, to the summit of the first range of mountains, ending at the northernmost point of cape Mendocino; thence along said summit to the Pacific Ocean; thence up said river in its windings to the place of beginning; together with the right of taking fish in any part of said river below the said place of beginning, and of fishing or digging for shellfish on any part of the coast. Said reservation estimated to be thirteen miles in length on the coast, and eighteen miles inland—average length fifteen miles; estimated width six miles.[36]

A considerable portion of the reservation along the coast consisted of salt marsh, and a portion along the river was subject to overflow. But between the river and the mountains, where Ferndale stands, patches of land were found to be suitable for cultivation.

Charles Robinson accepted McKee's offer to be subagent of this new reservation. McKee gave Robinson six head of cattle, flour, and presents for those Indians who would live peacefully on the reserved lands. Robinson was instructed to break up six acres of land within the reservation; then he was to plant potatoes sometime during the coming fall. McKee gave the subagent $140 to buy a "large prairie plow, ox-yokes, chains and a half a dozen axes and hoes," so that the agent "may obtain as much labor from the Indians as possible." Robinson's use of the oxen and tools to farm his personal lands would be his remuneration, but all items were to be held in trust as the property of the United States. To insure the intent of the Indian Agent's instructions, or in the event Robinson had an accident, "Messrs. Howard, Dobbins, and Durpren" from Humboldt City were to watch Robinson. There is no doubt that the cattle and equipment were desired by Robinson and other men to develop their homesteads, forgetting their obligations to the government and the Indians. When the news that the government had rejected the Eel River Reservation reached the Humboldt Region, any semblance of an existing reservation was lost, and the lands were taken up by homesteaders. Regardless, before McKee left the Humboldt Area he had sent a duplicate copy of the reservation plan to Howard, Dobbins, and Durpren to "be posted in some conspicuous place, so as to prevent anyone settling upon said land through mistake."[37]

McKee journeyed to Trinidad Bay as he had promised the Trinidad citizens in San Francisco in June. The Indians at this port called themselves the Kori Indians, with Oq-qua as chief. McKee assembled about fifty of these Indians, and "requested them to remove to and settle upon the reservation of land near the mouth of Eel River. Presents were distributed among them in the name of the President. But they made no reply." McKee only remained at Trinidad four days. He returned to Union September 21 because Indian hostilities along the Klamath River demanded his immediate attention. He had received reports that Indians were killing mule drivers and stealing mules from pack trains bound to and from the Trinity mines. In retaliation, the men traveling with the caravans shot all Indians they saw, the innocent being killed more frequently than the guilty. Citizens warned McKee not to attempt to make a treaty with these hostile natives, "until a war party of whites could be sent against

them, and until the Indians sue for peace." McKee, confident of his
ability and relying on his past success with the Indians, felt that he
could quiet the disturbances without resorting to war. Securing the
services of a Mr. Thompson as interpreter, McKee sent him off to
visit the Indians and to induce them into meeting the "treaty maker"
from the "Great White Father" at the forks of the Klamath and
Trinity rivers on October 1, 1851. The Treaty of Klamath, October
6, 1851, resulted, and hostilities were ended for the time being.[38]
Had this treaty been honored by the federal government, the resulting Indian wars could possibly have been avoided.

Before McKee could finish his expedition because of the rains
and before he could retrace his steps back to the Humboldt Coast, he
concluded his fifth and sixth treaties with the Indians at the mouth
of Salmon River: the Treaty of Coratem on October 12, 1851, and
the Treaty of Scott's Valley on November 4, 1851. At Scott's Valley,
several men from Shasta Butte City and Scott's Bar attended the
council to witness the treaty making. As part of the agreement between the Indians and the whites, the tribes had two years to move
to either the Klamath or Scott's Valley reservations. In the meantime
the miners would be allowed to work their mining claims, and the
farmers and ranchers would have time to remove themselves elsewhere. All the gentlemen present expressed their gratifications at the
conclusion of the council, and they believed that the whites and the
five thousand Indians would observe the treaties.[39]

Finishing his business, McKee retraced his steps to the coast. He
arrived at Union on November 21 and spent three days disposing of
the mule train and breaking-up the party. Thereafter, McKee proceeded to Humboldt City. No opportunity presented itself for leaving this city until December 8, when the steamer *Sea Gull* arrived on
her way to Portland, Oregon. This vessel proved to be the last opportunity to leave Humboldt for a while, and McKee concluded that he
should proceed north to Portland to meet the *Columbia* on her way
down the coast to San Francisco. The agent arrived in San Francisco
on December 28, 1851.[40] Thus, a five month journey of exposure
and great labor ended.

Reminiscing, McKee declared:

Considering the results which must happily follow, the expenses are trifling.
Taken as a whole I doubt whether ever in the history of Indian negotiations in
this or any other country as much work has been done as much positive good
effected and as many evils averted with such comparitive *[sic]* means at command.[41]

McKee's optimism proved to be disastrous for the Indians. His
idealistic program "to feed the whole flock for a year than to fight

for a week" only materialized after much destruction. McKee secured temporary peace by making presents and promises to the Indians—at times surpassing his limited powers to make and not execute treaties.

Well pleased with his expeditions, McKee suggested in a letter to the Commissioner of Indian Affairs that he return to Washington. He would bring the eighteen treaties that Barbour, Wozencraft, and he had made with the California Indians and explain them in person. The commissioner disagreed, even though he endorsed the treaties, but advised McKee to send the treaties posthaste to Washington.

The commissioner received the treaties, approved and delivered them to President Fillmore who signed and transmitted them with a message to the Senate where they were read June 7, 1852.[42] The Senate rejected the treaties, however, because of the immense claims against the federal government incurred by the agents. Furthermore, the attitude of the California legislature and its memorial to Congress that criticized the treaties persuaded the Senators to exclude them.

What had developed in California was an antitreaty coalition in the legislature. The Committee on Indian Affairs established by the assembly requested Redick McKee to appear before the committee to defend his reasoning for giving valuable lands to uncivilized Indians. Assemblymen charged McKee with giving the Indians large amounts of the finest farming and mineral lands in the state. In supporting his position, McKee berated their accusations, telling the committee that it was uninformed and that all the reservations together would not probably exceed 1 percent of the whole area of California. The agent further expressed to the committee that

he had endeavored to exclude in every selection some goods lands, capable of subsisting the Indians; and it would have been a wretched policy as well as gross injustice, to have done otherwise. My object had been to give them lands which they could work, and upon the product subsist.[43]

The committee told McKee that the reservations he had given the Indians "would prove most ruinous to the prerogatives of both the Indian and white population." It was obvious to the assemblymen that when the white men wanted the reservation lands they would take them and the "Army of the United States could not expel the intruders."[44] McKee left Sacramento when the committee adjourned for the time being and retired to San Francisco to await another chance to force the issue at hand—the ratification of his treaties. The opportunity came in early March; but again the committee opposed his policy, and the assemblymen became quite "savage" in attacking McKee for giving valuable lands to "bloody savages." They would not change their attitude.

The California senators were waiting in Washington for the decision of the legislature.[45] Only the appeals of McKee and Edward F. Beale prevented the Senate from endorsing the assembly's motives and drafting a joint resolution completely rejecting the treaties. What the state legislature adopted was a memorial to Congress on the subject of the disposal of the treaties: in place of reservations, missions should be established throughout California, where the Indians could receive supplies and could farm the mission lands.[46] This design seemed to entertain that which had been attempted in the past. The result of this memorial would then be that Congress would reject the eighteen treaties. Edward F. Beale, the new Superintendent of Indian Affairs in California received a request from Washington to express his views as to the expediency of ratifying or rejecting the treaties. He stated what he believed:

> To reject them without an effort to retain the Indians confidence and friendship would undoubtedly involve the State in a long and bloody war, disastrous and ruinous to her mining and commercial interests, and affecting, more or less, the prosperity of our whole country.[47]

Regardless of McKee's and Beale's arguments, the Act of August 30, 1852, rejected the eighteen treaties. In place of the treaties, Congress appropriated $100,000 for "the preservation of peace with those Indians who have been disposed of their lands in California, until permanent arrangements be made for their future settlement."[48]

President Fillmore was not satisfied with the Senate's decision: in his message to Congress he called attention to the fact that because "the Senate not having thought proper to ratify the treaties which had been negotiated with the tribes of Indians in California, our relations with them have been left in a very unsatisfactory condition." He continued: "the Indians are mere tenants at sufferance and are driven from place to place at the pleasure of the whites. Justice alike to our own citizens and to the Indians requires the prompt action of Congress."[49] Congress, which alone is vested with the power of disposing of the public domain, should have made the necessary provisions for reservations. The agents had attempted to conciliate the Indians by kindness and their efforts would have been successful in preventing to a degree the ensuing hostilities. But the consequence of rejecting the treaties was bloodshed, and the relation between the settlers and Indians appeared precarious.

Out of the $100,000 appropriation to pacify the Indians, $25,000 was specified for the purchase of suitable presents for the displaced Indians: small white, red, and blue porcelain beads; large colored glass beads; turkey red prints; and gay colored shawls.[50] Without assuming too much, it should be evident that these goods would be almost useless to poor, hungry, California Indians who needed supplies of food which ultimately would keep them from committing depredations against the white settlements. These supplies were not authorized, and the settlers continued pushing the Indians.

A new political movement to end the Indian problem in California evolved while the controversy within the government over ratification of the treaties progressed. Governor John Bigler directed this movement to remove the Indians entirely from the state. One would wonder to what place? A move east of the Sierra Nevada Mountains would be proof of the ignorance of those people advocating this measure. The region and country was counterpart to the coastal Indians' mode of living. Most of Nevada is waste and barren desert, where only a few Indians survived. A move north would add thousands of Indians to the already overflowing population of Oregon. A move south would place the Indians directly in line of southern immigration, thus preparing the way for increased hostilities. The white man's treatment of the California Indians was no better and perhaps not much worse than in other parts of the United States. But the attitude of Bigler, however, was not a humane means of solving the Indian problem in California. The governor's message to the legislature in 1852 is not a happy one:

The Indians ought to be removed beyond the confines of the state. . . . I condemn the reservations established by the commissioners as wrong, fraught with evil to the Indians and to the whites, and calculated to produce constant collisions and impose heavy burdens upon the government.[51]

The state senate committee on Indian Affairs approved Bigler's message, and it supported his policy until the actions of Senator John J. Warner of San Diego, "one of the best qualified men in the state to speak to the Senate upon the subject of Indians," aroused the public. Many citizens supported Warner who recommended a careful re-examination of the treaties and of the reservation system. He added, that there were many areas in the state suitable for Indian reservations and that enough land existed for Anglo-Americans and for the Indians.[52]

The governor's policy had been regarded as unfavorable by the public. But on April 6, 1852, two senators presented a memorial to Bigler that gave additional support to his policy of extermination. James W. Denver, senator from Klamath and Trinity counties, and

Royal T. Sprague, senator from Shasta County, wrote in the memorial that the problem of Indian affairs in the north forced the citizens to demand

more prompt, efficient and constant resistance, which they are no longer able to make. . . . This state of affairs cannot continue much longer. . . . We call on you as the Executive of the State, to demand from the commander of the United States forces in California troops sufficient to afford protection and to punish the depredators, or if that cannot be done, then order out the militia for that purpose.[53]

This communication gave Bigler grounds to start his campaign against the Indians. If he could not remove them, he could exterinate them. The governor sent this memorial and his personal letter to General Ethan A. Hitchcock, Commander of the United States Army on the Pacific Coast at San Francisco. In his letter, the governor told Hitchcock that the California Indians had the ferocity of South Sea cannibals and that they were born with a hatred for the white race. Furthermore, the two races could not live together and have peace, and the solution to the problem was the evacuation or destruction of the Indians, to be done by the central government because the Constitution guaranteed this service to the people. If the central government was neglectful in this duty, there was one alternative: the people would fight their own battles "to maintain their independence as a sovereign State and to protect themselves from intestine troubles, as well as from the incursions of merciless and savage enemies."[54]

These statements, precipitated by Bigler's prejudices and the memorial, are examples of his enmity towards the Indians. They are based upon emotionalism and not investigation by the government. One observation that the governor could have made would have been acknowledgment of the fact that immigration into California had not been gradual. The Indians had been pushed before a rapidly advancing civilization and every part of the country had suddenly been penetrated and explored, leaving the natives in the immediate proximity to the whites. Consequently, the Indian endured great sacrifices and loss of property. But the new settler's experiences dealing with Indians in the East no doubt justified this development.

General Hitchcock, in his reply to the governor on April 10, 1852, wrote that he had not been aware of extreme Indian problems in the northern counties. He realized that all parts of the state had problems, but he had believed that there was no need for additional troops in any one section of the state. He was thoroughly convinced of this notion, until several citizens from Humboldt Bay informed him that a military post was desperately needed somewhere near the bay or near the Klamath River. The citizens stated that "such a post would be most favorable for holding in check not only the Indians, but the whites who are ready to create disturbances on the slightest provocation."[55] The general sympathized with the citizens and promised them that at his earliest opportunity "he would establish a military post at some suitable point within those northern counties."[56]

In addition, Hitchcock disclosed to the governor that Redick McKee had also been told in correspondence from the Humboldt Bay region informing him of brutal outrages committed by whites upon the generally harmless and inoffensive Indians living near the Bay and the Eel River. McKee understood that these bloody massacres of the Indians would continue unless Hitchcock sent a small detachment of troops to establish reservations near the Eel and Klamath rivers; that a depot for supplies should also be established on Humboldt Bay; and that by means of small pack trains regular communications could be maintained between the reservation every two or three weeks.[57] The general included McKee's remarks in his letter of April 18.

Hitchcock, however, agreed with the governor that the Indians and whites could not live together and that the whites must come into full possession of the country. He also realized that he could not give full protection to the isolated northern counties because his troops were too few in number. He had received five hundred men, but he feared their desertion if they were stationed at isolated coastal posts. Bigler was pleased with what he read in Hitchcock's letter and wrote a lengthy reply on April 12, 1852, manifesting appreciation for the general's attitude and requesting the general to make the best use of military force under his command to protect the citizens until additional troops arrived. The governor closed his letter by asking Hitchcock to keep the capitol informed of what steps the military would take to terminate the difference in the northern counties. [58]

While the correspondence between Bigler and Hitchcock progressed, McKee attempted once again to help the Indians and to have reservations and a military fort established in the Humboldt Region.

By letter he informed Governor Bigler, as he had informed Hitchcock, of the problems between the whites and Indians on the Eel River, but from a more reasonable point of view. The Indians on the Eel had been accused of killing two white men living in an isolated place, but no investigation of the murders had been made. Nonetheless, the whites had organized into several parties and planned to destroy the Indians. A communication to the citizens of Union and Humboldt Bay makes evident their plans:

The Indians have murdered two of our citizens, under circumstances truly horrible, and at a meeting of the citizens of the valley it was unanimously agreed to commence war upon them immediately, and we the undersigned were chosen to devise some plan by which we can strike an effective blow upon them. On Monday 19th of the present month at the break of day is the day we have decided to make the attack on them. By attacking them at all points simultaneously one party moving up while the other moves down the Eel River until we meet. We hope to clear the river of them entirely. Lets thoroughly break up this den of thieves and murderers.

Very Respectfully Yours

B.F. Jameson
T.D. Felt
Kennerly Dobyns[59]

Attacking the Indians near the bay, the whites slaughtered many of them. The party then proceeded to Eel River and renewed their work of death and killed fifteen or twenty more defenseless natives. Not one of them had been suspected of being involved in the murder of the two white men. McKee related other cases of "wanton murder" of the Indians to Bigler, which, wrote McKee, "if it did not endanger the peace of the northern frontier, it had at all events brought lasting disgrace upon the American name."[60] He suggested to the governor that some measures were necessary to vindicate the laws of the country as well as those of humanity by bringing some of the white desperadoes to punishment.

Governor Bigler gave McKee's letter to the senators whose counties were involved in the Indian problem. These senators did not accept McKee's notions of "wanton murder of the Indians by the whites." McKee believed that the activities of the whites were purposely not noticed by those senators who wanted the Indians removed or exterminated. The agent proposed that the senate make an investigation of the massacres which would prove the validity of his statements. The senators countered by stating that they were well informed as to what was taking place in the north. If there was any contradiction, any special credit should be given to the statements of gentlemen because "they happened to be members of the legislature which was a position in which McKee's experience did not lead him to concur." McKee denied that he had made unsound reflections against the character of the senators; but his final remarks to them suggested that "nothing was to be expected of the government, except the old state of affairs and the war of extermination will continue."[61]

Redick McKee and the politicians exchanged words over the controversial issue of the Indians, while Edward F. Beale and General Hitchcock worked towards a plan of permanent arrangement for the Indians and whites—based upon McKee's reservation plan. Beale submitted a detailed proposal for a new program to Washington in October, 1852. In part it contained the following proposals:

A system of military posts to be established on reservations, for the convenience and protection of the Indians; these reservations to be regarded as military reservations or government reservations. Each reservation to contain a military establishment, the number of troops being in proportion to the population of the tribes.[62]

This program was eventually adopted by Washington and California. The federal government appropriated $250,000 towards the formation of five military reservations, garrisoned by federal troops and California volunteers: Nome Lackee, Klamath, Tejon, Mendocino, and Fresno.

The humanitarian efforts of McKee, Beale, and several citizens of Humboldt County, as opposed to the destructive efforts of McDougal, Bigler, and several members of the California legislature, were soon to be realized: the War Department would respond with ample troops so that General Hitchcock could fulfill his promise to the citizens of Union and Humboldt City. He would send two companies to Humboldt Bay in January, 1853, to test the new policy that had evolved from the work of Beale and Hitchcock and from McKee's suggestion to Hitchcock that there was a need for reservations and for a supply depot to be established on Humboldt Bay.

NOTES

1. U.S. Congress, *House Executive Documents*, 1848, Doc. 17, Serial 573, pp. 182-345.
2. Herbert Howe Bancroft, *History of California* (San Francisco, 1884), VII, 482. By December, 1853 the war debt amounted to $771,190.
3. John W. Caughy, *California* (New Jersey: Prentice-Hall, Inc., 1940), p. 325. A Democrat Congressman remarked, "the three agents were entirely ignorant, not only of the country, but especially of the native and the habits of the Indians. The agents were to protect the people of California from the Indians."
4. *9 U.S. Stat. At. L.* (1850), 558.
5. U.S. Congress, *House Executive Documents, 1850*, Doc. 1, Serial 595, p. 152; U.S. Congress, Senate, *Department of Interior Report, 1853*, Doc. 4, Serial 688, pp. 8-9.
6. *9 U.S. State At. L.* (1850), 572; U.S. Congress, *Senate Executive Documents, 1853*, Doc. 61, Serial 620, pp. 1-2; Alban Hoopes, *Indian Affairs and Their Administration, 1849-1860* (Oxford, 1932), p. 44.
7. Serial 688, *op. cit.*, p. 52.

8.   *Ibid.*, p. 53; U.S. Congress, *Senate Miscellaneous Documents, 1866*, Doc. 37, Serial 1239, p. 1.
9.   William H. Ellison, "The Federal Indian Policy in California," *Mississippi Valley Historical Review*, IX, 48; Charles Coan, *Federal Indian Policy in The Pacific Northwest, 1849-1870* (Berkeley, 1920); Bancroft, *op. cit.*, VIII, 456; Hoopes, *op. cit.*, p. 42.
      Because of the high cost to subdue the Indians, the California Legislature authorized $1,100,000, as bond issues, payable semiannually, to liquidate the $924,295.65 debt accumulated fighting the Indians by 1854.
10.   *California Statutes* (1851), p. 530.
11.   Serial 688, *op. cit.*, p. 225; Chad L. Hoopes, "Fort Humboldt" (Master's Thesis, Brigham Young University, Provo, Utah, 1963), pp. 37-48.
12.   Hoopes, "Fort Humboldt," p. 43.
13.   *9 U.S. Stat. At. L.* (1851), p. 572.
      This act also provided $6,750 pay for each Commissioner from October 1, 1850 to June 30, 1851.
14.   *Ibid.*
15.   U.S. Congress, *Senate Executive Documents, 1852*, Doc. 16, Serial 613, p. 486.
16.   Serial 688, *op. cit.*, p. 82.
17.   Serial 613, *op. cit.*, p. 486.
18.   *Ibid.*, p. 497.
19.   Serial 688, *op. cit.*, p. 79.
      "Many Indians had been dispossessed of their old homes. These unfortunate victims of white man's land hunger and congressional inefficiency were poorly provided for by an appropriations of $50,000 until permanent arrangements be made for their future settlement." Hoopes, *op. cit.*, p. 46.
20.   Serial 688, *op. cit.*, p. 86.
21.   *Ibid.*, p. 91.
22.   *10 U.S. Stat. At. L.* (1852), p. 56.
23.   Serial 688, *op. cit.*, p. 120.
24.   Ellison, *op. cit.*, pp. 58-59; Hoopes, *op. cit.*, p. 46.
      In 1854, Congress allowed the claim of John C. Fremont for $183,825; in 1856 the claim of O.M. Wozencraft for $7,000; in 1860 the claim of Samuel J. Hensley for $96,276. Other claims were not allowed. And only part of McKee's claim was allowed.
25.   U.S. Congress, *House Miscellaneous Documents, 1871*, Doc. 102, Serial 1463, p. 4.
26.   U.S. Congress, *Senate Report, 1870*, Report 20, Serial 1409, pp. 1-3; U.S. Congress, *Senate Miscellaneous Documents, 1866*, Doc. 37, Serial 1239, pp. 1-3.
27.   Journal of Major W.W. Wessells in U.S. Congress, *Senate Executive Documents, 1853*, Doc. 76, Serial 906, pp. 59-68.
28.   The itinerary of McKee's expedition is shown on a map in the National Archives, No. 47—"Sketch of the Northwestern parts of California accompanying a journal of the expedition of Redick McKee, compiled by George Gibbs in 1851." Thomas Seabring had been a member of the Gregg party in 1850. He had attempted to return to Humboldt Bay the Spring of 1850 with wagons that he was forced to abandon along the route along the Eel and Russian rivers. This route became the Sonoma Trail and used extensively for opening the Humboldt Region.
29.   Henry R. Schoolcraft, *History, Condition and Prospects of the Indian Tribes of The United States, Part III* (Philadelphia, 1853), 99-177.
      George Gibbs' Journal of the McKee Expedition is in this volume. Gibbs was attached to the Indian Commission in Oregon and was acquainted with the Chinook language. He was also a practical topographical engineer.

30. Serial 613, *op. cit.*, p. 498.
31. John McKee's "Journal of Minutes" of the expedition from Sonoma through Northern California—August 9, 1851 to December 29, 1851. *Alta California* (San Francisco), September 3, 1851, "Account of The Doings of Major General Estill and his staff of The California State Militia."
32. Journal of Minutes, *op. cit.*, August 18, 1851.
33. The "Big Bend of the Eel River," according to the Gibbs' Map, was located in the present area of Fortuna, where Rohner Creek empties into the Eel River. McKee called it Communion Creek. M.A. Parry, "The History of Loleta" (Master's Thesis, Humboldt State College, June, 1963), pp. 1-4.
34. Journal of Minutes, *op. cit.*, September 11, 1851.
35. *Ibid.*, September 12, 1851.
36. Journal of Minutes, *op. cit.*, September 16, 1851.
     The George Gibbs' Map gives a clear outline of the reservation plat.
37. Journal of Minutes, *op. cit.*, September 16-17, 1851.
     The Journal gives the details of the three men's duties.
38. Journal of Minutes, *op. cit.*, September 18, 1851.
39. *Ibid.*, November 4, 1851.
40. Schoolcraft, *op. cit.*, p. 177.
41. Serial 688, *op. cit.*, p. 284.
42. Rockwell D. Hunt, *California and Californians* (San Francisco, 1930), II, 448.
43. Serial 688, *op. cit.*, p. 248.
44. *Congressional Globe*, 33rd Congress, 1st Session, Pt. 3, p. 2173.
45. Serial 688, *op. cit.*, p. 296.
46. *Ibid.*, p. 308.
     McKee wrote to President Fillmore, "My opinion is, that unless our general policy is carried out in good faith, there will very shortly be a general Indian war on the frontiers of the state. The Indians must be fed for awhile or killed off." California, *Journal of the Senate, 1852*, pp. 44-64.
47. *Ibid.*, p. 329.
48. *10 U.S. Stat. At. L.*
     In January, 1905, the injunction to secrecy of the Treaties was removed. The unratified treaties had quietly reposed in the archives of Congress, forgotten by everyone but the Indians. At present, all eighteen of them are in a bundle in the Office of Indian Affairs, General Files, California, I 76/1852. Clipped to each treaty is a letter of rejection by the Senate. Hoopes, *op. cit.*, p. 44.
49. U.S. Congress, *Senate Executive Documents, 1852.* "President's Annual Message, December 6, 1852. Serial 673, p. 10.
50. Serial 688, *op. cit.*, p. 360.
51. *Journal of the Legislature of the State of California, 1852*, pp. 21-74.
52. *Ibid.*, pp. 537-604.
53. *Ibid.*, pp. 703-704.
54. *Ibid.*, p. 705.
55. *Alta California*, March 21, 1853.
56. *Journal of California Legislature, 1852*, p. 708.
57. Serial 688, *op. cit.*, p. 318.
     This suggestion evolved to the birth of Fort Humboldt and many smaller camps and posts, supplied by Fort Humboldt.
58. *Journal of California Legislature*, 1852, p. 711.
59. Copied from the original letter dated January 15, 1852, Mendocino Valley and addressed to "Fellow Citizens and People of Union town and Humboldt Bay." Clark Museum, Eureka, California.
60. Theodore H. Hittell, *History of California* (San Francisco, 1852), 708.
61. *Journal of California Legislature*, 1852, pp. 396-397.
62. Serial 688, *op. cit.*, p. 274. Hoopes, *op. cit.*, pp. 47-68.

FIGURE 3-1. Humboldt City. Courtesy Humboldt County Historical Society.

CHAPTER

4

Bret Harte in Union
(1857-1860)

Lynwood Carranco

Although he was born in New York State and lived most of his life there and in Europe, Bret Harte is remembered as the man who made the West a favorite realm of fiction. As a young man he went to California, had a brief experience as a miner, and then became a San Francisco journalist. His real fame came while he was editor of *The Overland Monthly*, and it was in this periodical that his most popular works first appeared.

"The Luck of Roaring Camp" made an immediate appeal, and it is still the favorite among his stories. Not only was it one of the first literary presentations of a colorful section of the country, but it exploited the popular conception that rough exteriors hide hearts of gold. Harte's other two successful stories followed this formula of nobility coming out in desperate characters. The sacrificial deaths of a prostitute and a gambler are told in "The Outcasts of Poker Flat," and in "Tennessee's Partner" Harte relates the beautiful friendship between a highway robber and his rough partner.

Where did he get much of his information and background for his stories? Union—now Arcata, Humboldt County—was the town in Northern California where Bret Harte spent three years—1857 to 1860. This period has been described as the "Three Lost Years of Bret Harte's Life."[1] Here in Union Harte gained much experience in writing and frontier life, but for the remainder of his life he cared little to discuss this part of his life because of the unfortunate circumstances which had occurred.

At the age of twenty-one Harte came by steamer to Union from San Francisco to see his sister, Margaret Wyman.[2] The settlement, numbering approximately five hundred inhabitants, was called Union or Uniontown, although later in March, 1860, the name would be changed to Arcata. The town stood at the northern end of Humboldt Bay, snuggled against the first ridge of the Coast Mountains, and in

1857—only seven years removed from the wilderness—consisted of one brick building and many of wood. There were the usual dirt streets, a church or two, stores, saloons, and a long pier extending out across the tide flats. A few tall redwoods stood in the outskirts, and some great stumps—ten to fourteen feet in diameter—studded the town. To the south were the mud flats and the bay. On the other sides there was a narrow fringe of cleared land and beyond that one of the most magnificent forests in the world—unbroken miles of gigantic redwoods.

There were some logging, farming, and cattle raising in the vicinity, but the town really existed as a point of reshipment. Goods were unloaded from the steamers and forwarded by pack train to the populous mining district on the Trinity River.[3] This traffic, however, was already declining and the town was threatened with ruin because shippers had discovered a cheaper route by way of Red Bluff, the head of navigation on the Sacramento River.[4]

The people of Union were a varied group. Indians lounged about, peaceful and dirty, demoralized by the sudden disruption of their normal life. Rough cattlemen and mule packers loitered in the saloons. Miners passed through on their way to the mines, or came to town to spend their gold on a drunk. There was also a small class of stable and respectable people who carried on the business and professional life, went to church, sent their children to school, attended the Lyceum debates, and worked toward the establishment of a civilized community.

What were the conditions in this rugged country of northwestern California? The struggle between the Indian and the white man was long and bloody and raged from 1851 to 1865. The peak of the Indian "wars" in Northern California was reached during the Civil War, and did not come to a climax until 1865.

The frontier has always had a noble, vigorous, intelligent, hardy pioneer population, but at the same time it has had a mean, shiftless, ignorant, vicious, and treacherous element of brutes, who boasted that they were white men and were armed ready to back up their assertions. This class on all our frontiers has been the main cause of many of the Indian troubles, and Humboldt County was no exception. They ran rough-shod over all the Indians' rights: they stole and outraged his women, and they shot him down if he raised the slightest objection. Some Indian tribes had vigor enough to resent such mistreatment and took revenge. In such cases innocent whites often suffered severely for their inability to control the vicious element of their own race.

Here in Humboldt County the Indians made but little resistance, yet were frequently killed for the most trivial of causes. Not only was there the occasional killing of small numbers of Indians, but between 1850 and 1873 a considerable number of slaughters, either by state troops or by unauthorized "volunteer companies," occurred on such a scale as to be dignified by the term of "Indian Wars."[5]

A common practice of these companies was to make a daybreak attack on some Indian rancheria and kill all its inhabitants without regard to age or sex, unless perhaps they spared one or two of the younger females of pleasing appearance to take along with them.

Often a few men followed these companies for the special purpose of taking possession of young women or children whose parents were killed, and selling them in the centers of population either for immoral purposes or as servants.[6] According to a state law Indians could be made apprentices or indentured to citizens for terms of ten to fifteen years. It may or may not have been intended for the good of the Indians to teach them the arts of civilization, but in practice it encouraged the kidnapping and sanctioned virtual slavery for the young and able-bodied, while the old and worn-out were left to shift for themselves.

Humboldt County had its full share of hunters, cattle thieves, and kidnappers; and several campaigns, similar to examples given, were conducted in the Bald Hills—northeast of Humboldt Bay—during the years from 1858 to 1864. These campaigns led to the undoing of the Wiyot or Coast Indians who lived on the land in and around the bay.

The Indians in the mountains east of the bay were described as having more spirit than the Indians about Humboldt Bay. These Indians committed depredations in order to survive. The Americans had slaughtered their game, and then had brought cattle to their prairies which ate up their supply of seeds for food.

Campaigns by volunteer companies, state troops, and federal troops continued for several years against the Bald Hills Indians because of their depredations on the stock. Prisoners were taken to the reservations and starved and abused until they returned to their native haunts, only to be chased off again to some reservation in a fresh campaign.

Reports can be found of one white man on the Van Duzen River who boasted of having killed sixty infants with his own hatchet at different slaughtering grounds.[7] This vicious white man was a leader and model of a certain class of settlers on the Van Duzen and Eel rivers, just south of Eureka. These men not only went about the

country attacking villages at early dawn and slaughtering the inhabitants of all ages and sexes, but they threatened and terrorized their
more peaceable white neighbors.[8] The sheriff and the editor of the
Humboldt *Times* of Eureka, the county seat, were their friends; and
they became so bold that certain of their number threatened to
"clean out" the small number of federal sodiers who had been sent
to Eel River in answer to a petition of the better class of citizens
desiring protection for both themselves and the friendly Indians.[9]

Such were the conditions between the whites and Indians when
Bret Harte lived in Union. Charles A Murdock recalled their association at that time:

> He was twenty one and I was sixteen, so there was little intimacy, but he
> interested and attracted me as a new type of manhood. He bore the marks of
> good breeding, education, and refinement. He was quiet of manner, kindly, but
> not demonstrative, with a certain reserve and aloofness. He was of medium
> height rather slight of figure, with strongly marked features and an aquiline
> nose. . . . He had a very pleasant voice . . . and never talked of himself. . . . He
> was dressed in good taste, but was evidently in need of income. He was willing to
> do anything. . . . He was simply untrained for doing anything that needed doing
> in that community.[10]

At first Harte found occasional work in the drugstore, and for a
time he had a small private school. He had little mechanical ability,
according to Murdock, who recalled an incident: "He bravely dug
postholes, but they were pretty poor, and the completed fence was
not very straight."[11] Harte was an agreeable guest, and was fond of
playing whist. He also had a sense of humor. One day while Harte
and Murdock were walking together, they passed a new house "des-
titute of all ornaments or trimming" which resembled a packing box.
"That," Harte remarked, "must be of the Iowan order of architecture."[12]

In October, 1857, he went to the Liscom ranch in the "bottom" at the head of the bay and became the tutor of two boys,
fourteen and thirteen years of age. He had a forenoon session of
school and in the afternoon enjoyed hunting on the near-by sloughs.
For his convenience in keeping lessons he kept a brief diary. George
R. Stewart, in his biography, *Bret Harte Argonaut and Exile*, reveals
most of the important information.[13] The diary is of interest both in
the little he recorded and from the significant omissions. It shows a
very simple life of a young man who did his work, enjoyed his
outdoor recreation, read a few good books, and generally "retired by
9:30 p.m." His entries were brief and practical, and he did not write
to express his feelings.

Socially, Harte continued to enjoy himself and to get along well. He was not popular with the rougher part of the population. His diary shows that he liked to drink whiskey with his friends in their homes, but he did not patronize the saloons and drink with the cattlemen and packers. Because of this they sneered at his fine clothes and thought him a snob as well as effeminate. But Harte had many friends among the leading citizens: Charles Murdock admired him, and he was a welcome guest at the home of Alexander Brizard, whose trading posts were scattered throughout the mountainous country of Humboldt County.[14]

In 1858 the leading citizens of Union began to view with alarm the decline of their town and the advance of its rival, Eureka, eight miles to the south. Union had enjoyed the early lead among the Humboldt Bay towns. The first consideration had been the facility in supplying the mines on the Trinity and the Klamath rivers. All goods were transported by pack trains, and the trails over the mountains were nearer the head of the bay. Lumber soon became the leading industry, and the mills at Eureka were on deep water at the center of the bay, making that the natural shipping point. Two years before, Eureka had captured the county seat; now the county's only newspaper followed. The people of Union decided that they needed some type of journal to make up for the lost Humboldt *Times*, for even a small weekly would increase their town's prestige and give publicity to the project of a wagon road to the Trinity River, which might restore to Union the reshipment trade. Colonel S.G. Whipple and Albert Hamilton Murdock founded *The Northern Californian*, a small four-page country weekly, which had a brief but colorful existence. The office was in a small frame building facing the Plaza which was approximately in the center of town.[15]

Bret Harte at twenty-two was hired as a printer's devil, but later began to help with the editorial work. Murdock told how this happened:

My father was a half owner, and I coveted the humble position of printer's devil. One journeyman could set the type, and on Wednesday and Saturday respectively, run off on a handpress the outside and inside of the paper, but a boy or a low-priced man was needed to roll the forms and likewise to distribute the type. I looked upon it as the first rung on the ladder of journalism, and I was about to put my foot thereon when the pathetic figure of Bret Harte presented itself applying for the job, causing me to put my foot on my hopes instead. He seemed to want it and need it so much more than I did that I turned my hand to other pursuits, while he mounted the ladder with cheerful alacrity and skipped up several rungs, very promptly learning to set type and becoming a very acceptable assistant editor.[16]

⟨Within a year Harte was almost an associate editor, since Colonel Whipple had to leave often on business. Harte was left in full charge and accepted the responsibility willingly. He was very happy in his surroundings, and he wrote constantly. While much of his writings during this time was unsigned, it can easily be identified by one familiar with his style.[17] And across the stage of this frontier town passed the miners, the gamblers, the traders, the prostitutes—the outcasts.

Harte's peaceful writing days on the paper were suddenly interrupted in a dramatic manner. Harte was left in charge when Colonel Whipple went to San Francisco on business trips. Whipple left for San Francisco again at the end of February, 1860, leaving Harte in charge as usual. There had been disturbing news from Eureka on Sunday, and on Monday the Colonel stopping there en route sent back a report for the paper. What had happened was the climactic act of barbarity and inhumanity on the part of a half dozen vicious whites from the southern part of the country.

From the earliest times of settlment in California and Oregon, Indians had been killed for the most trivial of causes. All the newspapers during the years previous to 1860 teemed with the words "annihilation" and "extermination."[18] The popular doctrine of Manifest Destiny supported this philosophy. This meant that the Anglo-Saxons—the chosen people—should kill the original inhabitants and possess the land.

The Indians had their friends among the newspapers as well as among individual whites, and these people tried to protect the Indians. On the other hand there were newspapers that openly advocated extermination. These poisoned public opinion by developing race prejudice and charging every possible crime against the Indians. Thus shielded and encouraged, the rougher element among the whites gradually went from bad to worse.

The storekeepers and stable townspeople remained on good terms with the peaceful Wiyot Indians, but back in the mountainous country both whites and Indians were growing bitter and violent in action. The sight of an occasional murdered settler gave the cattlemen and the general riffraff of the frontier ample excuse for shooting Indians.

The Wiyot tribe on the coast were harmless, but were thought to be allied with the belligerent mountain tribes. Nevertheless, an Indian was an Indian. There was a large ranchería of peaceful Indians on an island—now called Gunther Island—separated from the town of Eureka by only a narrow channel. At the end of February the inhabitants of the island and nearby rancherías celebrated a religious festival which called for a three-day feast and a dance. At the end of the ordeal the exhausted Indians lay down to sleep.

About four o'clock Sunday morning five or six men came to the island armed with guns, hatchets, and knives. The tired Indians were caught sleeping in their houses. Mercilessly the men used their hatchets on the old and young: women, children, and infants. The men knew—apparently for religious reasons—that most of the men had left the island. Their work was rapid and efficient. They killed approximately sixty Indians, mostly women and children, either sleeping or attempting to escape.[19] Two other rancherías, one on the South Beach near the entrance to the bay and one near the mouth of Eel River, were visited on the same night, in the same stealthy manner and with the same result. This was the famous massacre of February 26, 1860, reports of which were even printed in the newspapers of New York City.

When Colonel Whipple sent back his report and continued on to San Francisco, he placed Harte in a desperate situation. Harte did not visit the island which could be seen from Union, but he saw the mangled corpses unloaded from canoes as the remnant of the Mad River Indians passed through Union bearing home their dead. He was shocked when he saw the brutally mutilated bodies, and it made him furious to think that people of his own race could be such barbarians.

The excitement was intense. Could Harte publish what he felt? In the absence of his boss, he could decline to comment editorially on the shocking event. The massacre was on Sunday, and the paper was to appear on Wednesday. Harte knew the situation: he could expect some support from the townspeople, but the packers, miners, cattlemen, and loggers disliked the Indians and cared little for him. And the rougher element would not hesitate to shoot or lynch a writer who dared to oppose them.

On February 29 *The Northern Californian* left no doubt of what Harte thought of the massacre and its perpetrators. He bitterly attacked the whites responsible for the outrage. In bold type he headed his editorial:

INDISCRIMINATE MASSACRE OF INDIANS
WOMEN AND CHILDREN BUTCHERED[20]

The names of the murderers were not mentioned in the account, but the words used left no doubt of Harte's feelings:

Our Indian troubles have reached a crisis. Today we record acts of Indian
aggression and white retaliation. It is a humiliating fact that the parties who may
be supposed to represent white civilization have committed the greater barbarity. But before we review the causes that have led to this crowning act of
reckless desperation, let us remind the public at a distance from this savage-
ridden district, that the secrecy of this indiscriminate massacre is an evidence of
its disavowal and detestation by the community. The perpetrators are yet unknown.

The friendly Indians about the bay have been charged with conveying arms
and ammunition to the mountain tribes, and receiving slaughtered beef as a
reward. A class of hard-working men who derive their subsistence by cattle
raising have been the greatest sufferers, and if in the blind fury of retaliation
they spare neither age or sex, though they cannot be excused, a part of the
blame should fall upon that government which places the responsibility of self
defense on the injured party. . . . If the deed was committed by responsible
parties, we will give place to any argument that may be offered in justification.
But we cannot conceive of no palliation for women and child slaughter. We can
conceive of no wrong that a babe's blood can atone for. Perhaps we do not
rightly understand the doctrine of "extermination." . . . What amount of suffer-
ing it takes to make a man a babe-killer, is a question for future moralists. What
will justify it, should be a question of present law. . . . An "irrepressible conflict" is really here. Knowing this, was the policy to commence the work of
extermination with the *most peaceful?* And what assistance can be expected
from a legislature already perplexed with doubts and suspicion, in the face of the
bloody record we today publish? . . . But when the facts were generally known,
it appeared that out of some 60 or 70 killed on the Island, at least 50 or 60 were
women and children. Neither age or sex had been spared. Little children and old
women were mercilessly stabbed and their skulls crushed with axes. When the
bodies were landed at Union, a more shocking and revolting spectacle never was
exhibited to the eyes of a Christian and civilized people. Old Women wrinkled
and decrepit lay weltering in blood, their brains dashed out and dabbled with
their long grey hair. Infants scarce a span long, with their faces cloven with
hatchets and their bodies ghastly with wounds. We gathered from the survivors
that four or five white men attacked the ranches at about four o'clock in the
morning, which statement is corroborated by people at Eureka who heard pistol
shots at about the same time, although no knowledge of the attack was public.
With the Indians who lived on the Island, some thirty from the mouth of Mad
River were staying, having attended a dance the evening previous. They were all
killed with the exception of some few who hid themselves during the massacre.
No resistance was made, it is said, to the butchers who did the work, but as they
ran or huddled together for protection like sheep, they were struck with hatchets. Very little shooting was done, most of the bodies having wounds about the
head. The bucks were mostly absent, which accounts for the predominance of
female victims.

On Monday we received a statement from our Senior, at Eureka en route
for San Francisco. He says that about nine o'clock he visited the Island, and
there a horrible scene was presented. The bodies of 36 women and children,
recently killed, lay in and near the several ranches. They were of all ages from
the child of but two or three years to the old skeleton squaw. From appearances
most of them must have been killed with axes or hatchets—as the heads and

bodies of many were gashed, as with such an instrument. It was a sickening and pitiful sight. Some five or six were still alive and one old woman was able to talk, though dreadfully wounded. Dr. Lee visited them and dressed the wounds of those alive. . . . It is not generally known that more than three bucks were killed, though it is supposed there must have been 15 or 20. It is thought that the bodies of the men were taken away by Indians early this morning as four canoes were seen to leave the Island.

On the beach south of the entrance it is reported that from 30 to 50 were killed. It is also reported, that at Bucksport, all were killed that were there. I passed in sight of them about 11 o'clock and saw the ranches on fire. It is also said that the same has been done at the several ranches on Eel river.

No one seems to know who was engaged in this slaughter, but is supposed to have been men who have suffered from depredations so long on the Eel river and vicinity.

Indian Island is scarcely one mile from Eureka the County seat of Humboldt County. With the exception of the conjectures that the Indians on this Island offer aid and assistance to mountain Indians, they are peaceful and industrious, and seem to have perfect faith in the good will of the whites. Many of them are familiar to our citizens. "Bill," of Mad river,[21] a well-known and intelligent fellow, has proven a faithful ally to the white men on several occasions and has had his wife, mother, sister, two brothers, and two little children cruelly butchered by men of that race whom he had learned to respect and esteem.[22]

It was never publicly known who the white men were who were engaged in the crime, since none were brought to trial. Many were suspected, but they were shielded by persons of position and authority. No one dared to accuse these men openly. The most that was ever done to promote justice was the writing of numerous anonymous letters to the San Francisco newspapers. From these letters it appeared that some of the murderers were from the Eel River region and some were members of Seaman Wright's Company of Volunteers.[23]

An incident which occurred three days later did not help Bret Harte's situation. This was an article on the massacre which was published in The Humboldt *Times* in Eureka. The editor, Austin Wiley, was prejudiced against the Indians, and he wrote the following:

There are men in this county, as there may be elsewhere, where the Government allows these degraded diggers to roam at large, and plunder and murder without restraint, who have been perfectly desperate, and we have here some of the fruits of that desperation. They have friends or relatives cruelly and savagely butchered, their homes made desolate, and their hard-earned property destroyed by these sneaking, cowardly wretches; and when an attempt is made to hunt them from hiding places in the mountains, to administer punishment upon them, they escape to the friendly ranches on the coast for protection. When appeals are made for aid in protecting their lives and property, they are met by contumely and reproach. Their brethren in other parts of the State, many of whom approve of hanging up white men without "due process of law" for much less crimes than these diggers have committed, heap ridicule upon them and shed crocodile tears over the "poor Indians."[24]

Colonel Whipple, who hurried back to Union, found it impossible to stem the tide rising against his associate who dared to take the part of the Indians against the whites. Within a month Harte left Union for San Francisco. There can be little doubt that he probably departed by request. There are many stories which cannot be documented. One popular story in Arcata which old timers still tell is that he waited with two pistols for a mob that was going to lynch him. Another story is that a troop of United States Cavalry arrived just in time to drag Harte from the vengeance of a mob who were going to lynch him.[25] Charles A. Murdock, the best source, mentioned that "Harte was seriously threatened and in no little danger."[26] On March 26, 1860, Harte left Union and Humboldt County on the steamer *Columbia.*[27]

On March 28, Editor Whipple printed the following in his editorial column:

Mr. F.B. Harte—This young gentleman, who has been engaged in this office from the commencement of the paper, left for San Francisco a few days ago, where he intends to reside in the future. In addition to being a printer, Mr. Harte is a good writer. He has often contributed to the columns of this paper, and at different times when we have been absent, has performed the editorial labors. He is a warm-hearted, genial companion, and a gentleman in every sense of the word. We wish our friend, the success to which his talents entitle him, and cordially commend him to the fraternity of the Bay City.[28]

Harte profited by his experiences here in Arcata, gaining the local color which was different from that of the Sierra foothills. His newspaper experience was a great advantage to him because he had learned a trade in which there was a demand. When Harte returned to San Francisco from Arcata, he obtained employment with *The Golden Era* as a typesetter, and within a few weeks began to contribute. This magazine became the doorway to his career. He later joined the *Californian* where he became the star contributor.

In 1868 Anton Roman, a San Francisco bookseller and publisher, selected Harte editor of *The Overland Monthly*, a new magazine to be written entirely by local talent.[29] "The Luck of Roaring Camp," "The Outcasts of Poker Flat," and "Tennessee's Partner," the best stories that he was ever to write and the ones responsible for his reputation to this day, were printed in this magazine.

NOTES

1. Sophie Whipple Root, "Three Lost Years of Bret Harte's Life," *The Over-land Monthly* (October, 1932), p. 229. Mrs. Root's father was Colonel S.G. Whipple, one of the founders of *The Northern Californian*, the news-paper for which Bret Harte worked at Union, now Arcata.
2. Charles A. Murdock, *A Backward Glance at Eighty*, p. 73.
3. The Humboldt *Times*, October 4, 18, 1856.
4. Isaac Cox, *The Annals of Trinity County*, pp. 29-30.
5. Hubert Howe Bancroft, *History of California*, XXIV, 477, says that California "cannot grace her annals with a single Indian war bordering on respectability. It can boast, however, a hundred or two of as brutal butcherings, on the part of our honest miners and brave pioneers, as any area of equal extent in our republic."
6. San Francisco *Bulletin*, July 23, 1857.
7. *Ibid.*, March 13, June 1, and June 4, 1860.
8. *Ibid.*, June 1, 1860.
9. *Ibid.*, March 13, 30, 1860.
10. Murdock, *op. cit.*, p. 73.
11. *Ibid.*
12. *Ibid.*, p. 74.
13. George R. Stewart, *Bret Harte Argonaut and Exile*, pp. 61-83.
14. Root, *op. cit.*, p. 246.
15. *Ibid.*, 229.
16. Murdock, *op. cit.*, p. 76.
17. George R. Stewart made a study of his writing in *A Bibliography of the Writings of Bret Harte in the Magazines and Newspapers of California 1857-1871*, published by the University of California Press in 1933.
18. As early as October 1852, the Superintendent of Indian Affairs in California recommended to the government the quartering of troops on the reservations for the protection of the Indians against lawless whites. General E.A. Hitchcock, commander of the Department of the Pacific, endorsed the plan as "perhaps the only one calculated to prevent the extermination of the Indians." See 33 Cong. spec. sess., serial no. 688, doc. 4, p. 377.
19. Owen C. Coy, in *The Humboldt Bay Region 1850-1875*, said that Gunther, the owner of the island, in his *Autobiography, MS.*, repeated the report given by others, but later said that there were probably forty killed on the island. A.J. Bledsoe, in *Indian Wars of the Northwest*, used the files of The Humboldt *Times*, and he placed the total number killed at 250. Hittell, in *California III*, followed Bledsoe's account. In 1916 Lucy Thompson, a full-blood Yurok of Pekwon, published in Eureka a little-known book called *To the American Indian*. In the book she mentioned that the massacre nearly exterminated the large tribe, and that in 1916 there were not more than twenty of the Wiyot Indians living. Llewellyn L. Loud, in *Ethnogeography and Archaeology of the Wiyot Territory*, used the files of the San Francisco *Bulletin*. He stated that "nobody ever knew with any exactness the precise number killed on the island," and he quoted Editor Whipple's report as written by Bret Harte.
20. *The Northern Californian*, February 29, 1860.
21. Mad River Bill was the son of "Old Mauweema," the leading Indian of the village north of Arcata on the bend of Mad River. He was honored with a burial in the Arcata cemetery when he died in 1918 at the age of seventy-six. The community endeavored to pay back the debts due him for what he had suffered.

22. *The Northern Californian*, February 29, 1860.
23. Llewellyn L. Loud, *Ethnogeography and Archaeology of the Wiyot Territory*, p. 332.
24. The Humboldt *Times*, March 3, 1860.
25. Root, *op. cit.*, p. 249.
26. Murdock, *op. cit.*, p. 77.
27. Stewart, *Bibliography of Writings of Bret Harte*, p. 139.
28. *The Northern Californian*, March 28, 1860.
29. Franklin Walker, *San Francisco's Literary Frontier*, p. 259.

FIGURE 4-1. An early picture of Arcata about 1885—twenty-five years after Bret Harte was forced to leave town. *Ericson Photo.*

FIGURE 4-2. The issue in which Harte wrote his controversial editorial. Courtesy of The Huntington Library, San Marino, California.

88

Figure 4-3. Bret Harte shortly after his meteoric rise to fame. Courtesy of the Society of California Pioneers.

CHAPTER

5

Two Men and a Mill

H. Brett Melendy

The California redwood lumber industry is one of the oldest industries in the state and yet one that has been largely ignored by the state's historians. This industry has been an important contributor to the economy of California for over one hundred years; the uniqueness of its product and its location makes its history a fascinating story. Because of the habitat of the coast redwood, the *Sequoia sempervirens*, the industry has been confined to northern California coastal counties. Since 1850 many men have tried to launch careers as mill men but only a few have succeeded. Two such successful entrepreneurs were John Dolbeer and William Carson. Together they overcame the stupendous obstacles of moving the red giants from the woods to the mill. There they solved the problem of finding equipment sufficiently strong to handle the gigantic logs. They were also successful in finding suitable markets for their lumber throughout the Pacific area.

These two men and their mill are representative of that handful who were successful in the redwood lumber industry in the last half of the nineteenth century and the early years of the twentieth century. In following their career and the company that they founded, one can gain an insight into the complex problems that faced all who attempted to establish themselves in the redwood industry, particularly in the three coastal counties of Del Norte, Humboldt, and Mendocino.

John Dolbeer and William Carson became partners in 1864, forming the Dolbeer & Carson Lumber Company.[1] This organization lasted until 1950. Its beginnings and its life span much of the industry's first one hundred years. Both Dolbeer and Carson were already old hands in the business of producing redwood lumber by 1864. Their joining forces was one of those happy circumstances which proved to be mutually beneficial.

John Dolbeer, the senior partner, was born in Epsom, New Hampshire, March 23, 1827. He arrived in California with other gold seekers in 1850. He joined a rush then underway to the Gold Bluffs along the coastline just north of Redwood Creek in Humboldt County during 1851.[2] In August, 1853, he made his first connection with the Humboldt Bay redwood industry when he joined Martin White, Isaac J. Upton, Dan Pickard, and C.W. Long to form the Bay Mill, which was located below the bluff at the foot of what is now N Street in Eureka.[3]

Martin White, the moving spirit of this enterprise, was an important figure in the history of the industry, for it was he who built the first sawmill, the Pioneer, on Humboldt Bay in September, 1850, at the foot of what is now M Street at Second Street. This first mill was operated until 1855.[4] White was also instrumental in organizing seven Humboldt Bay mills into the Humboldt Lumber Manufacturing Company in 1854 to solve the common problem of how to sell lumber at a profit. Unfortunately this organization immediately ran headlong into a declining lumber market and was soon in financial difficulty. Most of the mill owners, including Martin White, lost their holdings.[5]

The Bay Mill was one of the seven mills involved in the collapse of the ill-fated association. However, there appeared to be some irregularity in the actual transferring of the Bay Mill property to the association and John Dolbeer, alone, was able to retain his holdings in that mill while the other partners lost their shares.

The Bay Mill in 1854 was typical of the several sawmills located on Humboldt Bay. It had one sash saw, a rip saw mounted vertically in a frame. It could produce 15,000 feet of lumber and 6,000 laths daily. The mill employed ten men in its operations. According to the *Humboldt Times*, its capital investment was $25,000.[6]

By 1856 the Bay Mill had weathered the storm occasioned by the failure of the Humboldt Lumber Manufacturing Company, and Dolbeer had allied himself with Charles McLean. McLean became the San Francisco partner of the firm; it was his job to take care of securing orders for the mill at Eureka. The two men made their venture a successful one. It prospered for it was not involved in costly litigation to clear its title as were the other mills of the defunct Humboldt Lumber Manufacturing Company.[7] On September 2, 1860, the Bay Mill was destroyed by fire. (Fire was always one of the big hazards of the industry and it was doubly costly. Not only were mills and their stock destroyed, but these early ones were not covered by insurance, as the rates were prohibitive.) This fire was

called the first big mill fire of the county by the *Humboldt Times.*
By September 22, Dolbeer had started reconstruction. He seized the
opportunity to bring his equipment up-to-date, installing a double
circular saw head rig. This was the first use of such equipment in the
county, and one of the first on the coast. The new mill was in
operation by November, 1860.[8]

In 1863 a not too common occurrence took place on the bar of
Humboldt Bay when the tug *Merrimac*, on its way from San Fran-
cisco, capsized and sank. Among those drowned was Charles
McLean.[9] The death of McLean left Dolbeer again without a partner.
It was at this time that the partnership was offered to William
Carson, who purchased McLean's half-interest in the Bay Mill. The
next year the new organization, the Dolbeer & Carson Lumber Com-
pany, came into being.[10]

William Carson was born near Saint John, New Brunswick. It
was in this region that he became acquainted with the lumber trade.
He, too, joined the rush to California, arriving at Humboldt Bay in
October, 1850. Both Carson and Dolbeer present a common picture
of what happened to many of the gold seekers. Upon arrival in San
Francisco or after only a short visit to the gold fields, many men, like
Carson and Dolbeer, became convinced that prospecting was a most
difficult and uncertain livelihood and turned shortly to their former
occupations. In the fall of 1850, Martin White was busy building his
Pioneer Mill and Carson obtained the contract to supply logs for that
mill. In November he established a logging camp on Ryan Slough and
cut the first log on Humboldt Bay which was sawn into lumber.
These first logs were spruce. The first years of the redwood lumber
industry saw selective logging practiced because the primitive mills
could not handle large logs. For the first two or three years at
Humboldt Bay redwood was not commonly logged because of its
size. Those logs that were sent to the mills were split with black
powder in order that the saws could handle them. In March, 1851,
Carson set out for the Trinity mines but returned to Eureka in 1852.
In 1853 Carson, J.T. Ryan of the Eureka Mill, and Colonel W.H.
Kingsburg of the Modena Mill were members of a committee to
decide upon a uniform scale for sawlogs. The adopted scale was
designed for spruce, fir, pine, and redwood, the major timber species
of the redwood area. With the advent of logging of redwood timber
in great quantities, this scale became very important to the early
loggers. It remained in vogue for many years.

In the summer of 1854, William Carson leased the Mula Mill,
which was located at the foot of I Street at the bay's edge. His

enterprise here shows the great efforts that many of these men made to gain success. He not only managed the mill's several operations, but also served as head sawyer every day and on alternate night shifts. It was through his work at the Mula Mill that the first redwood logs were successfully cut and sawn into lumber. The first cargo of redwood, priced to sell at $12.50 per thousand, was shipped from this mill under Carson's direction. In 1855 he gave up the Mula Mill and leased the Vance Mill at the foot of G Street. The next few years saw him working in various lumber activities until he became Dolbeer's partner at the Bay Mill.[11]

Following the announcement of the partnership, Dolbeer and Carson hastened to timberlands in the Elk River area. The heavy investment in mill equipment and logging equipment meant that a firm had to be assured of long life if the owners were to make a profit in their venture and long life in the redwood industry was closely tied up with the size of one's timber holdings. It was commonly believed that a mill needed from twenty to thirty years of standing redwood timber to insure success. By 1875, the partners had bought up the heavily forested area of Lindsay Creek, five miles north of Humboldt Bay.[12]

Ordinary mill equipment, common throughout the rest of the country, was ill-suited to the handling of the giant redwood logs. Thus, during the first decades of their existence, the redwood mills underwent a time of trial and error as the owners tried to find adequate machinery that could stand up under the burden of the heavy logs. Owen C. Coy pictures some of the difficulties that these early mills faced in sawing the large logs, and cites the example of two logs handled at the Bay Mill. They were twelve feet and fourteen feet respectively in length and from eight to nine feet in diameter. These two logs produced 11,000 board feet of clear lumber.[13] Translated into dollars and the prices of that era, the lumber from those logs sold for about $1,700, which was a high gross return. It was this opportunity for seemingly high profit that lured many men into the redwood region. The inherent risks remained hidden to most lumbermen until they were too deeply involved. Only the persevering survived.

In 1878 fire destroyed the second Bay Mill. In planning the rebuilding job, Dolbeer and Carson secured the services of an outstanding millwright, David Evans. Evans was one of the giants in the redwood industry in the Humboldt Bay area. He had invented a special headrig which utilized circular saws in such a manner as to enable the mills to cut logs of very large diameter. On the ordinary double circular saw headrig, the diameter of a log that could be sawn was limited by the distance between the axles of the two circular saws. In 1869 Evans had invented his "third saw" process by which two small circular saws were placed at right angles to each other and suspended above and ahead of the two major circular saws to cut off the top of the log as the main body was fed through the larger saws.[14] Evans designed and rebuilt the Bay Mill with his special third saw headrig installed. The next year saw the installation of gas lights at the mill, which made it the first in the county with such a facility. The *Humboldt Times* said the new mill was "complete in every respect."[15]

Dolbeer and Carson expanded their Humboldt County lumbering activities in 1878 when William Carson purchased the Salmon Creek mill at a sheriff's sale for $23,650.[16] This mill, located near the southern end of Humboldt Bay, had been one of David Evans' several ventures that had come to naught. It was to prove a good investment for Dolbeer and Carson. On February 11, 1879, the partners filed articles of incorporation under the name of the Milford Land and Lumber Company. Control of the mill was divided between the two, with Carson holding 406 shares while Dolbeer had 250.[17] The Milford name was chosen to avoid confusion with the Salmon Creek Mill Company, then operating in Mendocino County. The Milford mill was capable of producing about 45,000 feet a day with its standard double circular headrig.

During the first thirty years of the industry, most of the logs had been cut near tidewater or along river banks. As a result, log drives of various sorts were utilized. (Here again is a reflection of the loggers' experiences in the forests of eastern North America.) The redwood logs had such a high water content that many simply sank to the bottom of the river and stayed there. Nevertheless with the primitive mills of that period, a sufficient quantity of redwood logs and logs of other species did reach the saws. As the mills improved their sawing techniques, there were heavier demands to move the logs at a faster rate. Thus the railroad came into fairly common usage during the late 1870's and the 1880's. The next pressure felt by the industry was to find some means by which logs could be moved from the woods to the railheads more quickly.

It was in this phase of redwood logging that the ability of John Dolbeer came to the fore. One of his talents was mechanical aptitude. His skill was shown in May, 1863, when he applied for a patent on a mechanical tallying machine to count the number of board feet cut by the mill for any given length of time.[18] And it was Dolbeer

who created the first invention that enabled the redwood logging
crews to keep up with the mills and the railroad. The Dolbeer Steam
Logging Donkey made its appearance in August, 1881, and totally
revolutionized logging in the United States. It paved the way to
modern logging, replacing man power with machine power for the
heavy task of moving the logs through the forests. The donkey was
able to pull in logs from the ravines and hillsides to be arranged so
that the oxen teams could move the string of logs to the railhead.
The first Dolbeer donkey had an upright boiler with a horizontal
single cylinder which turned a gypsy head mounted on a horizontal
shaft. Dolbeer received a patent on this machine April 18, 1882. It
proved an immediate success on the logging claims of the Milford
mill.

In 1883 Dolbeer came out with his "Improved Logging Engine"
which received a patent on December 25, 1883. The new machine
had an upright spool, replacing the horizontal gypsy head. Both
types were used in the redwood region until about 1915 when larger
and more efficient donkeys, brought in from the Pacific Northwest,
took over.[19]

Dolbeer's donkey was mounted on a wooden skid platform.
Around the gypsy head a four and one-half inch diameter manila
rope line was turned two or three times and then played out to the
log. A block and tackle system was used to increase the pulling
power of the line to move the logs into position. The line, about 140
feet long, was played off the spool onto the ground as it was pulled
in, instead of being wrapped on the spool. To operate the Dolbeer
donkeys, three workers were used: an engineer, who operated the
steam engine; a spool tender, who handled the line; and a boy, who
had the unenviable job of supplying the hungry boiler with water and
wood. The crew was under the supervision of the head chain tender,
whose main responsibility was to make up the log strings to be
moved out by the oxen teams.[20]

In 1883 Dolbeer made still another invention, a "logging locomotive," whereby logs near the railroad could be readily pulled in
and the handling of the giants at the landing be facilitated. The
locomotive had an unmilled cog wheel drive. The large central cog
ran both the wheel drive, which was geared to neutral, forward and
reverse gears, and a pull-in winch. The locomotive would run to the
spot of operations and the wheel gears be placed in neutral. The
pull-in winch, simply a gypsy head on a horizontal shaft, then operated in the same manner as the Dolbeer donkey engine. These logging
locomotives were used in Humboldt County for the next several

years, with high success.[21] Thus did the inventive genius of John Dolbeer contribute to the advancement of logging techniques in the West.

A problem most mills faced was that of building a railroad to move the logs to their saws. In order that this movement might be at a constant and dependable rate, William Carson in 1884 invested in the Bucksport & Elk River railroad. It was a narrow-gauge affair twelve miles long, and cost $146,284.[22] This road was used by the Bay Mill until 1950. At the Bay Mill's other logging claim of the 1880's, Jacoby Creek, there was a small standard-gauge tramway operating on the principle of the inclined plane. The loaded cars rolled to tidewater by their own momentum, a distance of more than three miles. Horses then pulled the empty cars back to the head of the line.[23]

In 1885 the first bandsaw on the coast was installed at the Bay Mill in the industry's continuing effort to improve milling techniques. This installation was not a headrig but a recutting saw. The importance of this saw to the industry was quickly proven in a sawing demonstration between it and a circular pony saw. With the bandsaw there was about thirteen percent less loss through sawdust. Out of every 1,200 feet of lumber cut, the bandsaw produced 160 feet more than did the circular saws.[24] This fact spelled the doom of circular saws in the industry. An additional fact of the utmost importance to the redwood lumbermen was that a bandsaw could cut through logs of larger diameter than could the circular saw headrigs and do it more quickly.

The earliest surviving copy of Articles of Incorporation for the Dolbeer & Carson Lumber Company dates from 1886. It lists the Board of Directors as William Carson of Eureka, 998 shares; John Dolbeer of San Francisco, 998 shares; George D. Gray of Oakland, two shares; William D. Mugan of San Francisco, one share; and John Carson of Eureka, one share.[25] This of course shows quite clearly that the enterprises of the Bay Mill was a two-man partnership and that Dolbeer and Carson directed the destinies of the concern. John Dolbeer resided permanently in San Francisco after 1866. The responsibility of handling the sales and marketing aspect of the firm was his. It was common among the several partnerships in the industry in its early stages, when communication was slow between the redwood coast and San Francisco, to have one partner reside in San Francisco, the major financial center of the West, to secure orders and handle sales. The other partner resided at the mill site and looked after the logging and milling operations.

William Carson, as manager of the woods and plant facilities, made his home in Eureka. In doing so, he created for himself a mansion that was to become one of the outstanding monuments to the Victorian style of architecture. The house, built in 1885-1886, incorporated in both its exteriors and interiors the height of architectural fashion of the day. Located on the bluff overlooking the Bay Mill and standing at the head of Second Street, the Carson mansion with its ornate tower dominated the skyline of that part of Eureka.

Throughout most of its career, the Dolbeer & Carson Lumber Company was known to the millman and the logger as a good firm for which to work. An examination of the company payroll books at the Bancroft Library, University of California at Berkeley, reveals the benevolent attitude of the employers. In September, 1890, William Carson took the unprecedented step of voluntarily cutting the working day of the mill crew from twelve hours to ten hours without cutting wages. The other mills of Humboldt County quickly followed, reflecting the general paternalistic attitude prevalent at that period in the area.[26] Behind this paternalism there was also the hard fact that the lumber market was not very stable and all mills were faced with the problem of overproduction.

The position that the Dolbeer & Carson Lumber Company held with the working man was demonstrated in 1907, when the first industry-wide strike occurred in Humboldt County. Dolbeer and Carson, as employers, together with the Elk River Mill & Lumber Company, were excluded from the strike by the union for they were already meeting the working and wage demands of the strikers.[27]

In 1891 the Bay Mill turned to a lumbering technique that was to become a specialty of that mill for the next two decades, that of air drying and curing redwood lumber. Large drying yards were built to the east of the mill where the lumber could be stacked for curing.[28] The use of dry kilns and an understanding of their operation was just beginning in the industry. Redwood lumber was of the highest quality when cured for some two years by the salt air and then milled into a finished product. The drawback was the length of time that the stock was tied up in the yard. For this reason, the kiln, which accomplished drying in about a two-week period, gained widespread acceptance by the turn of the century.

In 1895 the firm closed down its logging camp on Elk River and moved into the Lindsay Creek region, where it had 9,000 acres ready for immediate logging. In one year a logging crew of sixty men had three and one-half million feet of logs down and the area ready to be burned.[29] The standard logging practice in the redwood forests at that time was to fell the trees, cut them into logs, and then set the area on fire to burn away the debris, leaving the fire-resistant redwood logs relatively undamaged. This was done just prior to the rainy season, allowing the rain to wash away the soot and ashes. Burning was usually done a year in advance of the need of the logs at the mill. The first trainload of logs from Lindsay Creek arrived at Humboldt Bay in May, 1897.[30]

The Milford Land and Lumber Company was producing about one million board feet a month in 1897. It still utilized river drives of a sort. The logs from the Salmon Creek claim were placed in the stream bed behind sluice dams. When there was a sufficient quantity of water, the dams were opened and the logs were floated with good success to the log pond.[31] The Milford mill was sold in 1902 and the equipment was moved by the new owners to Fields Landing. Carson felt that with the opening of the Lindsay Creek camp and the Bay Mill running at top capacity, there was no further need for the mill at Salmon Creek to supplement the filling of orders for the Dolbeer & Carson Lumber Company.[32]

An indication of why only a few were successful in the industry and some measure of the capital required to operate a redwood lumber concern by the last decade of the nineteenth century are given in a survey made by David Evans of Eureka. His report shows that the Dolbeer & Carson Lumber Company held some 16,270 acres (about twenty-four square miles) of timberland, worth $1,093,128. The Bay Mill and its equipment were valued at $160,000. The log dump at Samoa on the bay was worth $3,000. The logging equipment consisted of two bull engines worth $4,500, five Dolbeer donkey engines worth $5,000, and logging supplies worth $5,000. A shingle mill at Samoa was valued at $12,000, while the Bucksport and Elk River Railroad was worth $60,000. John Dolbeer and William Carson had assets in the Bay Mill and its affiliated operations totaling $1,342,628.[33]

John Dolbeer died in San Francisco in August, 1902. He was survived by a daughter. His wife had died in 1879 and his only son had been killed in a wagon accident in 1886. The daughter, Bertha Dolbeer, was a reported suicide in New York City a few years after her father's death. The Dolbeer estate, valued at $400,000, was involved in lengthy litigation.[34]

The firm continued to follow the policies established by the partnership. In early 1912 the mill stopped shipping its own lumber. This was in anticipation of the Northwestern Pacific railroad, which was under construction, and also because there was a large volume of maritime business in and out of the port of Eureka. By March, 1912, the lumber schooners *Lottie Carson* and *Bertha Dolbeer*, built in 1881, had been sold.[35]

On February 19, 1912, William Carson died. His remaining in Eureka at the head of a successful company had made him one of the town's leading citizens. He was at the time of his death associated with the Humboldt County Bank, the Bank of Eureka, and the Savings Bank of Eureka. He had been an incorporator of the Eel River & Eureka Railroad, the Bucksport & Elk River railroad, the Milford Land & Lumber Company, the San Diego Lumber Company, the West Coast Lumber Company, and the Humboldt Lumber Manufacturers' Association.[36] With the passing of William Carson, the "golden era" of the redwood lumber industry in Humboldt County came to its end. He was the last of the individual giants who had worked long and hard to make a success of his enterprise. It is important to note the outstanding role that such men played in the economic life of the United States. Not only did he have a major role in managing an important mill but he was also involved in the financial institutions and transportation facilities of the area. In this he was a typical redwood lumber entrepreneur.

Upon the death of William Carson, his interests passed to his family while the Dolbeer interests were vested in the Warren family, which had secured that block of stock through settlement in the courts. The new head of the concern was John Milton Carson. The two founders had been relegated to history but the Bay Mill continued in the mainstream of the redwood lumber industry.

In the early 1920's the company found that its ability to compete with newer organizations was limited by its older facilities. The turn of the century had seen the influx of lumbermen from older timber areas such as the Great Lakes and Oregon and Washington. They brought with them the latest logging and milling techniques and the new mills soon surpassed the older ones. Plans were made to abandon the old Bay Mill and build the first all-electric mill on the Pacific coast. The new plant was designed to double the capacity of the old mill. The new mill had two bandsaw headrigs capable of cutting 150,000 feet daily and was equipped with dry kilns. Construction started in 1922 and the plant was ready in 1924.[37]

The mill met the expectations of its owners and competed on equal terms with others during the remainder of the 1920's. As was the case for most concerns, the depression years hit the Bay Mill hard; however, it was able to withstand the collapse of the lumber market during the 1930's.

The firm prospered during the Second World War and survived the industry-wide strike of twenty-six months. On December 16, 1950, the Dolbeer & Carson Lumber Company, the oldest redwood firm then operating, came to an end when the Bay Mill and the timber holdings were sold to The Pacific Lumber Company. This closed a business career of ninety-six years.[38]

By 1950 a new era had started in the Humboldt County Lumber industry. The pioneers were long gone and in their place stood a few giant business consolidations. A third generation of lumber operators were upon the scene. Nevertheless this new group was deeply in the debt of such men as John Dolbeer and William Carson for their contributions to the redwood lumber industry.

NOTES

1. Humboldt County Recorder, *Deeds, Book D*, p. 641.
2. *Wood and Iron* (San Francisco), XXXVIII-3 (Sept. 1902), 18.
3. *Humboldt Times* (Eureka), Sept. 16, 1854, 2.
4. Humboldt County Recorder, *Chattel Mortgages, Book A*, pp. 19-24.
5. Owen C. Coy, *The Humboldt Bay Region, 1850-1875* (Los Angeles, 1929), p. 119.
6. *Humboldt Times*, Sept. 16, 1854, 2.
7. *Ibid.*, Aug. 2, 1856, 2.
8. *Ibid.*, Sept. 8, 1860, 2; Nov. 10, 1860, 3.
9. *Ibid.*, August 4, 1904, 4.
10. Humboldt County Recorder, *Deeds, Book D*, p. 641; *Humboldt Standard* (Eureka), Feb. 20, 1912, 1.
11. *Humboldt Times*, Dec. 31, 1899, 3; Humboldt County Recorder, *Deeds, Book B*, p. 332.
12. Humboldt County Recorder, *Deeds, Book F*, p. 656; *Book I*, p. 758; *Book P*, pp. 252-261.
13. Coy, *op. cit.*, p. 261.
14. *Humboldt Times*, April 27, 1878, 3; United States Commissioner of Patents, *Annual Report, 1869*, p. 528.
15. *Humboldt Times*, Nov. 22, 1879, 3; interview with Peter J. Rutledge of Eureka, former superintendent of the Bay Mill, Aug. 20, 1949.
16. *Humboldt Times*, March 29, 1878, 3.
17. Humboldt County Clerk, *Articles of Incorporation.*
18. *Humboldt Times*, May 16, 1863, 3.
19. *The Timberman* (Portland, Oregon), XXXIV-5 (March, 1933), 9.
20. *Humboldt Times*, Oct. 24, 1889, 2; Nov. 7, 1899, 3.
21. Interview with Peter J. Rutledge of Eureka.
22. Lillie E. Hamm, publisher, *1890-1 History and Business Directory of Humboldt County* (Eureka, 1890), p. 69.
23. *Wood and Iron*, VII-7 (July, 1887), 69.
24. *Humboldt Times*, Oct. 31, 1885, 3.
25. Humboldt County Clerk, *Articles of Incorporation.*
26. *Humboldt Times*, Sept. 2, 1890, 2.
27. *Ibid.*, March 31, 1907, 1; April 30, 1907, 1.
28. *Ibid.*, March 19, 1891, 3.
29. *Wood and Iron*, XXV-5 (May, 1896), p. 180.

30. *Humboldt Times*, May 13, 1897, 3.
31. Redwood Lumber Manufacturers' Association, *The Home of the Redwood* (San Francisco, 1897), p. 47.
32. *Wood and Iron*, XXXVIII-3 (Sept. 1902), 1.
33. "David Evans' Survey." Manuscript in possession of Peter J. Rutledge, Eureka, California.
34. *Wood and Iron*, XXXVIII-3 (Sept. 1902), 18.
35. *Humboldt Standard* (Eureka), Jan. 29, 1912, 5; March 19, 1912, 8.
36. *Humboldt Standard*, Feb. 20, 1912, 1. The San Diego Lumber Company and the West Coast Lumber Company are indicative of a common practice in the industry. Mill owners secured interests in retail concerns elsewhere in the state to guarantee an outlet for their lumber.
37. Interview with Peter J. Rutledge.
38. *Humboldt Times*, Dec. 15, 1950, 1.

FIGURE 5-1. The Donkey and the Mule in the 1880's. The early Dolbeer donkey with a horizontal single cylinder turned a gypsy head on a horizontal shaft. The mule was used to carry water to the buckets placed at intervals along the skidroad. Wire rope later replaced the Manila rope. Ericson Photograph.

FIGURE 5-2. The Bull Buck and Choppers in the 1890's. Bull Buck Norman Graham (sitting to left) sitting in the undercut of a huge redwood. Both choppers worked together, using double-bitted axes, which were the biggest and heaviest in the United States. Ericson Photograph.

FIGURE 5-3. World Famous Carson Mansion. This mansion, built by William Carson in 1885 and 1886, is one of the outstanding monuments of Victorian architecture in the United States. Photographer Ericson took this picture in 1892.

6

California's First Railroad: The Union Plank Walk, Rail Track, and Wharf Company Railroad

Lynwood Carranco *and* Mrs. Eugene Fountain

Although the lure of gold first drew men to the wilds of the virgin region of Humboldt County, the lumbermen soon followed in the wake of the pioneer gold hunter, and soon the brawny men from the Atlantic Seaboard began to lay the foundations for many fortunes by following the principal vocation which they and their forefathers had followed in the East.

The early mill-owners logged the timber easily around Humboldt Bay because the land sloped towards the bay, which served as a natural log pond to the mills on the shore. The first railroads in the State of California were constructed in Humboldt County in 1854 to haul logs to the water's edge. Horses or mules furnished the motive power. In 1854 there were more than twenty miles of good, graded, substantial railroads built by loggers.[1]

These early logging railways were very primitive in form and construction, yet they were railroads and are entitled to consideration. The trucks that hauled the logs were fitted with big axles, and large flanged wheels were hewed to fit the track or rails which usually were made of two parallel straight saplings.[2]

The Union Plank Walk, Rail Track and Wharf Company constructed the first enduring railroad in California. The Sacramento Chamber of Commerce has repeatedly publicized that the Sacramento Valley Railroad was the first to be constructed in California.[3] Let us examine the two early railroads.

The Sacramento Valley Railroad filed Articles of Association in October, 1853,[4] a year before the Union company was incorporated. The Sacramento company commenced work on February 12, 1855.[5] The Union company, having begun in December, 1854, was using its wooden railroad in January, 1855, although the wharf was not completed until May of that year.[6] The Sacramento Valley Railroad used the first locomotive, a small one of eighteen tons called the

"Sacramento," and began to operate on two miles of track in September, 1855,[7] seven months after the Arcata railroad.

Thus the first railroad in California was the Union Plank Walk, Rail Track, and Wharf Company—later the Arcata and Mad River Railroad—even though the rails were of wood and horses served as the motive power. Following is a history of this line, the first railroad in California.

Union (Arcata), on the north shore of Humboldt Bay, grew steadily from 1850 to 1856. For a number of years the town had been the leader both in population and business activity. Located at the head of the bay, with a direct route to the mines, Union soon became the center for trade with the mining district.

One disadvantage was the difficulty with which shipping was carried on. The town was located near tidewater, but extensive mud flats separated it from navigable waters. A number of sloughs came to the southern edge of town, and the east boundary was on the margin of a large salt water slough called Big Slough. It was difficult for the large ships to dock here, and only small boats could get up the slough. Almost every business firm in Union had a warehouse on Big Slough; these buildings were built from the main landing on Front Street to the upper landing near Fifth and A Streets.[8]

The Tilley and Murdock Livery Stable ran an "omnibus" from this first steamboat landing on Big Slough to Union in November, 1854, a month before the Union Plank Walk, Rail Track, and Wharf Company was incorporated.[9] Big Slough was used even after the new Union wharf was built.

In 1854 permission to remedy this problem was obtained from the State Legislature in a law authorizing the building of a wharf. The Union Plank Walk, Rail Track, and Wharf Company was incorporated December 5, 1854. This railroad was paid for by money raised by popular subscriptions and most of the stockholders were business and professional men of Union. The contractors—Stillman Daby, Byron Deming, and Henry Walker—were to receive one-half of their payment in stock, and three thousand dollars in cash.[10]

The Union Plank Walk, Rail Track, and Wharf Company—Daby, president; Deming, secretary; and Walker, treasurer—made an agreement with Titlow and Averill and Company to construct the plank walk in payment of fifteen hundred dollars. Titlow and Averill were to furnish the lumber.[11] Construction began in December, 1854.[12]

Vessels began to use the unfinished wharf in January, 1855, although it was not completed until May. A railroad or tramway two miles in length connected the wharf with the town.[13]

The first rails used were six-by-six redwood timbers, with a running surface of pepperwood two-by-fours. Strap iron was added later. The deck of the trestle was covered with planks to provide footing for the first "locomotive" in California—an old white horse named "Spanking Fury." One four-wheel car comprised the rolling stock. The citizens named the pike the "Annie and Mary."[14] The local paper mentioned an incident which occurred on the railroad:

> On Wednesday a mare attached to one of the cars on the railroad ran away, and while kicking she broke her right hind leg. The male passengers jumped off, one of them falling into the mud. There were two ladies aboard, who exhibited much more coolness than the "lords of creation," as they made no attempt to get off, but sat still, as good sensible folks would do. The mare was one of the most valuable animals in the county, but is now ruined.[15]

It is not known whether the mare was the legendary "Spanking Fury." Many horses must have served as locomotives from 1855 to 1875, but only the name "Spanking Fury" seems to have endured the test of time. Another railroad accident occurred in May, 1856, when the "locomotive" went off the track. The following story appeared in the local newspaper:

A LOCOMOTIVE OFF THE TRACK

> Saturday last, as the car was on its way down, loaded with passengers, express, etc., for the Goliath, lying at the wharf at the lower end of the road, one of the reins of the horse attached to the car, caught in the wheel and the locomotive was thrown off the track. It so happened that the car, at the time, was crossing the gulch, just below town—over which the road passes, at an elevation, in the centre, of about fifteen feet—and "Old Gray" was suspended midway between the track and the water and mud beneath, until he was dropped by cutting the traces. One of the passengers, who said he had never seen a railroad before, was seized with panic, and jumped off in the opposite direction and brought up in the brush and mud in the middle of the gulch. The moment he struck he sung out lustily for fear the car and all the passengers were coming down on top of him. The horse was led out of the mire on one side, and "greeny" was helped out of the brush and mud on the other. No bones, either horse or human, were broken, and the car was soon on its way again. Thus ended the first locomotive accident.[16]

On February 16, 1856, the stockholders of the Union company elected the following officers: Byron Deming, president; H.W. Walker, secretary; A.H. Murdock, treasurer; and the following directors: J.E. Wyman, A.H. Murdock, W. Van Dyke, H. Walker, and Byron Deming.[17]

A year later the company had financial troubles—a debt of over six thousand dollars to various citizens. There were no funds available to pay the creditors, but property was assigned to them commensurate with the debt. The creditors selected M. Spencer and J.E. Wyman, and the company chose Byron Deming to have sole custody and management of the company,[18] and by 1859 the company announced a dividend of twenty percent.[19] In 1860 the town of Union was renamed Arcata.[20]

George Tilley, part owner of a local livery stable and one of the founders of Eureka, is said to have purchased the Union Plank Walk, Rail Track, and Wharf Company when the company again fell into debt. He sold out to G.W.B. Yocum in 1871.[21]

In the 1870's, a passenger service was established from Arcata to Eureka. The first passenger car to run out of the dock was a four-wheeler with a canvas top; later an enclosed car was constructed with two benches running the length of the car. When business put too great a burden on the horse, two steam locomotives were built. The first was a small one with an upright boiler developing three horsepower. The second, called Number One or the "Black Diamond," was somewhat larger and consisted of a horizontal boiler with two oscillating pistons. The "Black Diamond" could pull six cars having a total capacity of two thousand five hundred feet of lumber.[22]

No documentary evidence can be found that can throw light on the builder of the "Black Diamond." Some writers say that Lou Parsons of the Eureka Iron Works built the first engine. W.J. Hunter, a retired superintendent of the Northwestern Pacific Railroad, stated in 1926 that G.W. Yocum personally supervised the building of the engine, and that a local man named Sharp did the actual work and operated the engine after it was completed.[23]

In June, 1875, a new company was formed. The stockholders and directors were G.W. Yocum, S.M. Buck, C.B. Stone, H. Metz and S. Haun.[24] At this time the railroad was extended from Arcata to Falk and Minor's mill, the Jolly Giant, a distance of almost a mile. The two men had secured a lease of ten years from A.M. Preston of four hundred ninety acres of fine timber lying in the vicinity of Arcata.[25] In 1876 the roadbed was again extended a mile to the Dolly Varden mill, also owned by Noah Falk and Isaac Minor,[26]

Two years later the railroad was taken over by the Arcata Transportation Company which was organized on June 15, 1878.[27] In 1880 Isaac Minor built his Warren Creek mill, and the railroad, constructed by a gang of Chinese earning $1.50 a day, was extended three and one-half miles to the mill.[28] A big picnic was held on the river bank near the mill to celebrate the new mill and the new railroad extension. The railroad was "overworked" by hauling crowds from Eureka to Arcata. The picnickers were hauled on the bob-tailed lumber flats with loose benches placed for seats. W.J. Hunter, a retired railroad man, in his reminiscences, had the following to say about the ride home from the picnic:

> I will never forget the perilous ride home that afternoon. There was not a hand brake on the train, not even on the engine, nothing but the reverse lever. An engine air pump was unknown in Humboldt County at that time. When we were coming down the grade over the Falor Flat by the Janes' place, the train reached a pretty high speed for that kind of train and the bob-cars with loose seats and no railings to get over to the engine, but failed on account of the long drawbars and of course not being a good enough tight rope walker. It was a miracle that one of the cars did not jump the track. You can imagine what the result would have been.[29]

In 1881 G.W. Yocum and Richard Fernald acquired all the stock of the Arcata Transportation Company.[30] The Arcata and Mad River Railroad Company filed articles of incorporation on July 22, 1881.[31] The company was to construct a single track narrow-gauge railroad to be operated by steam and horse power. This track was to be built from the main channel at the northerly end of Humboldt Bay, to the North Fork of the Mad River, passing through the town of Arcata for the transportation of freight and passengers. This road was an extension of the Arcata Transportation Company's road. The directors were G.W. Yocum, R.M. Fernald, B. Deming, Austin Wiley and E.S. Deming. The capital stock was $60,000. The wharf at that time was said to be the longest wharf in the United States.[32]

The "Black Diamond" was no longer suitable and had to be scrapped. The new company purchased a new locomotive in 1881 from the Porter Locomotive Works of Pittsburgh, Pennsylvania. It was an 0-4-0 tank and was named the "Arcata," but the local people called it the "Coffee Pot."[53] The strap rail was replaced with 35-pound "T" rail, and a steamboat was put into service from the wharf to Eureka, a distance of five miles, to carry passengers, freight and lumber.[34]

The Korbel brothers—Frank, Antone and Joseph—from Sonoma, purchased timber holdings on the North Fork of the Mad River in 1883, and shortly afterward they bought the Arcata and Mad River Railroad, extending the road through to their mill on the north fork of the river, a distance of five miles.[35]

The Korbel brothers bought two more locomotives: No. 3, an 0-4-4 tank, named the "North Fork," and No. 4, an 0-4-2 tank, called the "Eureka." Both locomotives were built by the Golden State and Miners Iron Works of San Francisco. The company also made extensive improvements on the wharf at Arcata. The trestle and wharf covered a combined distance of more than two miles.[36]

In 1885 a branch about one-quarter of a mile long was built to Isaac Minor's new mill at Glendale.[37] In 1886 another branch, also about one-quarter of a mile long, was constructed to the Riverside Lumber Company's mill at Riverside, down-stream from North Fork.[38]

The "Annie and Mary" did a booming business in 1885. Twenty-one million feet of lumber, thirty-eight million shingles, and twenty-two thousand fence posts were shipped to the wharf. During the year one hundred forty-two vessels were loaded at the company's wharf, averaging about twelve a month. Passenger traffic averaged two thousand tickets a month.[39]

The "Annie and Mary" had passenger problems in 1886. A local Eureka newspaper stated:

> It is not an uncommon thing for the steamer Alta, on her trip on the afternoon of Sundays to be boarded by a lot of drunken men who live in the direction of Mad River. On several occasions the profane language of such passengers has terrorized women and children and shocked the ears of decent people. To keep order on the boat, Captain Cousins has been invested with a Deputy Sheriff's badge and has made a few arrests. But it is impossible for him to be at the wheel and to know what is going on in other parts of the boat at the same time. These disgraceful occurrences have become so frequent that ladies do not travel Sunday afternoon if they can avoid it.[40]

In 1888, another locomotive, a 2-4-0, No. 5 called the "Blue Lake," was purchased from Baldwin. The Arcata and Mad River Railroad locomotives were also used by the Humboldt Lumber and Mill Company for logging in the woods.[41] In 1891 the Humboldt Lumber and Mill Company owned one mile of 45 1/4-inch gauge track and one locomotive, an 0-4-0 tank, named the "Gypsy." The name of the town of North Fork was changed to Korbel. The railroad was extended up Mad River to Canyon Creek the same year, making it three miles from Riverside and four miles from Korbel.[42]

In 1893, five mills used the railroad for shipping, and the towns of Glendale, Blue Lake and Korbel furnished regular traffic. A local newspaper advertisement at this time stated that the railroad passed through a section of untold wealth of agricultural lands and timber:

> Nature has endowed this section with far more than ordinary attractions. The road all the way from Arcata presents the passenger a pleasing picture of well-cultivated fields, willows, hedges, and forest growth, but arriving at Korbel, the long reaches of maple groves that have been cleared up give an irresistibly enchanting scene that makes one wish to get out and wander through these primeval groves. The stream is alive with handsome silver-side salmon, trout;

pure sparkling water is running on every side; wild flowers and berries are in profusion—all framed in a setting of abrupt and rugged hills. Such is the town of Korbel.[43]

Tragedy struck the railroad in 1896. At five o'clock in the evening, Sunday, September 13, the northbound Arcata to Korbel train crashed through the Mad River bridge. Falling forty feet, the engine, one box car, and two passenger coaches hit the dry river bed—splintering the cars to pieces. Seven persons died, and only three out of the thirty-three persons aboard escaped injury.[44]

The year 1898 was a bad one for the lumber business. The annual report of the "Annie and Mary" showed a deficit of nearly thirty thousand dollars—earnings were thirty thousand dollars and the expenses were twice that sum.[45] In 1899 redwood timber land was bought in Humboldt County at six dollars an acre.[46] Two years later the outlook was entirely different. In 1901 records were broken. Capitalists began to buy redwood holdings, and there was almost a lumber famine in the county as a result of the unprecedented building boom. Special trains had to be run daily on the railroad to supply the great number of vessels anchored at the Arcata wharf.[47]

In 1901, the Eureka and Klamath River Railroad was built, crossing the A & M R R R at Arcata and at an interchange called Korblex, a distance of seven and one-half miles from Korbel and near Arcata.[48] A Baldwin locomotive, a 2-4-0, was purchased at this time; it was No. 6, and named the "Hoopa."[49] In 1906 the "Coffee Pot" was temporarily brought out of retirement to help repair a number of trestles near the Mad River.[50]

In February, 1903, the Korbel brothers sold all of their holdings, including mills, timberlands, and the A & M R R R to the Northern Redwood Company. The Riverside Lumber Company was purchased also, but continued to operate as the Riverside Mill. The locomotives were renumbered because No. 1 had been left vacant years before with the retirement of the "Black Diamond." Numbers 2, 3, 4, 5 and 6 became Numbers 1, 2, 3, 4 and 5, respectively.[51] In 1905, the second No. 6, a 2-4-2, named the "Northern," was bought from Baldwin.[52] Also in 1905 the San Francisco and Northwestern Railroad opened a line from Eureka to Arcata, crossing the A & M R R R near the wharf.[53]

In 1906, the Northern Redwood Company, now the Northern Redwood Lumber Company, bought a two-truck Heisler locomotive; it was now No. 2—the "Gypsy" was renumbered as No. 1. In 1910, a two-truck Heisler locomotive, No. 3, also a 4-4, was purchased. Only the "Arcata" operated on the wharf during the twenty years that Korbel brothers owned the railroad, but now the wharf was reinforced so that all the locomotives of the A & M R R R could operate on it.[54]

In 1908 the Northwestern Pacific Railroad took over the San Francisco and Northwestern Railroad, and in 1914 the north and south sections were joined so that products could now be shipped by rail to any part of the country.[55] The Humboldt Bay region had waited more than sixty years for a railway communication with the outside world, the ocean furnished the only highway for commerce. The many rugged mountains between Humboldt Bay and the other settled sections of California caused this isolation. In a region so detached, independence in thought and action developed to such a degree as to affect the ideals and political opinions of the people. Before World War II the local self-consciousness of the Humboldt Bay people was an interesting characteristic of the region.

In 1911 the Northwestern Pacific took over the Oregon and Eureka, which had taken over the Eureka and Klamath River Railroad in 1904.[56] The Charles Nelson Steamship Company had the controlling interest in the Northern Redwood Lumber Company, and it was not until 1925 that an interchange with the A & M R R R was made at Korblex with the Northwestern Pacific. A third rail for standard gauge cars was laid from Korblex to Korbel so that standard gauge cars could be brought into Korbel. Up until this time all locomotives had to be equipped with three coupler pockets, the lower center one being used for the narrow gauge cars while the two upper pockets were used for standard gauge cars. The automatic coupler was used in the proper pocket depending on which way the engine was facing. Automatic couplers were installed on most of the double-truck narrow gauge cars, but some of them carried link couplers to the end. The narrow gauge automatic couplers had a slot in the knuckle to take the link and pin couplers.[57] In 1917 Heisler locomotive No. 4, a 4-4, was bought and shortly afterwards, Heisler No. 5, also a 4-4 tank, was purchased.[58]

In 1921, the Northern Redwood Lumber Company purchased a two-truck Heisler, No. 4. To avoid mistakes on train orders the first Heislers were numbered H-2 and H-3, but this also proved confusing because both the Arcata and Mad River and Northern Redwood Lumber Company locomotives were used on the main line and the logging line. A figure 2 was placed before the regular numbers, making them now Numbers 22, 23 and 24. In 1922 another two-truck

Heisler was purchased and it became No. 25. In 1925 the company replaced the rail laid in 1881 with 50-pound steel.[59]

In 1928 the Northern Redwood Lumber Company bought a large standard gauge 2-8-2 tank locomotive from the Charles Nelson Lumber Company and named it the N.R.L. Co. No. 7. Old No. 1, having served faithfully for forty-eight years, was scrapped in 1929 and, in 1930, No. 2 was also scrapped. Because No. 7 was too heavy for the 50-pound rail, the line was relaid with 70-pound rail.[60]

Although the redwood industry was severely hit by the depression, one mill was kept running. Fewer lumber boats were running so that most of the lumber was shipped by rail. On June 6, 1931, the company discontinued all passenger service.[61]

Locomotive No. 3 was no longer needed to handle passenger trains, and it was scrapped in 1932.[62] Business went from bad to worse, and in 1933, the company closed down the mill. A few men were kept on to look after the mill, and No. 25 was used as a stationary boiler to supply steam for the fire pumps. The engines, Numbers 4, 5, 6, 7, 22, 23 and 24, were run into the "barn" at Korbel to wait for further developments. In 1937, the Hammond Lumber Company leased No. 7 and renumbered it No. 14.[63]

In 1941, the company scrapped No. 4 and burned all the narrow gauge cars.[64] In 1942, the government granted the company a loan, and the company began to get the railroad and mill back into working order. Locomotives No. 5 and No. 6 were scrapped in 1942, and most of the narrow gauge rail was removed.[65] Thus the curtain dropped on the story of the narrow gauge with its odd 45 1/4-inch gauge. The narrow gauge had served faithfully through the years. At one time the main line had run from the crowded wharf, where connections were made with the company's boat, the *Alta*, running between Eureka and the wharf, to Korbel, a distance of just under thirteen miles. There was also the one-quarter-mile branch at Glendale to Isaac Minor's mill, a six-mile logging line up the North Fork of the Mad River, and a line of four and one-half miles up Mad River. At one time, counting sidings, spurs, and yards, there were over thirty miles of narrow gauge truck in use. A roundhouse with turn table, car shops, and a station was also located at Arcata. Block signals were used to protect the crossings with the N.W.P. at Arcata just north of Korblex.

The Hammond Lumber Company returned No. 7, and it was sold to the United States Government. The company bought a two-truck Shay from the Lampson Logging Company and this became A

& M R R R No. 7.[66] When the Northern Redwood Lumber Company resumed operations, the A & M R R R track of only the seven and one-half miles between Korbel and Korblex was used, plus ten miles of Northern Redwood Lumber Company track to the woods up the North Fork of the Mad River.

A bad accident occurred on January 24, 1943. Heisler No. 24, working near Camp No. 8, fell through a trestle, killing the engineer and injuring the fireman.[67] The Heisler was later scrapped. In 1945, a three-truck Shay was bought from the Yosemite Sugar Pine Company to replace No. 24. The new locomotive became N.R.L. Co. No. 5 and actually replaced No. 23, which was then scrapped.[68]

The company tried out a Baldwin seven hundred fifty horsepower diesel-electric and a General Electric six hundred sixty horsepower diesel-electric on the railroad in 1950, but they were not successful. No. 5 could pull more logging cars up the grade to the woods than either of the diesels; also, both diesels were too heavy for the 50-pound rail. In 1951, Heisler No. 22 was sold for scrap, and it was replaced by No. 12, a 2-6-6-2 tank mallet which was purchased from the Hammond Lumber Company. This steam locomotive, the largest one in the county, was used between Korbel and Korblex because it was too large for the tracks in the woods.[69]

Two years later, in 1952, the last of the faithful Heislers was scrapped. The following year in July, No. 23, a 2-6-2, was bought from the McCloud River Railroad and was redesignated A & M R R R No. 11. This engine was used to help No. 12.[70]

In October, 1953, a three hundred eighty horsepower diesel-electric was purchased from the Pine Flat Dam contractors and numbered 101; No. 101's mate, No. 102, was bought from the same source in February, 1954. At this time Nos. 5 or 7 worked the lines in the woods, and Nos. 101 and 102 handled the A & M R R R line.[71]

After World War II business increased steadily. Many lumber mills were built along the A & M R R R right-of-way. The railroad became little more than a switching line with spurs and served fifteen shippers at the height of the lumber boom. The round trip of fifteen miles took nearly eight hours to pick up the loaded cars from Korbel to Korblex and to spot the empties on the return. The daily average car loadings were enough to place the road among the highest paying railroad properties per mile in the United States. The "Annie and Mary" handled 7,241 outgoing cars during 1953, which was an increase of 1,717 cars over the total handled in 1952. Of this total, 6,917 were cars of lumber, 153 were cars of chips, and 171 were cars of logs. The record number of cars handled per day was fifty loads which occurred in December, 1953.[72]

The "Annie and Mary" celebrated its one hundredth anniversary on May 30, 1954. A large crowd composed of local people and railway fans from as far as San Jose enjoyed a trip on the A & M R R R from Arcata to Korbel. From Korbel the large group changed to the woods' train to travel up to Camp No. 9, a distance of twelve miles from Korbel.[73]

On April 1, 1955, the Simpson Logging Company from the State of Washington, which had bought extensive timber lands along the Klamath River after World War II, purchased the Northern Redwood Lumber Company's operations—timber, mills and the A & M R R R.[74]

In the fall of 1955, Engineer Archie Ambrosini made his last run up to the woods. All the rails were ripped out so that the roadbed could be converted into a motor truck road.[75] The conversion to diesel-electric motive power is now complete. At the present time (1964) there are three diesel-electrics operating from Korbel to Korblex and serving twelve shippers on the railroad of seven and one-half miles. Nos. 101 and 102 have been synchronized and can be handled from either control.[76]

Locomotive No. 11 was sold to Lerner's Junk Yard in Eureka in 1956. About the same time No. 12 was sold to the Northwest Lumber Mills in Flagstaff, Arizona. No. 7 was given to the City of Arcata and is now on public display, along with two flat cars and a caboose—a reminder to all of the "good old days."[77]

Thus the Arcata and Mad River Railroad, the first railroad in California, which was incorporated as the Union Plank Walk, Rail Track, and Wharf Company in 1854 and began operating in January, 1855—seven months before the Sacramento Valley Railroad—has had a long and exciting history.

On September 26, 1970, official recognition came to the Arcata and Mad River Railroad in Blue Lake. The California State Landmarks Commission approved the "Annie and Mary" for Landmark status as "the oldest railroad on the North Coast." A handsome bronze plaque identifying the "Annie and Mary" as State Historical Landmark No. 842 was unveiled. Principal speaker was Lynwood Carranco, Humboldt County historian who traced the history of the railroad. Other participants were Andrew Genzoli, historian for *The Times-Standard* and a member of the California Historical Landmarks Commission; Henry Trobitz, California timberlands manager of Simpson Timber Company, owner of the "Annie and Mary"; John

Thompson, general superintendent of the line, and Richard Harville of the Humboldt County Historical Society.

NOTES

1. *Humboldt Times*, September 9, 1854.
2. William Lindsey, *Statement of Reminiscences* (1914), as quoted in Owen C. Coy, THE HUMBOLDT BAY REGION, 1850-1875 (Los Angeles: 1929), p. 287.
3. *Romance of California*, Sacramento Chamber of Commerce publication, 1938, p. 10.
4. Gilbert H. Kneiss, BONANZA RAILROADS (Stanford, 1941), p. 7.
5. *Ibid.*, p. 9.
6. *Humboldt Times*, April 14, 1855.
7. Kneiss, *op. cit.*, pp. 11-12.
8. *Alta California*, August 5, 1850.
9. *Humboldt Times*, November 4, 1854.
10. Howard Melendy, ed., *Newsletter*, Humboldt County Historical Society publication, April, 1954, as quoted from BOOK A—*Miscellaneous*, in the office of the Humboldt County Recorder.
11. *Ibid.*
12. *Humboldt Times*, January 20, 1855.
13. *Ibid.*, April 14, 1855.
14. *Ibid.*, April 7, 14, May 5, August 11, September 15, 1855.
15. *Ibid.*, October 6, 1855.
16. *Ibid.*, May 17, 1856.
17. *Ibid.*, February 16, 1856.
18. Melendy, *op. cit.*
19. *Northern Californian*, June 18, 1859.
20. *Humboldt Times*, March 24, 1860.
21. *Siskiyou News*, January 8, 1897.
22. Interview with Mrs. Ogilwy, April, 1954. The late Mr. Ogilwy was superintendent of the A & M R R R from 1920 to 1931.
23. *Headlight*, May, 1926.
24. *Weekly Times Telephone*, July 14, 1883.
25. *Humboldt Times*, May 15, 1875.
26. *Headlight*, *op. cit.*
27. Files of the Northern Redwood Company, March, 1954.
28. *Humboldt Times*, August, 1881.
29. *Headlight*, *op. cit.*
30. *Weekly Times Telephone*, July 14, 1883.
31. Wallace Elliott, HISTORY OF HUMBOLDT COUNTY (San Francisco, 1881), p. 139.
32. *Ibid.*
33. Files of Northern Redwood Lumber Company.
34. *Ibid.*
35. *Weekly Times Telephone*, March 24, 1883.
36. Files of the Northern Redwood Lumber Company.
37. *Ibid.*
38. *Ibid.*
39. *Weekly Times Telephone*, August 1, 1885.
40. *Ibid.*, February 13, 1886.
41. Files of the Northern Redwood Lumber Company.
42. *Ibid.*
43. *Watchman*, June, 1890.

44. *Blue Lake Advocate*, September, 1896.
45. *Ibid.*, August 27, 1898.
46. *Ibid.*, December 15, 1899.
47. *Ibid.*, December 10, 1901.
48. Files of the Northern Redwood Lumber Company.
49. *Ibid.*
50. *Blue Lake Advocate*, February 10, 1906.
51. Files of the Northern Redwood Lumber Company.
52. *Ibid.*
53. *Ibid.*
54. *Ibid.*
55. *Humboldt Standard*, October 22, 1914.
56. Files of the Northern Redwood Lumber Company.
57. *Ibid.*
58. *Ibid.*
59. *Ibid.*
60. *Ibid.*
61. *Blue Lake Advocate*, June 11, 1931.
62. Files of the Northern Redwood Lumber Company.
63. *Ibid.*
64. *Ibid.*
65. Interview with the late Mr. Louis Sundquist. Mr. Sundquist retired as the chief engineer of the "Annie and Mary" in 1958, after working on the railroad for forty years.
66. *Ibid.*
67. *Ibid.*
68. Interview with Archie Ambrosini. Mr. Ambrosini is the present (1964) engineer for the A & M R R R, succeeding Mr. Sundquist in 1958.
69. Interview with Louis Sundquist.
70. Interview with Archie Ambrosini.
71. *Ibid.*
72. *Blue Lake Advocate*, May 27, 1954.
73. *Arcata Union*, June 4, 1954.
74. Files of the Simpson Logging Company.
75. Interview with Archie Ambrosini.
76. *Ibid.*
77. *Ibid.*

FIGURE 6-1. Mr. V. Zaruba, superintendent of the Humboldt Mill Company at Korbel from 1895 to 1903, inspects the Arcata and Mad River Railroad wharf out in Humboldt Bay. This picture was taken on the Arcata Wharf on June 1, 1893. *Ericson Photograph.*

FIGURE 6-2. The Blue Lake crossing the North Fork of Mad River leading to the Riverside Lumber Company about 1901. Ericson Photograph.

FIGURE 6-3. Arcata and Mad River Railroad. This picture was taken at the Arcata Roundhouse about 1885. Left to right, the engines are No. 3, the North Fork; No. 4, the Eureka; No. 5, the Blue Lake; and No. 2, the Arcata. Ericson Photograph.

FIGURE 6-4. Arcata and Mad River Railroad Company Wharf. Sailing vessels—three- and four-masters—tied up at the Arcata and Mad River Railroad Company's wharf at Arcata in the 1890's. The stern-wheeler "Alta" carried passengers and freight between the Arcata wharf and Eureka. The two-mile railroad trestle can be seen extending far out into Humboldt Bay. A.W. Ericson Photograph.

CHAPTER

7

The Samoa Peninsula

Lynwood Carranco

A series of fascinating sand dunes, long beaches, and aging growth all help to make the Samoa Peninsula, opposite the City of Eureka, one of the most unusual and attractive stretches of Humboldt County to visit and enjoy. The peninsula has seen a large share of history and has played an important part in many maritime chapters. Unfortunately through the years, the dreams of those who would like to see the peninsula develop into a Cape Cod has never materialized, and instead it has become principally an industrial site. The Samoa Peninsula is approximately seven miles long and one mile wide at its broadest point.

The Humboldt Bay area, before the coming of the white man, was the home of the Wiyot Indians. The Wiyot territory fell into three natural divisions: lower Mad River, Humboldt Bay, and the lower Eel River; the Indian names were Batawat, Wiki, and Wiyot. Wiyot, only a name of a district, was used for the entire people by most neighboring groups.[1]

The Wiyot resided near the Pacific Ocean, yet they used the ocean very little for either subsistence or travel. Although the towns at the mouths of the two rivers could look out on the ocean, they faced the rivers like the settlements upstream. The Indian houses on the two spits were on the bay side; farther north they were on Mad River Slough, not on the parallel beach.[2]

The main line of north-south communications avoided the beach and ran along inland waterways which, except at a few spots, could be traveled either by boat or along the shore on foot. Although the Wiyots rarely slept beyond the smell of salt water, they managed their lives so as to avoid more than an occasional putting out to sea. But with all their proximity to the ocean, the Wiyots had made the pattern of their life attach to still water and its shores.[3]

In the Wiyot area, there were approximately thirty to thirty-five towns with about thirty persons in each, which totaled approximately 1000 people. The main towns were near the mouth of Mad River, on the peninsula, on Gunther Island (now Indian Island), at intervals around the bay, and on Eel River to where the town of Scotia is now located. The bay villages seemed to be more or less in a line, like those on the Eel and Mad rivers and those of the neighboring tribes. The line ran north and south, cut across the bay at Gunther Island, and was apparently the trail of main travel.[4]

There were evidences of twenty-four villages on the peninsula, extending from the end of Mad River Slough near Mad River to the end of the North Spit. Some of the sites were abandoned for one reason or another some time previous to 1850.[5]

When the white man came in 1850, there were three major or regular settlements and a minor one on the peninsula proper, from the North Spit to the entrance of Mad River Slough to the north. Two of the regular rancherias were on Mad River Slough. The first village was situated on a sand dune point reaching down through the marsh to the slough. The location was about three hundred yards north of the Emmerson Fir Mill, on the slough, and near the present huge water pipe. The spot is now used as a storage area for logs. Before the company purchased the property, farm buildings occupied the site, and a deposit of shell mussels could be seen.[6]

The second village was a mile and a half north of the Emmerson Mill on the slough, and near the old Carson Railroad bridge, backed by a twenty-foot hill and surrounded with beach pine and huckleberry bushes. There was a graveyard here, and up to 1900 mourners came by annually from Mad River in canoes.[7]

Another large village was located just south of the Simpson Plywood mill in Fairhaven. When the Gregg party came down the peninsula on December of 1849, they stopped for two days near this village. When the entrance to the bay blocked their advance southward, an Indian from this village, who was killed by the whites some years later, guided the party around the north end of the bay.[8]

A minor village was just southwest of the old Georgia-Pacific sawmill, located in the mill yard.[9] In the early 1950's construction workers uncovered skeletons, indicating the location of a graveyard. Located north of Samoa and about three hundred yards north of where the new Samoa Bridge meets the peninsula is one of the largest shell mounds of the region, and was said to be a regular rancheria one hundred and fifty years ago. In more recent times Indians living on Mad River when visiting Gunther Island used to walk down the

North Spit as far as this site and then shout or make a smoke signal to attract attention. Then the Indians on the Island would cross in a canoe to get them as soon as the tide was favorable. Robert Gunther, who used to live on the Island, mentioned that dances used to be held at this place.[10]

The peninsula, which is one half to almost a mile wide, with elevations reaching eighty-five feet (Hammond Lumber Company leveled two of the highest hills in order to build a drying yard), is composed entirely of sand cast up by the combined action of wind and wave. Here there are fresh dunes nearly sixty feet in height, half burying and killing spruce trees which measure two and three feet in diameter where they reach above the sand. Approximately only half of the width of the peninsula is covered with drifting sands, and the bay shore, being protected from cold ocean winds by the high sand ridge and a belt of beach pine, is a desirable place for habitation. Many villages were probably established from time to time in the past along the shore between Samoa and Mad River Slough, only to be later rendered uninhabitable by encroaching sands.

In the early part of the nineteenth century the Russians in Alaska engaged a number of American "tramp" ships in trapping sea otters on the coast of California. In May, 1806, Captain Jonathan Winship went to Sitka with an American ship, and the Russian Governor made a contract with him to take one hundred Aleuts with fifty small boats on a ten-to-fourteen months' hunting trip to California. On this trip Humboldt Bay was discovered and charted. This chart was combined with that of Trinidad Bay made by Vancouver, and published in an atlas compiled by Tebenkof in St. Petersburg in 1848.[11]

Arriving at Trinidad, the expedition spent twelve days hunting and trading with the Indians for furs, and it was at this time that a group of Aleuts discovered the bay. Winship left Trinidad and discovered the entrance, which he named "Resanof" in honor of the Russian Imperial Chamberlain. He found a depth of fifteen feet, which was enough to float his ship. Crossing the bar, Winship came up the channel, which was about the same as the present one. He anchored his ship, the *O'Cain*, at the southern end of what is now known as Indian Island, halfway between the island and the peninsula and called the bay the "Bay of Indians." He made a map of the surrounding country, which is remarkably correct (see Map).[12] Ships of the Russian-American Company made visits to the area between 1806 and 1812. In 1809 Winship made another voyage to the "Bay of Indians."[13]

In 1849 Dr. Josiah Gregg and his party set out from Rich Bay on the Trinity River and discovered the South Fork of the Trinity River. This they followed, and then headed across the mountains on a straight line for the coast. They emerged from the almost impenetrable redwood forest at the mouth of Little River, forty days from the starting date. Traveling south, they reached a stream which they named "Mad River" because of a disagreement in the party.[14]

On December 20, David Buck, who was as usual in advance of the party, discovered the bay, which they named "Trinity Bay" because they thought it was the bay shown on the Spanish maps. At daylight of the next morning, December 21, they moved their camp to the bay on a sandy beach now known as the peninsula. The discovery that they were on a peninsula was made somewhere in the vicinity of Fairhaven. The Indians from their nearby rancheria came to their camp, curious to see the white men. The Gregg party learned that they could not travel south because of the entrance to the bay, which was just below them. David Buck went south to explore, and when he returned, he confirmed the statements of the Indians. He also said that it would be dangerous to attempt to cross to the opposite shore.[15]

They retraced their steps up the peninsula and arrived December 24 on the site of Arcata, at a spring about two hundred yards east of the present plaza. Two days later they started around the southern side of the bay, and camped that night on the site of Bucksport. A few days afterward they continued south, and eventually reached Sonoma.[16]

A large number of gold miners had gone to the many streams in Trinity and Siskiyou Counties in the winter of 1849 and the spring of 1850. These miners were dependent on the slow and expensive interior route up the Sacramento Valley for travel and transportation of supplies. At this time it was believed that a coast route by water would divert this traffic, and in the hope of discovering coastwise communications with the mines by some navigable stream, several expeditions were fitted out. One of the first was that sent out under the auspices of the Laura Virginia Association. The schooner *Laura Virginia* left San Francisco in the latter part of March, 1850, with Captain Ottinger in command.[17]

Sailing up the coast, the men saw the waters of Humboldt Bay from the masthead, but the bar was breaking so heavily that the entrance was not discovered. The *Laura Virginia* arrived April 4 at Trinidad after the group explored to the north. A party of six went ashore to explore the Bay which had been seen. They came down the coast and camped that night under a tree on the peninsula, at a point near where the lighthouse was subsequently erected. While the party gathered around the campfire that night, the members decided to name the body of water "Humboldt Bay," which lay spread out before them. Alexander von Humboldt was a distinguished German scientist whose writings on Spanish America had attracted wide attention at this time. The six members of the party were E.H. Howard, H.W. Havens, S.B. Tucker, Robert La Mott, L.W. Shaw, the famous San Francisco painter, and a Mr. Peebles. The group returned to Trinidad the following day. They were taken aboard, and the vessel returned to the entrance of the bay.[18]

On the following day, a small boat was launched in order to obtain more definite information regarding the channel, before the larger vessel could attempt a crossing. H.H. Buhne, the second officer, succeeded not only in making the entrance, but in repeating the performance later the same day with two of the ship's boats loaded with passengers and supplies. A temporary camp was made on the peninsula and the following morning all moved over to the high point of land (Buhne's Point) lying opposite the entrance, which they named "Humboldt Point." On April 14, the *Laura Virginia* entered the bay. Humboldt Point was looked upon as the central location, and here it was decided to establish a city. An imposing array of tents and buildings soon sprang up, and for a year or more Humboldt City kept in advance of any other town on the bay.

Another town, not recorded by any historian, was laid out on the peninsula about the latter part of June, 1850. "West Humboldt," as the town was called, was two miles north and on the opposite side of the bay, approximately where the United States Coast Guard Station now stands. The extent of the city was one mile and a half on the bay and a half mile in width. The low-water mark was from twelve to fifteen feet. Wharves were to be constructed on this excellent frontage to load and unload cargo.[20]

West Humboldt seems to have died, being unable to compete with the other towns: Union, founded April 21 by the Union Company, which included members of the Gregg expedition; Eureka, founded May 13 by the Union and the Mendocino Companies; and Bucksport, founded in the summer of 1851. In February of 1851, a reporter from San Francisco visited Port Trinidad and Humboldt Bay on board the *Sea Gull*, piloted by Captain Tichenor, and reported the following:

Having been a passenger in the "Sea Gull" on her late trip to Port Trinidad and Humboldt Bay, I give a description of that part of the country that is attracting the attention of a large portion of the people of California. Humboldt Bay, situated about 15 miles to the southward is a most beautiful sheet of water, of 18 miles in length; varying from one to three miles in width.

The town of Humboldt is located near the entrance, it contains from ten to fifteen small houses, and does not appear to be improving much. About two miles up, and on the opposite side of the bay, is what is called West Humboldt, which contains one house and from its location, being on the outer side of the bay, cannot amount to much. About four miles further up we come to "Eureka," containing about 20 houses and one steam sawmill about completed.[21]

During the 1850's settlements spread over the open agricultural lands near the bay, and even began to crowd into the more remote valleys and prairies lying in and beyond the redwood belt. The white men seemed to come from every direction at once. All parties entered the real estate business and began to stake out town sites lining the shores of Eel River, Humboldt Bay, Trinidad Bay, and Klamath River. And the Indians had to take what was left.

Among the earliest arrivals at Humboldt Bay was a Methodist preacher, A.J. Heustis. He is supposed to have conducted the first public religious service on Humboldt Bay, at Bucksport early in the summer of 1850.[22] The camp meeting, always associated with frontier Methodism, was not lacking here. The peninsula offered an excellent place for these services. In August, 1855, the first camp meeting was held there, and boats came from Eureka at regular intervals. The attendance at later services was large, for the meetings served both a religious and a social need, offering a chance for friends to meet and families to reunite.[23]

Fort Humboldt was established in 1853 to protect the settlers from the Indians, even though Colonel Redick McKee had addressed a letter to Governor Bigler severely blaming the whites for their unjustifiable hostility toward the Indians.[24] The press from 1855 to 1865 was filled with a bitter controversy concerning the mismanagement and official misconduct in office exhibited by the Federal agents. These officers charged with the care of the Indians were a bad group. Among their bad habits in neglect of duties was a tendency to neglect the food supply of their wards, through crookedness, neglect, or plain stupidity. Not until the middle 1860's was any consistent scheme set in operation to ensure an adequate year-round food supply. Meanwhile, thousands of Indians had been gathered in droves and herded like cattle from home-sites to some unfamiliar and unpromising reservation. Many of these people escaped at their first opportunity and made their way across the forests toward home. A food supply was not available and even if the raw materials could have been obtained, there was no opportunity to process and store them. Rancheria after rancheria was destroyed in Humboldt County to wear down the Indians by keeping them moving, and preventing them from laying in supplies of food.[25]

The four basic staples of Indian diet were fish, game, acorns, and various seeds. The Indians never did depend greatly for food on the larger fur-bearing animals or the deer. The destruction and disappearance of small rodents was a great misfortune. The rabbit was utilized very much, to some extent, ground squirrels.[26]

Perhaps the greatest anguish was caused by the white man's own domestic animals, particularly cattle and hogs. The fencing-in of free range made trespassers of people who from time immemorial had gone wherever they wished in search of food, particularly acorns, seeds, and green plants. Under the protection of the whites, the cattle ate the grasses which produced the Indians' seeds, and the hogs ate the acorns. The white man recognized that now the Indians were prevented from exercising their normal biological reactions, but they preferred to sacrifice the Indians rather than their livestock.[27]

When the Indian turned to the white man for food, he found one admirable source ready at hand—livestock. The problem of stock raiding had existed since Spanish times. The Indian, faced with starvation, attacked the race responsible for his condition. For a period, until utterly defeated and exhausted, the Indians instinctively demonstrated the primitive, automatic struggle for survival. The main reason for the Indian "wars" and difficulties in northern California up to 1865 had as their basic cause the depletion of the Indian food supply.[28]

Although the regular military forces from Fort Humboldt maintained an appearance of activity in 1860, the Indian depredations continued in the remote valleys and settlements. The soldiers were successful in capturing a large number of prisoners. Because of the crowded conditions at Fort Humboldt, the Indians were removed to the peninsula, across from Bucksport, which during the month of August was converted into a temporary reservation. Captain Gibbs, with twenty men from Fort Humboldt, was able to command the situation by placing sentries across the northern limit of the reserve, and allowing the Indians, who appeared more or less contented, to have considerable freedom over the southern end. This prison camp accomodated between eight and nine hundred Indians.[29]

James Henry Brown is given credit for being the first permanent settler on the peninsula.[30] He lived an adventurous life before finally settling on the peninsula in 1865. Born in Quincy, Illinois in 1830, he left at the age of twenty to join the thousands on their way to the gold fields in California. After mining the streams around Hangtown (Placerville), he headed north with a party. In January of 1851 the party passed through Eureka and Union on their way to Weaverville to again engage in mining. In September of the same year he traveled to San Francisco from where he sailed to Nicaragua. In 1853 he returned to Hangtown and finally came back to Eureka where he opened a blacksmith shop. He sold out the following year and bought some acres on Kneeland Prairie where he tried his hand at farming and stock-raising. In 1859 he moved to Elk River. In 1865 he sold his ranch and moved to the peninsula where he continued to farm and raise stock.[31] The Brown ranch was on the bay side of the peninsula, and on the present site of Samoa. His ranch was then jokingly called Brownsville, and for years the only buildings were the house and barn of the Brown ranch.[32]

Shipbuilding on the bay began almost with the settlement of the country since there was a need for a quick and safe means of communication among the towns of Eureka, Union, and Bucksport, and wood was available from the many different kinds of trees that grew down to the bay. The first sea-going vessel was supposed to have been built about 1854 on the peninsula on the present site of Louisiana-Pacific warehouse 14, but there is no specific documentation.[33]

The Fay Brothers were early shipbuilders on the bay. Early in 1860 they built the *Pert* at Bucksport, which was used for service on Humboldt Bay by Captain H.D.P. Allen.[34] In 1861 the Fay Brothers were on the peninsula across from Bucksport approximately on the site of the Gillette Marine Ways. A report of November, 1861, showed that they were building a vessel seventy feet long by twenty feet, six inches in the beam, and was about eighty tons. During the summer of 1864, the *Phoebe Fay*, a schooner of eighty tons, was launched at their new site.[35]

About 1867 the Fay Brothers converted their shipbuilding plant to a shingle mill. Redwood was found to be an ideal wood for the making of shingles, which to a large extent became a separate industry apart from the sawmills. About 1867 the first documented shingle-sawing plant in the county was constructed by George M. Fay & Brother, or popularly called the Fay Brothers. This mill contained two upright machines, and sawed about 12 million shingles each year. Later this plant was enlarged by the addition of a second mill, and in 1873 its output was about 30 million. Up to this time, this plan produced practically all the sawed shingles manufactured in

Humboldt County, and had a virtual monopoly of the coast market, which at that time meant San Francisco only.[36]

There was a huge demand for shingles in 1879 and the early 1880's because of the Southern California real estate boom. Mills sprang up in all parts of the county and the output of shingles reached nearly 300 million. But in 1892 and 1893, a depression and a glutted market closed many of the shingle mills when the price of shingles on the coast market dropped to little if any above the cost of production.[37] The Fay Brothers closed down their operations, and in 1902 were operating another shingle mill on Kneeland Prairie near the timber.

In 1871 Hans Bendixsen, the foremost shipbuilder on Humboldt Bay, moved his shipyard from the foot of L Street in Eureka to Fairhaven on the peninsula.[39] In the thirty years that he was engaged in ship construction at Fairhaven, he built over one hundred vessels of all classes.[40] In 1892 the largest sailing vessel built in California at that time was launched from this shipyard. This was the *Jane L. Stanford*, having a lumber capacity of 1,250,000 feet. The shipyard had a well-equipped sawmill, which was designed for sawing timbers and other construction work. The shipyard employed over one hundred men, and the daily wage was from $1.00 to $3.50.[41]

Rather than commute each day to work, the Bendixsen employees began to construct homes, and the town of Fairhaven came into being. *The History and Business Directory of Humboldt County* of 1890-1891 had the following to say about Fairhaven, "The Alameda" of Humboldt County:

This beautiful and prosperous village is situated on a peninsula, and is destined to be one of the brightest jewels in Humboldt's crown, bounded on the north by Mad River, east by Humboldt Bay, south by the Humboldt Bay lighthouse, and west by the Pacific Ocean. Can you imagine a lovelier spot for health and pleasure? . . . Fairhaven is connected with Eureka by the Ocean Beach Ferry. Every fruit, grain, grass and shrubbery that grow in any portion of the country will thrive and flourish here without irrigation. The town is beautifully laid out, with a regular street system. At one end of the village on the banks of the bay, is situated Bendixsen's shipyard, constantly employing many men. The north end is occupied by the Fay Bros. Shingle Mill, employing from 30 to 40 men. Its proximity to Eureka, the natural position it occupies as a shipping point, its transportation facilities, its level tracts of land along the bay, all point it out as the place where most of the great manufactories of this country will one day be situated. In the rear of Fairhaven lies one of the grandest ocean beaches in the world. For a stretch of 18 miles you can spin along this magnificent shell-marbeled, ocean-crowned highway and inhale the vigorous sea breeze. . . . We see a grand and pleasing future for this maiden village.[42]

In 1901 Hans Bendixsen sold his shipbuilding plant to a stock company organized by J.C. Bull, netting him close to a quarter of a million dollars.[43]

Experiments in growing tobacco on the peninsula, near Fairhaven, were successfully made in 1888. In 1892, 62,927 pounds of tobacco were produced. Thirteen men were employed, and 2,309,250 cigars were made. The value of the product was $89,783. About 1900 the tobacco industry on the peninsula and along Eel River closed down because the local men could not compete with the cheap tobacco grown in the southern states.[44]

In 1892 a group of Eureka business men formed the Samoa Land and Improvement Company, and purchased the James Brown property and adjacent property. The directors of the company were Dan Murphy, George Miller, G.R. Gibson, S.E. Allard, David Cutten, T.W. Power, and R.W. Rideout. The property, which consisted of two hundred and seventy acres of land and nearly one mile of waterfront, extended from the bay to the ocean. The land was surveyed and lots were to sell from $75 to $300. The Company advertised that this town would be the "Oakland of Humboldt Bay."[45]

At this time, two rival chiefs were fighting for supremacy in the Samoan Islands. They were owned by several European nations that planned to seize part of the islands when the Samoans had exterminated themselves. News of the Samoan Revolution occupied a prominent place on the front pages for some time, and the town builders chose the then popular name. Since then the original tract and the land south along the bay, including the Brown property, have been known as Samoa.[46]

A booklet, called *Samoa or West Eureka*, which was published and circulated by the Company, mentioned the following:

The soil is very productive, and at the present time large quantities of all varieties of garden truck are grown for Eureka markets. . . . The ocean beach is one of the best on the coast of the Pacific, hard and wide. . . . One of the largest shipyards on the coast is now located, opposite Eureka, near the south boundary of the townsite of Samoa and employs about one hundred men continuously. . . . The large lumber mills of the Excelsior Redwood Company are situated on Indian Island in Humboldt Bay, less than one half mile from Samoa.

A large lumber mill (Carson Mill) is nearly completed on the North boundary of the townsite, which will employ quite a number of operatives. Arrangements have been perfected whereby the Vance Estate will locate their railroad, now having a terminus northeast about five and a half miles to the town. The mill of this concern will be the largest of the kind on the Pacific coast and will cost in the neighborhood of $150,000 to construct, and will give employment to nearly two hundred men. . . . Samoa has a climate nearly seven degrees warmer than that of Eureka, and building sites being much higher priced in the latter place, many business men of that city have already purchased lots in Samoa for the building of their homes; plans for several fine residences are now in the hands of architects, and before long many of the best families now living in Eureka will move across the bay to their homes. . . . The Company have rescued six blocks and are now improving and laying grounds, and a large hotel will soon be constructed, with additional salt water bathing facilities adjacent thereto.[47]

The promoters did build three cottages and a huge bath house. The bath house, which was built by Dan Murphy, proprietor of the Western Hotel of Eureka, was located on the bay shore. The bath house had a large swimming tank which was filled with heated water from the bay, and was popular for several years.[48]

Besides the Carson Mill to the north and the proposed Vance Mill, another mill, called the Consumer Mill, was built on the bay, approximately just east of the present new Louisiana-Pacific redwood mill. The D.R. Jones Mill on Gunther Island closed down, and a group of local men bought the machinery and moved it to the peninsula. The new mill did not prove profitable, but it did help to publicize the proposed town.[49]

John Vance, the pioneer lumberman, died on January 23, 1892, and left his estate to his nephew and two sons. The mill at the foot of G Street burned, and the two sons decided to build across the bay where there was plenty of cheap land available for storage space. In 1893 the Vance brothers bought the frontage area on the bay from the Samoa Land and Improvement Company. The old Big Bonanza Mill on Mad River was dismantled and moved to Samoa on the peninsula for temporary use until equipment arrived. The railroad was extended from Mad River Slough down the bay side of the peninsula to the mill. The Samoa mill in 1895 produced 60,000 feet a day and employed 320 men.[50]

Andrew B. Hammond, the founder of the Hammond Lumber Company, began his meteoric rise to the top in Montana, where he began by taking a contract to furnish all the ties, trestle, and tunnel timber for the Northern Pacific Railroad, which was to connect Montana with the East. He later began lumbering operations on the Big Blackfoot River which proved successful. After acquiring the Missoula Water Works and the First National Bank, he bought the Oregon Western and Pacific Railroad. Mr. Hammond then built the Astoria and Columbia River Railroad. Before 1900 he had secured valuable timber lands near Astoria and in the Cascade mountains, and was operating three sawmills in Oregon.[51]

A.B. Hammond was anxious to buy the Vance properties which were for sale at this time. The deal, involving the Vance properties, consisting of several thousand acres of redwood timber, a sawmill, a shingle and shake mill, the Eureka & Klamath River Railroad, a steamer and several lumber schooners, and 1200 feet of waterfront, was completed at the price of $1,000,000. In 1900 the John Vance Mill was incorporated in New Jersey by A.B. Hammond. On September 1 of that year the Samoa mill, the largest redwood mill of that time, began producing lumber as the Vance Redwood Lumber Company. From this time on, as president of the company, Mr. Hammond devoted all this time to developing and enlarging his new enterprise until his death in 1934 at the age of 85.[52]

In 1905 the Vance Redwood Lumber Company expanded its California operations by purchasing property in Los Angeles, and in 1912 the name was changed to the Hammond Lumber Company. Soon after 1912, the Company began to acquire the private homes, lots, and unpurchased land from the Samoa Land and Improvement Company when their dream failed to materialize. By 1924 the Company owned and operated the entire town.[53]

In 1931 The Little River Redwood Company, which began operations in 1908, was merged with the Hammond Lumber Company whose interests controlled the two firms. The name was changed to Hammond and Little River Company, Ltd., but two years later the name of the corporation was again changed to Hammond Redwood Company. The company purchased the Humboldt Redwood Company Mill, located on the southern end of Eureka, in 1937 and this mill became Plant No. 2.[54]

About 1904 Captain W. Coggeshall started his "Coggeshall Launch Company, Ferry to Samoa," at the foot of F Street in Eureka. He purchased his first little boat, the *Island Home*, from William McDade, the Humboldt Bay shipbuilder. By 1914 Coggeshall had eleven ships. Included was the popular stern-wheeler Antelope which was built at the Bendixsen shipyard.[55] The Antelope was used until World War II to ferry the mill workers to the Hammond Mill.

The Coggeshall Launch and Towboat Company took over the New Era Park about 1910 when the former owners failed to make a profit. This park was on the bay shore, and about one hundred yards north of the northern end of Fairhaven (just south of the present Georgia-Pacific Plywood Mill). In 1910 there was a broken down wharf, a redwood open dance platform, and several acres of pine trees. Within three months from the date of transfer, the New Era Park opened with a casino. At that time this was the best recreational park and casino north of San Francisco. The first Chautauqua ever held in northern California had its headquarters on these grounds, the casino being used as the auditorium. In those days the gala event of the year was the May Day Picnic, when schools closed for the day and hundreds of people came over to the park.[56]

In the early part of 1917, James Rolph, Jr., the mayor of San Francisco and later Governor of California, and head of the Rolph Coal and Navigation Company, purchased the southern yard of the old Bendixsen shipyard at Fairhaven and the northern yard of the old shipyard from the Hammond Lumber Company. The new company built many wooden ships here, and the shipyard employed over one thousand men. Fairhaven was renamed Rolph, and at this time the town was a bustling community.[57] When World War I ended and the demand for ships ceased, Rolph developed into a ghost town, inhabited mostly by commercial fishermen. Later the town was renamed Fairhaven. The Hammond Lumber Company also built a shipyard during 1917 and 1918 (just south of boat slip), and constructed seven liberty ships for the United States Government.[58]

One of the most spectacular ship disasters on the Pacific coast occurred on the peninsula in the early morning of January 13, 1917. The cruiser *U.S.S. Milwaukee* ran aground when Captain Newton attempted to pull the submarine *H-3* from the Samoa beach.

The Northern California coast, often called the "graveyard of the Pacific," has always been a dangerous one. During the winter season, gale chases gale, lashing the coast with pounding and slashing combers. Before the *H-3* went aground, twenty-seven vessels had, in the preceding years, gone ashore in the area, many with loss of life.[59] Because of the treacherous waters, the U.S. Government, in 1879, established the U.S. Lifesaving Service Rescue Station at the southern end of the peninsula. Later in 1936 the Humboldt Bay Coast Guard Station was built on the same location.[60]

The *H-3*, under the command of Lieutenant Harry Bogusch, was returning to San Francisco from the Columbia River when the submarine had battery trouble. The sub had experienced bad weather farther north, but on the way south she had been running through fog with few navigational fixes. Visibility was low when a diesel was temporarily disabled, leaving only one engine running.[61]

Bogusch decided to head into the calm waters of Humboldt Bay. The subs of that day had short conning towers which afforded little visibility, and navigating equipment was crude. Landmarks were difficult to recognize, and the tall brick chimney of the Hammond mill might have been mistaken for a beacon on the south jetty that guarded the entrance. The sub was already inside the first line of breakers when Bogusch realized his mistake. But the one engine was not strong enough to move the sub back out, and soon the *H-3* was broadside in the breakers about 300 yards offshore, pounding and rolling fearfully, opposite the southern end of the town of Samoa. The date was December 15, 1916.[62]

A crew from the Humboldt Bay Life Saving Station arrived in answer to the S.O.S., hauling their surfboat on a cart along three miles of sand. The crew first shot a line from a Lyle cannon to the sub, the first step in rigging a breeches buoy. One man appeared from below to brave the heavy surf breaking over the sub, and he managed to secure the line to the conning tower. Then the sub rolled seaward on her side, and the line parted.[63]

Another line was shot across, but no one on board had strength enough to fight the breaking waves topside. The crew finally decided to risk launching their boat, fearing the worst for the men trapped inside. The boat, although nearly swamped, finally made it to the sub, where a crewman with a line tied around his middle managed to jump aboard, while the boat sheered clear of the sub. Making his way along the wavelashed deck, he climbed the conning tower and secured his line, on which he hauled the breeches buoy block aboard. More of the men boarded the sub to help the first man, and one by one, the twenty-seven battered, half-conscious officers and men were hauled safely ashore.[64]

A short time before the beaching of the submarine, the destroyers and submarines of the Pacific Fleet had been combined in a task command called the Coast Torpedo Force under a single Force Commander, who was also commanding officer of the Force Flagship and tender, the first class seven-million-dollar *Milwaukee* of 10,000 tons.[65]

The *Milwaukee* was then at Mare Island, getting an overhaul which included installation of heavy machine tools, fitting her as a tender with ship equipment capable of all routine repairs to the coast torpedo vessels short of a major navy yard overhaul. At this time the Force Commander had been detached because of the cruiser's long stay at the navy yard, and the senior officer Lieutenant Newton was in temporary command as Captain.[66]

The *H-3* had run aground at the Samoa beach before the new Force Commander arrived from the East Coast. At this time Captain Haislip, who was to play a major part in the futile salvaging of the sub, was ordered aboard the tug *Iroquois* to go with Captain Newton to Eureka to pull the stranded sub which was now lying on the sand. The monitor *Cheyenne* and the Coast Guard Cutter *McCullough* were standing by to assist in salvage operations.[67]

The *Iroquois* was not equipped for salvage operations, and none of the navy men were experienced in salvage work. Arriving at Eureka, the officers on board the *Iroquois* established communication with the crew of the *H-3* who had made camp on the sand near their vessel, which was now high and dry at low water.[68]

Attempts to run a line in to the shore failed. Then Harry Bogusch, Skipper of the *H-3*, borrowed a surfboat from the life saving station, and with a volunteer crew, brought out a light line through the rough surf to the *Cheyenne*, and soon a ten-inch Manila line connected the *Cheyenne* to the *H-3*.[69]

At high tide, with the *Iroquois* towing in tandem ahead of the *Cheyenne*, the pulling began, and the *H-3* moved a little until her bow was pointing seawards. After more pulling, the line broke between the sub and the monitor.[70]

Storm warnings were issued, and the sea was beginning to churn. Salvage operations had to be suspended, and the ships headed for Humboldt Bay to let the gale blow itself out. But huge rollers were breaking across the always dangerous entrance, and the ships proceeded to San Francisco.[71]

The Navy decided to turn the salvage operations over to civilian experts and called for bids. One major marine salvage company bid $150,000, and the Mercer-Fraser Construction Company of Eureka bid $18,000. The first bid was considered too expensive, and the other was too little to be taken seriously.[72]

Not happy with the bids, Captain Newton decided to try to salvage the *H-3* again. Only this time, in addition to the *Cheyenne* and the *Iroquois*, they would take the *Milwaukee* whose added 24,000 horsepower would be more than adequate to free the *H-3* from the beach. Captain Haislip was ordered to go aboard the *Milwaukee* for temporary duty as the navigating officer.[73]

The *Milwaukee* and the other ships arrived in a heavy sea and anchored opposite the submarine to begin the salvaging operation. Efforts to bring in a light line by a barge and by buoys failed, and the men on shore refused to take a line out because of the murderous breakers. Finally Haislip borrowed a surfboat from the cutter *McCullough*, which was at the scene. But the men from the Coast Guard refused to accompany Haislip, telling him that it was sure death to run the dangerous surf.[74]

Captain Newton refused to listen, and Haislip and a crew of volunteers moved from the *Milwaukee* to the *H-3* with a light line to haul back the heavier lines. On their way to the shore, two huge waves swamped the boat, throwing the men into the boiling surf. Some of the men, including Haislip, were pulled out unconscious by the many men on shore who formed a human chain into the surf when they spotted a swimmer or a man floating in a life jacket. One man drowned, and his body washed ashore near the harbor entrance.[75]

The capsized boat washed ashore with the line attached to it, and this line was used to haul two wire hawsers, five-inch and six-inch lines, which were fastened securely to a towing tackle in the sub's bow, reinforced by wire straps around the hull. In the meantime the *Milwaukee* had moved in dangerously beyond the breakers to take the ends of the lines.[76]

The local citizens and the Skipper of the Life Saving Station thought that the proposed rescue of the *H-3* was ridiculous and stupid, and that the big expensive cruiser would be lost if she ventured too close to the surf. The Mayor of Eureka and the Skipper pleaded with Captain Haislip to return to the cruiser and to warn Captain Newton that he was in great danger because of the heavy swells and strong current on this part of the coast. The people of the area were so sure that the *Milwaukee* would be lost that they had arranged a signal of five blasts on the Hammond Lumber Company steam whistle to announce to all that the *Milwaukee* was in the breakers![77]

The Skipper finally took Haislip and some of the crew members across the bar and back to the *Milwaukee* in his powered life boat. Once aboard Haislip told Captain Newton of the danger, but the Captain refused to change his mind. In the meantime, the *Milwaukee* and the other two ships had already attempted to pull the *H-3*, moving the sub a couple of feet on the sand. High tide would come the next morning at 3:00 a.m., and Newton was determined to try again.[78]

In the foggy darkness, between 3 and 4 a.m., on January 13, the three ships began simultaneously to pull the submarine: there were two lines from the cruiser to the submarine, and two separate lines from the bow of the cruiser, one to the tug *Iroquois* and the other to the tender *Cheyenne*. Suddenly the hawser to the *Cheyenne* broke, and the *Milwaukee* swung violently to port. Commander Frank Bruce on the tug tried desparately to hold the cruiser's bow toward the sea, but the tug was too small with inadequate horsepower. Although the *Iroquois* was being forced to the shore by the steady pressure of the waves and tide, Bruce held on as long as he could. But when he saw the first line of breakers in the darkness, he cut the hawser to the *Milwaukee*.[79]

With the aid of searchlights, Commander Howe on the *Cheyenne* saw what was happening, and he followed the *Milwaukee* in and attempted to shoot a line to the cruiser. His two attempts failed. The heavy cables, the big swells, and the strong current finally forced the *Milwaukee* into the breakers, her bottom plates touching the sandy bottom from time to time with each heavy swell. The men worked desperately to cut the lines, but the cruiser was trapped in the mechanism with which she had hoped to save the submarine. The strong current put such a strain on the towing cables that they could not be cleared. Soon about 4:10 a.m., the *Milwaukee* was in twelve feet of water, broadside to the beach, and tilting at a twenty-degree list.[80]

Captain Newton radioed the other ships to stay clear, that the *Milwaukee* was in the breakers beyond help. The message was intercepted by the nearby Table Bluff Radio Station, which in turn was relayed to the Humboldt Bay Life Saving Station on the peninsula. And soon after five shrill blasts pierced the cold morning air, announcing to all that the *Milwaukee*, a seven million-dollar, four-stack, first class cruiser, had come ashore to stay.[81]

Although many of the men were shaken in the rolling and lurching ship, only one man was injured. When daylight appeared, the seashore was wrapped in a dense blanket of fog. About 10 a.m., the fog lifted, and the men from the Life Saving Station succeeded in shooting a line to the cruiser which was secured to the main mast. The ship was rolling, causing the line on which a breeches buoy was attached to go slack and then jerk taut. The first two passengers, Haislip and another crewman, were jerked high into the air and then plunged into the surf. Even though the men ashore pulled as fast as they could, the men made most of the distance under water. Once the system was perfected, two men at a time were brought in.[82]

The system of the breeches buoy was too slow to bring in 450 men, so a boat had to be launched. The Skipper of the life saving crew refused to launch a boat in the dangerous surf. So Harry Bogusch, the Skipper of the *H-3*, borrowed a surfboat and asked for volunteers from the large number of men on shore. Many of the local citizens volunteered, and soon two surfboats were kept busy ferrying the navy men to shore, using relief crews to keep the oarsmen fresh.[83]

Bonfires blazed through the fog up and down the beach, and hundreds of citizens supplied hot coffee and sandwiches. Rescue operations went on all day while the surf kept moderating. By nightfall when Captain Newton came ashore in the last boat, he and those with him were not even splashed with spray.[84]

Eyewitnesses report that most of the people in Humboldt County rushed to the scene of the disaster. The Coggeshall Launch and Towboat Company was kept busy transporting people from Eureka to Samoa. Government and navy officials, as well as sightseers, kept the beach well populated during the entire winter.[85] And years later the cruiser was still a tourist attraction.

The Mercer-Fraser Construction Company of Eureka was finally awarded the contract to refloat the *H-3*. Timber balks were laid in a three-foot-high wooden double track across the half-mile sandy peninsula, and the *H-3*, cradled between two huge redwood logs, was pulled into the calm waters of Humboldt Bay. After a cleaning, the sub resumed her interrupted voyage to San Francisco, in tow of the *Iroquois*.[86]

A railroad spur was constructed over the sand dunes to the beach where a wharf was built to the *Milwaukee*. All that could be salvaged from the cruiser was taken away by train.[87] The once-proud *Milwaukee* was gradually obliterated by the elements and professional and amateur shipwreckers. The final act occurred during World War II when the remains of the *Milwaukee* were salvaged for scrap to help the war effort. A few years ago parts of the hull were still visible during a minus tide.

The writer was born and raised in the company town of Samoa, which was a stable community prior to World War II. The peninsula was a paradise for the youth: acres and acres of sand dunes, pine woods to the north and south of town, the Pacific Ocean to the west, and Humboldt Bay to the east.

Boredom was never a part of growing up. Wild strawberries, huckleberries, and blackberries grew in profusion; an over-supply of rabbits—both cottontails and jack rabbits—populated the lupine bushes and beach grass; many species of ducks and geese literally filled the bay on their way south; and during the summer, schools of salmon followed the smaller fish into the bay. At night or on rainy days there was always the huge gymnasium in which to play basketball and handball and to box, and nearby was the baseball diamond for baseball or softball. The Firemen's pool hall was always open for pool or billiards.

The Company was paternal in helping the older boys to get jobs, and after World War II veterans could work part-time and attend Humboldt State College. Bosses "Bud" Peterson and "Tony" Oliveira went beyond the call of duty in helping the local students in quest of an education.

Soon after war was declared on December 7, 1941, the U.S. Government established a sea plane base and a blimp base, between the Coast Guard Station and Fairhaven, to patrol the ocean for enemy submarines and to protect the shipping lanes off the coast. Long-range guns were placed at strategic positions along the peninsula, and men from the Coast Guard Station patrolled the Pacific beach on horses.[88]

After the war the City of Eureka purchased the blimp base, which became the Eureka Airport. Since the war, many homes have been built on the northern end of the peninsula, and the new community is called Manila.

After the war a nation-wide demand for lumber, pent up by more than a decade of depression and war, drove the country's demand to the highest levels in forty years. At the same time easily available old growth timber in the Pacific Northwest was being depleted. This meant that lumbermen had to look for undeveloped timber areas in order to meet the swelling demand. Many of them came to Humboldt County, attracted by the untapped stands of Douglas fir. The result was spectacular. By 1953 lumber production in the county was four and one half times more than it had been in 1940, and the number of sawmills had multiplied eightfold.[89]

On April 1, 1955 the Simpson Logging Company (now the Simpson Timber Company) of Washington, which had bought extensive timber lands along the Klamath River after World War II, purchased the Northern Redwood Lumber Company. The company built a new mill at Klamath, and also built a huge remanufacturing plant, which included a planing mill and drying yards, just west of Arcata near the ocean. On October, 1967, the Simpson Timber Company acquired the Mutual Plywood Plant at Fairhaven from the U.S. Plywood Champion Papers, Inc., which was built in the late 1940's.[90]

On Thursday, May 24, 1956, the local newspapers carried the big news that the Hammond Lumber Company had been sold to the Georgia-Pacific Corporation of Atlanta, Georgia, for $80 million. The sale of the Hammond Lumber Company, one of the two largest redwood mills in the United States, was the biggest private financial deal in the history of Humboldt County.[91]

In July of 1963 the Georgia-Pacific Corporation at Samoa, in addition to constructing a plywood mill, built a $3,500,000 new redwood mill operated by a highly automated push button system. The old mill, originally built by the Vance Lumber Company in 1894, was shut down December 18, 1964. The new mill began production August 14, 1965. This mill produces 160,000 board feet of lumber each eight-hour shift. The automated mill eliminated fifty jobs, including the popular setter or ratchet setter who operated the set works on the carriage.[92]

The bleached kraft pulp mills on the Samoa peninsula are the big news in the lumber business today. The huge plants dominate the peninsula and can be seen for miles. The Georgia-Pacific Corporation, which built the first pulp mill to be designed and constructed to utilize redwood chips as a raw material source for bleached kraft pulp, began to operate in 1965.[93]

In 1966 the Crown Simpson pulp mill was built at Fairhaven, just south of the Georgia-Pacific plant on the peninsula. This mill represents a partnership of two of the major forest product companies in the Northwest: the Crown Zellerbach Corporation of San Francisco, the second largest paper manufacturer in the world, and the Simpson Timber Company, with headquarters in Seattle. The Fairhaven mill, built at a cost of some $50 million, has a capacity of 500 tons a day of bleached kraft pulp. Simpson and Crown Zellerbach each receive half of the mill's production and sell it separately in the world market. Simpson supplies the chips and Crown Zellerbach personnel manage and operate the mill.[94] 94

The pulp manufactured by both pulp mills is produced entirely from wood chips generated by lumber and plywood mill operations in Northern California. These chips, both redwood and Douglas fir, were formerly burned as unusable material by the mills, and the pulp industry has provided the lumber and plywood interests with a major new source of revenue.

Since the 1930's there has been much discussion of a proposed bridge linking Eureka with the peninsula. This dream will become a reality on May of 1971 when the new Samoa Bridge, which cost more than $5 1/4 million and which is two miles in length, will be opened to vehicular traffic.[95] The span—actually three bridges—is built to the north of deep water and the shipping channels. The two-laned bridge leaves Eureka at R Street, crosses the Eureka channel, the north end of Woodley Island, the north end of Indian Island, the Samoa channel, and reaches the peninsula just north of Samoa to a new highway which was built in 1970 along the ocean, bypassing Samoa and meeting the old road near the Eureka Airport, south of Fairhaven.

Thus the peninsula, which has played an important part in the history of the county and which has fulfilled the prophecy of 1890 that "most of the great manufactories of this country will one day be situated on the peninsula," has become one of the most important areas in the Redwood Country.

FOOTNOTES

1. Owen C. Coy, *The Humboldt Bay Region* 1850-1875 (Los Angeles: The California State Historical Association, 1929), p. 12.
2. Gladys Nomland and A.L. Kroeber, "Wiyot Towns" in *Varia Anthropologica* (Berkeley: University of California Publications in American Archaeology and Ethnology, 1936), p. 45.
3. *Ibid.*, p. 46.
4. *Ibid.*, p. 45. Also Llewellyn L. Loud, *Ethnogeography and Archaeology of the Wiyot Territory* (Berkeley: University of California Publications in American Archaeology and Ethnology, 1918), p. 302.
5. Loud, p. 403.
6. Nomland, p. 47. Also observations by the writer.
7. Loud, pp. 265-266.
8. *Ibid.*, p. 269.
9. Nomland, p. 47; Loud, p. 403.
10. Loud, p. 274.
11. Coy, *Humboldt Bay Region,* p. 29.
12. Leigh H. Irvine, *History of Humboldt County California* (Los Angeles, 1915), pp. 27-28.
13. Chad L. Hoopes, *Fort Humboldt, Explorations of the Humboldt Bay Region and The Military Fort.* Published by California State Division of Beaches and Parks, 1963.
14. A.J. Bledsoe, *Indian Wars of the Northwest* (San Francisco, 1885), p. 88. Louis K. Wood, a member of the Gregg party, published the story of the discovery of Humboldt Bay in *The Humboldt Times* of April 26, 1856. The narrative appeared again in *The Humboldt Times,* February 7, 1863. The story can also be found in the *West Coast Signal* (Eureka, California) for March 20, 1873; *Quarterly of the Society of California Pioneers,* Vol. IX, No. I (April, 1932), p. 43; Irvine's *History of Humboldt County* (Los Angeles, 1915); and Chad Hoopes, *Lure of Humboldt Bay Region,* Dubuque, 1967), pp. 155-178.
15. *Ibid.*, pp. 89-90.
16. *Ibid.*
17. Coy, p. 45; Hoopes, *Lure of Humboldt Bay Region,* p. 32.
18. *Souvenir of Humboldt County* (Eureka: Times Publishing Company, 1902), pp. 6-7.
19. *Ibid.*, pp. 7-8.
20. San Francisco *California Courier,* July 10, 1850. Credit must go to Instructor Chad Hoopes of the College of the Redwoods, who discovered this important information in the Bancroft Library in Berkeley.
21. San Francisco *Daily Pacific News,* February 20, 1851. Courtesy of Chad Hoopes.
22. Wallace W. Elliott, *History of Humboldt County, California* (San Francisco, 1881), p. 213.
23. Coy, p. 306.
24. *Ibid.*, pp. 141-142.
25. S.F. Cook, *The Conflict Between the California Indian and White Civilization:* III (Berkeley, 1943), p. 31.
26. *Ibid.*, pp. 33-34.
27. *Ibid.*, p. 31.
28. *Ibid.*, p. 37.
29. *The Humboldt Times,* September 6, 1862; Coy, p. 174.
30. Mrs. Elsie Miller, "Samoa, Then and Now," *Redwood Log,* Vol. 6 (April, 1953), pp. 1-2.
31. Irvine, pp. 770-771.
32. Interview with Mrs. Elsie Miller, whose mother, Anna Whitaker, was an

early resident of Samoa. Mrs. Whitaker left a folder which contained information on the early history of the peninsula.

33. *Souvenir of Humboldt County*, p. 118.
34. *Ibid.*, p. 116.
35. Coy, p. 219.
36. *Souvenir of Humboldt County*, p. 70.
37. *Ibid.*, pp. 70-71.
38. *Ibid.*, p. 84.
39. Irvine, p. 810.
40. *Ibid.*
41. S.M. Eddy, *In The Redwood's Realm*, (San Francisco, 1893), p. 47.
42. *History and Business Directory of Humboldt County*, 1890-1891, p. 113.
43. Irvine, p. 810.
44. Eddy, p. 59.
45. Interview with the late Mr. James McArthur, Sr. of Samoa, January, 1947.
     Mr. McArthur was employed by Hammond Lumber Company and later
     Georgia-Pacific for more than 50 years.
46. Interview with Mrs. Elsie Miller, January, 1947.
47. Information from the booklet owned by the late Mr. James McArthur, Sr.
48. Interview with Mrs. Elsie Miller, January, 1947. There is a picture of the
     Samoa Baths in Eddy's *In The Redwood's Realm*, p. 96.
49. Earl G. Roberts, *They Called It West Eureka, The Humboldt Historian*,
     Vol. XVII, (September-October, 1969), p. 1.
50. Hyman Palais and Earl Roberts, "The History of the Lumber Industry in
     Humboldt County" *Pacific Historical Review*, Vol. XIX (February, 1950),
     p. 8; Howard Brett Melendy, "One Hundred Years of the Redwood
     Lumber Industry, 1850-1950," (unpublished Ph.D. dissertation, Dept. of
     History, Stanford University, Stanford, 1952), p. 72.
51. "Hammond's 50th Anniversary," *Redwood Log*, Vol. 3 (March, 1950), pp.
     1-2.
52. *Ibid.*
53. Elsie Miller, *Redwood Log.*
54. "Hammond's 50th Anniversary," *Redwood Log.*
55. Irvine, p. 301.
56. *Ibid.*
57. "Humboldt County California Wants Your Factory," *Industrial Edition of
     Humboldt Times* (Times Publishing Company, Eureka, 1917), p. 18.
58. Elsie Miller, *Redwood Log.*
59. Captain Harvey Haislip, "The Valor of Inexperience," *United States Naval
     Institute Proceedings*, Vol. 93, (February, 1967), p. 35.
60. *The Times-Standard*, May 16, 1970.
61. Haislip, p. 36.
62. *Ibid.*
63. *Ibid.*
64. *Ibid.*, pp. 36-37.
65. *Ibid.*, p. 37.
66. *Ibid.*
67. *Ibid.*
68. *Ibid.*, p. 38.
69. *Ibid.*, p. 39.
70. *Ibid.*
71. *Ibid.*
72. *Ibid.*
73. *Ibid.*
74. *Ibid.*, p. 41.
75. *Ibid.*, p. 44.

76.	*Ibid.*
77.	*Ibid.*, p. 45.
78.	*Ibid.*, p. 46.
79.	*Ibid.*, pp. 46-47.
80.	*Ibid.*, p. 47.
81.	*Ibid.*
82.	*Ibid.*, p. 48. Also Arthur L. Brickey, "The U.S.S. Milwaukee Story," Speech (Humboldt County Historical Society), April, 1963. Mr. Brickey was a member of the crew.
83.	Haislip, pp. 48-49.
84.	*Ibid.*, p. 49
85.	Interview with Mrs. Elsie Miller, January, 1947; interview with the late Mr. Wesley Dean, Sr., January, 1947.
86.	Haislip, p. 49.
87.	Interview with the late Mr. Wesley Dean, Sr., January, 1947.
88.	Interview with Eureka Fire Chief Ray Lay, March, 1971. Chief Lay, who was a radioman on a blimp crew, was stationed at the base during the war.
89.	Interview with John Sten former mill superintendent, March, 1966.
90.	Interview with James Hartley, March, 1971. Mr. Hartley is Public Relations man for the Simpson Timber Company.
91.	*The Humboldt Times*, May 24, 1956.
92.	Interview with Arthur "Bud" Peterson, March, 1971. Mr.Peterson is Public Relations man for Georgia-Pacific, Redwood Division.
93.	Interview with Bud Peterson, March, 1971.
94.	Interview with James Hartley.
95.	*The Times-Standard*, March 23, 1971.

FIGURE 7-1. Bendixsen's Shipyard at Fairhaven. In 1892 the Barkentine Jane L. Stanford was launched at the Bendixsen's shipyard at Fairhaven on the peninsula. At this time this was the largest vessel of this type ever built in California. A.W. Ericson Photograph.

FIGURE 7-2. The *U.S.S. Milwaukee* on the morning of January 13, 1917. Notice the crew on the decks. Courtesy Humboldt County Historical Society.

FIGURE 7-3. A picture of the peninsula, Humboldt Bay, and the city of Eureka. Above the two multi-million-dollar pulp mills on the left is the town of Samoa. The pilings for the Samoa bridge may be traced across the bay in the upper part of the photo. Courtesy David Swanlund.

FIGURE 7-4. An early photograph of Samoa, taken about 1910. Notice the sailing vessels in the background. Courtesy Georgia-Pacific, Redwood Division.

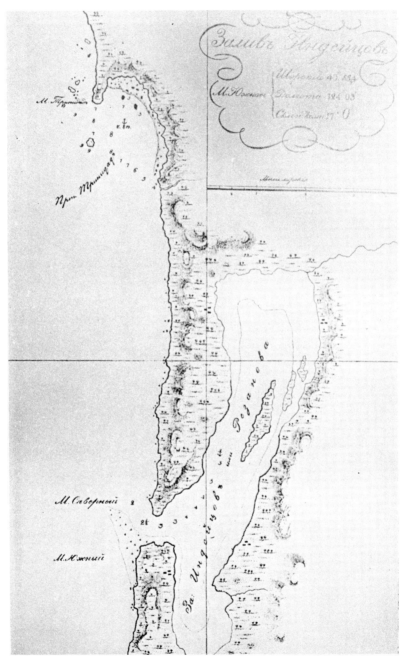

FIGURE 7-5. The Winship Chart of Humboldt Bay, 1806.

FIGURE 7-6. On March 1, 1907, the *Corona*, because of a mixup in orders, went aground on the north jetty. Only one person out of 154 aboard was lost in the disaster. Courtesy Humboldt County Historical Society.

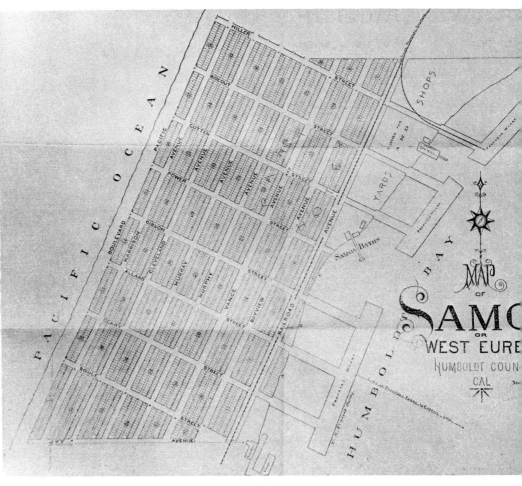

FIGURE 7-7. A map of the proposed town of Samoa which the Samoa Land and Improvement Company were going to develop. Courtesy James McArthur family.

CHAPTER

8

Seth Kinman

Chad L. Hoopes

Table Bluff, near the community of Loleta, overlooks the Pacific Ocean, and here I located Seth Kinman's grave in an ancient, run-down cemetery. The grave was covered with brush, wild grape and ivy, entangled and wild like Seth's spirit. Seth slept in a country where he enjoyed numerous adventures during his lifetime. He was not a mountain man—the lusty trailbreaker who pushed his way into each succeeding strip of wild country ahead of the settler and frequently left his bones as gruesome landmarks of his failure to survive the rigors of his calling—but a hunter and storyteller. Seth Kinman had set out into the wilderness, not to build an empire, but to hunt and to find some release for his wild, "romantic spirit," which had evolved from his contact with nature that developed in him expressions of brutality, viciousness, cunning, and good humor.

Born on the frontier on September 29, 1815, near Uniontown, Pennsylvania, Seth lived in the shadows of the Alleghenies where he explored the haunts of the Indians; here he trapped, fished, and hunted as a renegade white, perhaps more devilish than the Indians living there. He dressed in full backwoods toggery of buckskin that fitted well his tall, straight frame. At fifteen, he appeared a powerful and most formidable looking man who followed his father, James Kinman, to Pekin, Illinois. James Kinman, unlike his son, was an ambitious, speculative man, who secured a favorably located tract of land, laid out a cabin, and built a grist mill. Before the business enterprise could operate, Chief Blackhawk and his followers terrorized the new settlers. James Kinman joined the frontier army of militiamen who took the field against the Indians. Seth remained behind to defend his home, to help erect a fort, and to take, "with the other men, his turn standing guard with a long rifle."[1]

Seth always drove himself to work the family grist mill, while his restless, ambitious spirit was "hungry for the fruits of the hunt."

Often, Seth and his close companions hunted, fished, and trapped near the settlement, but game was not plentiful. Every time Seth heard a trapper or a teamster tell stories where the "game was more plentiful" he could not resist leaving his "artificial life." In 1836 Jacob Farnham sought "six or seven good, stout-hearty young men who were good shots with the rifle and good hunters" to accompany him to Oregon and California. But Seth's father needed his son at home and did not speak to Seth of Farnham's expedition.

Seth worked his father's mill until 1839 when his father died. He then sold the mill and purchased a farm. On January 14, 1846, Seth married Anna Maria Sharpless and tried farming, but "the lure of the hunt was still in his blood. He would rather hunt than plow." Game became scarcer; Seth became ill with consumption. Then in 1849 the "California Fever" spread. Unable to control his hunger for the mountains, Seth told his wife:

... I am going to California and see if I can't find a more healthy country than this, for if I stay here another year, the chances are you will plant me here. I am going to get out of this miserably sickly country and make arrangements to start as soon as possible. I hear that California is healthy, with plenty of mountains, good water, and lots of game.[2]

Dressed in buckskin, belted and bristling with hunter's arms, Seth and his mule Dave arrived at Independence in April. He met an old friend of the family; they purchased pack mules and equipment and left May 10 on the trail to California, arriving in Hangtown, now Placerville, in August.[3] Seth soon fled from Hangtown where he had watched the miners dig their graves as they exhaustingly dug for the elusive gold. "Not being much of a hand at digging in the ground," he wanted no part of this drudgery; he decided to hunt for game. By the following spring, he was in the Trinity River country north of Sacramento hunting game for the Pierson B. Reading expedition that was surveying the Trinity River. Reading supposed that the river, which he named, emptied into Trinidad Bay, as marked by the old Spanish charts. Seth went with Reading to Weaverville. While traversing the mountains of the Trinity country, he met Indians who described the Humboldt Bay Region. The descriptions, depicting the country "full of elk, grizzlies, a fine grass country and full of salmon," pleased Seth. He believed that this natural paradise would be an ideal one for his family which he had left in Illinois.

Anxious to move them to Humboldt country, Seth returned overland to Illinois in the fall of 1850. Upon his arrival, he discovered that malaria had taken its toll in Pekin, that his family had contracted the dreaded disease, and that they would be in no condition to travel to California for some time. Seth forced himself to farm for two years, during which time he lost two children to the fever.[4] He was dissatisfied with farm work, and he wanted to begin a new life in California. In the spring of 1852, Seth left his family a second time and went overland to California to locate a homestead in Humboldt country.

Seth took passage on a San Francisco steamer bound for Humboldt Bay. At Eureka, he met James T. Ryan who was impressed with Seth's remarkable shooting. "Mr. Ryan suggested that as he employed a good many men, and fresh meat was scarce, he would take all the fresh meat Seth could bring him." Kinman also took a government contract to furnish elk meat for the troops at Fort Humboldt.[5] Kinman built a cabin where present day Ferndale stands; later, he built another cabin on Bear River Ridge "for the reception of his family." He left a friend, George Hill, to clear land and plant crops while he returned to Illinois for his family. He left Eureka in September 1853. However, he was shocked to learn that his wife had died of the fever while he was in Humboldt country. According to one of Seth's friends:

Her death deprived him of the mainstay of the family, the mother. Her authority and care devolved on his aged mother, and Seth says: "never did mortal woman fulfill her trust better than she whilst she lived." The settled life in the Illinois home did not suit his taste, and he disposed of his property. So in May 1854, he started once more across the plains with his mother and three children. They joined a wagon train and brought with them 60 head of cattle. He had the cattle placed on a ship and taken to Table Bluff, and after much difficulty, 10 out of the 60 cattle reached the cabin on Bear River Ridge, near what is still known as Kinman Pond.[6]

Kinman had trouble with the Indians who burned his cabin three times. Seth, fearing that the Indians would kill all of his precious cattle, moved his family to Table Bluff in 1857. Since he was close to Fort Humboldt, he made new contracts to furnish meat to the soldiers.

The soldiers at Fort Humboldt greeted Seth when he delivered meat to the cookhouse, not so much for the meat, but for the pleasure Seth gave them with his yarns. Seth's close friend, George McClellan, described Seth's appearance that awed the soldiers:

Seth was a big man and physically strong, well over six feet in height and weighed 200 lbs. He had piercing blue eyes, heavy sandy whiskers and dressed as a typical frontiersman. He had the usual pioneer's contempt for the city dweller. In his mature years, he wore a full beard, which he kept tucked in his buckskin jacket. He wore a hunter's shirt, buckskin pants and coat with heavy boots, the tops of which he wore outside his pantaloons. On the sides of his pantaloons were strips of buckskin and on the sleeves and collar of his coat were rows of the same material. The skirts of his coat were bordered with it, and there were also strips of it on the seams and back of his coat, which with his long hair and beard gave him a very shaggy appearance. Over the whole costume, he wore a red flannel blanket in cold or rainy weather. He possessed a deep, melodious voice and even as an old man, was a great storyteller.[7]

Seth played a fiddle which he had constructed in part from the forehead of his favorite mule Dave, "whose spirit he hoped to meet in the beyond." Dressed in his full regalia of buckskin, Seth would jig his feet and bray out the "Arkansas Traveler" to the intense delight of the attentive soldiers. Because he played this tune, "the best ever heard," many people called him "Arkansas." Seth would also spellbind the soldiers with the exploits of his adventures with Indians and grizzlies. But, according to one eyewitness, Seth always needed a few glasses of liquor before he could shine in his particular sphere. Seth remarked about the Humboldt County Indians:

You can't trust an Injun, I know em. If they git the upperhand of you, they will cinch you sure. The only way to get along with them is to make them afeard of you. I told them Eel River Indians I was a conjurer, and couldn't be killed by a bullet or arrer, and to prove it I took my buckskin shirt off and set it up twenty steps off, and told them the man who could put a arrer through it might have it. They were more than a hour shooting at that shirt, and they couldn't faze it, because the shirt is well-tanned and tough, and I just stood it up on the edges, so that when a arrer struck it, it would naturally give away.[8]

On another occasion he told a story of how he had wounded a large grizzly that he and his Indian companion had trailed. The bear turned on them and it was a "nip and tuck race." Seth was a good runner, but the Indian was better. Seth realized that the bear was gaining on them, so he knocked the Indian down, and before he could get up and run, the grizzly had the Indian. Seth remarked that "the bare chawed him up awhile, and then left him, and the Injun finally got well. If it had of been me I would of died. Injuns can stand a great deal of hurtin and not die."[9]

Seth enjoyed hunting grizzly bears; at least his storytelling indicates the fact. According to this hunter, "you shoot a grizzly in his tender place—about the ear, then he goes round and round like a top until he drops. But if you only wound him, you spile his mind." Seth's dogs jumped a large bear in the brush near the Eel River—"a whooper he war." The hunter fired at the grizzly as it rushed by him, hitting the creature in the back and knocking it down the river bank into the grapevines and thick brush. The following morning Seth put his dogs on the bear's trail which was easy to follow because the bear was dragging his hind legs which indicated that its back was broken.

Soon the dogs began baying, and when Seth arrived on the scene, he found the bear sitting on his rump in a water hole. The storyteller said that the bear:

... was snappin his teeth at my dogs as they swum around him, barkin like fury. I thought I would have a little fun by aggravatin him awhile. I took some big rocks and went up close to him and hit him between the eyes. You out to have heered him yowl. His eyes actually turned green he was so mad, and his jaws champed like a sawmill, but he couldn't budge. Evertime he tried to get on his feet he fell back, the maddist bar I ever seen.[10]

Seth stated that four men pulled the grizzly out of the water, the animal weighed 1,300 pounds. Kinman also claimed to have killed more than 800 grizzly bears in his lifetime and slaughtered fifty elk in one month in Humboldt country. The soldiers at Fort Humboldt consumed 240 elk in eleven months.

The hunter's impressionable career eventually climaxed in Washington, D.C., where he attracted great attention and drew crowds of people, while the press had a field day. In 1857, 1864, 1865 and 1876, Seth Kinman presented an elk-horn chair of different character and shape to Presidents Buchanan, Lincoln, Johnson, and Hayes. Seth greatly admired James Buchanan and wished to flatter this "guardian of liberty" with a throne of elk horns. With the chair on his back, the strongly built and grizzly-bearded hunter made his way to Washington by way of San Francisco. He was dressed in one of his buckskin suits made by himself:

It was trimmed with fringe from an old red army sash. Around his waist dangled a huge pouch of bearskin, decorated with bears' claws. His cap was made of black bearskin, a band of brown bearskin, and a grizzly bear's tail looped across the top for an ornament.[11]

While in San Francisco he was persuaded to show his chair at a fair. Various people were so overcome by the colorful hunter's plan to present his novel gift to the President himself that they contributed money to pay Seth's passage to the nation's Capitol.

James Buchanan, courteous and business-like, accepted Seth's chair and, in exchange, Buchanan purchased the best rifle he could find in New York for Seth, together with two fine pistols. Since Seth was well-acquainted with the Humboldt Bay country, Buchanan appointed Seth as agent at a salary of $1,800.00 to help return the California Indians to their reservations.[12]

Perhaps more amusing and more dramatic is John Huntington's account of Abraham Lincoln receiving his chair from Seth. Huntington, Seth's cousin, recalled that when Kinman first met Lincoln, the hunter immediately related the sorrowful account of how his mule

Dave died on the plains; then he described how he had made a fiddle from the mule's skull, all the time displaying it to Lincoln, who was comfortably seated in his elk-horn chair. Lincoln remarked; "Mr. Kinman, you got my measure pretty well; it just fits me." The President asked Seth to play his mule-head fiddle. What followed has been described like this:

Mr. Lincoln, I will play you two tunes, one is the "Essence of Old Virginia," and the other is "Root Hog or Die." Well, when Kinman drew the bow across those strings, the music hit Lincoln hard; it took Old Abe down so, that he laughed until his stovepipe hat fell off on the floor. When the music ceased, Mr. Lincoln said: "Now Mr. Kinman, I will take the chair and you take the violin; for I can sit in the chair but I can't play that violin."[13]

The chair Seth Kinman constructed for Andrew Johnson is worth describing:

The four legs and claws were those of a huge grizzly and the back and sides ornamented with immense claws. The seat was soft and exceedingly comfortable, but the great feature of the chair was that, by touching a cord, the head of a monster grizzly bear with jaws extended, would dart out in front from under the seat, snapping and gnashing its teeth as natural as life.

As Seth prepared to present this chair to President Johnson, some government official offered to make a presentation speech for Seth; the hunter said: "No, sir, you can't. I ain't much posted on grammer nor Webster, but damned if I can't make the President understand me." Johnson was very amused, but requested Seth to explain why he had attached the grizzly head to the chair. Seth told him it was to keep the office seekers from getting too close.[14]

In a minor way, Seth was a national figure; but in 1888 he died in obscurity from complications resulting from a gunshot. Seth accidentally shot his leg bone below the knee; both break and wound did not heal, and, on January 24, 1888, the doctors amputated his leg. But his condition became worse, and he died Monday, February 24, 1888, and was buried in one of his buckskin suits in the Table Bluff Cemetery.

FOOTNOTES

1. Marshall R. Anspach, "The Lost History of Seth Kinman," *Now and Then*, VIII, (April, 1947), pp. 188-189.
2. Seth Kinman's Manuscript. In possession of Margaret James Anderson, Eureka, California.
3. Anspach, *op. cit.*, p. 191.
4. Seth Kinman Manuscript.
5. Leeper, *op. cit.*, p. 131.
6. Andrew Genzoli, "Seth Kinman," *The Grizzly Bear*, August, 1931.
7. Anspach, *op. cit.*, p. 190.

8. Simpson Letters, *op. cit.*, April 28, 1857. Chad L. Hoopes, "Seth Kinman—Man of the Mountains," *Mountain Men and the Fur Trade*, Vol. V, p. 227.

9. *Frank Leslie's Illustrated Newspaper*, June 3, 1857.

10. O. Fritzgerald, *California Sketches* (San Francisco: Palmer Company, 1898), p. 31.

11. Simpson Letters, *op. cit.*, April 28, 1857.

12. *Washington Dollar Star*, April 29, 1857. Anspach, *op. cit.*, p. 195.

13. John C. Huntington, *Reminiscences of a Pioneer of Kansas and the Two Mexicos* (Pennsylvania: Williamsport, 1897).

14. Kinman Manuscript. Anspach, *op. cit.*, p. 196.

FIGURE 8-1. Seth Kinman.

The Northern California Vendetta

Lynwood Carranco *and* Estle Beard

The Hatfield and McCoy clans of Pike County, Kentucky, were in the national spotlight for two decades, but there is another little-known feud that occurred in Mendocino County in northern California, some seventeen years before the beginning of the Hatfield-McCoy feud. Although the Frost-Coates feud of Mendocino County never assumed the proportions of the legendary one of Kentucky, there are similarities between the two.

One of the bloodiest and most fatal affrays that ever took place in California occurred at Little Lake Valley, fourteen miles north of Ukiah, the county seat of mountainous Mendocino County. And like that remote wilderness part of Kentucky and West Virginia, the Frost and Coates clans lived in another isolated area of the country, probably the last of the West to be settled.

Little Lake Valley was first settled in 1853. The Baechtel brothers brought a herd of cattle from Marin County in 1855, and the first beginnings of a town was at the Baechtel ranch where a public hall was built in 1860, and a dance was held on July 4th. A store was opened in 1865, but a rupture in business led to the establishment of an opposition town, Willits, which was located a mile north.[1]

The legend states that the famous Kentucky feud began when Floyd Hatfield stole two hogs from Randolph McCoy, chief of the McCoy clan who lived across the Little Tug River in Pike County. The Frost-Coates feud was the result of a quarrel between two school boys. The Frost clan had come from Missouri and the Coates from Pennsylvania and Wisconsin. The two clans settled near one another in Little Lake Valley. The hatred between the two clans finally erupted in one glorious fight with much blood spilled. The Hatfield-McCoy feud, which began in 1882 and ended about 1906, cost close to twenty lives, but no more than four persons were ever killed in any one of their battles.[2] On October 11, 1865 (given date in the old histories although the grave stones state October 16, 1867), six men were killed in the fight between the two groups: one Frost and five of the Coates clan.[3]

The children of both families attended the district school in the valley. One day the sons of the two families got into an argument and began to fight. The teacher then interfered and gave the boys a good thrashing for breaking the school rule of no fighting on the school grounds. When the parents heard of the incident, they all came to the school to reprimand the teacher for unjustly punishing their boys.[4]

The Coates family were finally convinced that the teacher was right in his actions and were willing to forget the incident. But Mr. Frost was not so easily pacified. The matter was finally taken to the Board of Trustees who supported the teacher. The Frost family's pride was hurt, and a hatred began between the two families. Mr. Frost removed his son from the school, and he decided on a plan of revenge to remove the teacher.[5]

The annual election for the new Board of Trustees was soon to take place, and Frost declared that no member of the Board should be elected again. He was one of the citizens who appointed the teaching staff, and he meant to have the offending teacher discharged. But there was now another group, who included the Coates clan and who were determined to keep the present Board in office and to retain the teacher.[6]

It soon became evident to the people of the valley that serious trouble would develop over a trivial matter. The Frost family had been one of the most prominent in the area. They were industrious but too aggressive when a fight occurred. Terrible threats were now exchanged between the two families. The Frosts threatened to kill every male of the Coates clan if they did not back out of the argument.[7]

A few days before Election Day, Wesley Coates, who liked to fight, met Frank Duncan, an older man and a brother-in-law of the Frosts, and they got into a heated argument. But at this time the friends of both families separated them, and the two left swearing vengeance. At this time the men of the country were always armed, for this was the last frontier in the West, and there were still angry Indians about who did not want to leave their homes to die on the reservations. And there was an unwritten law which gave every white man the right to shoot an Indian.[8]

On Election Day in Little Lake, Wesley Coates met Frank Duncan again, and, according to most stories, Frank started a nasty argument, and soon the two were fighting and wrestling on the dusty street near Baechtel's store. Among the spectators who had gathered were members of the Coates clan: Albert, Henry, Thomas, James, Abraham, and Abner.[9]

Wesley finally got the better of Frank and took his pistol away from him. But as he straightened up, he looked into the hatefilled eyes of the three Frosts—Elisha 40 years, and his two nephews, Martin 21, and Isom 16—who had approached unnoticed on horseback. The Frosts leaped from their horses, apparently thinking that Wesley Coates had gunned down their relative who was surrounded by the Coates clan.[10]

Abner Coates raised his shotgun and fired, breaking the explosive tension. Elisha Frost received both barrels at close range and fell. But as Elisha dropped, he fired at Abner Coates but missed and killed Abner's son Albert. Martin Frost opened up with his Navy Colt and Wesley, Abraham, and Henry Coates went down, dead or fatally wounded. Isom Frost killed Patriarch Thomas Coates instantly with his Navy Colt.[11]

When the smoke cleared, there were five dead and three wounded. The entire shooting did not take over twenty seconds, but in that short time twenty shots were fired, the noise sounding "like the rapid explosion of a string of fire crackers."[12]

It was never known who shot Abner Coates through the shoulder and James Coates through the right breast. Duncan was dangerously stabbed, supposedly by Wesley Coates whose bloody knife was found near his body. Five of the men were killed instantly except Abner Coates who exclaimed, "My God!" before he fell over dead. Abraham Coates died the next day. The doctor, when cleaning James Coates's wound, ran a silk handkerchief through his body, but James recovered as did Frank Duncan, who was stabbed in a dozen places.[13]

Those who were killed were Thomas J. Coates, age 63; Wesley Coates, age 25; Henry H. Coates, age 25; Albert Coates, age 21; Abraham Coates, age 21; and Elisha Frost, age 42. Thomas Coates left a widow and two children. Elisha Frost left a widow and six small children. All the rest were single men, except Abner Coates who had a family.[14]

But the Mendocino funeral that followed was not similar to most of those of the Kentucky feud. In 1882 Jonse Hatfield ran off with Rose Ann McCoy. In the battle that followed two members of each clan were killed. The next day the two funeral processions happened to pass each other. The bearers and mourners, rifles in hand, glanced stealthily at one another and were ready for any eventuality.[15]

The dead, after the Mendocino fight, were taken into the public hall and laid out side by side, where they remained until they were placed in their coffins. Before the funeral procession moved to the cemetery, the parents, children, wives, brothers, and sisters of the slain and their slayers cried together over those who but a short time before were struggling in fierce combat, but who were now cold and still, lying peacefully side by side.[16]

The feud between the two clans seemed to have come to a halt, since most of the male Coateses were killed. But the Frost clan, like the Hatfields, took up the fighting among themselves.

Cap Hatfield was his father Anse's right-hand man, next to his father, the most powerful and crafty member of the tribe. He specialized in slaughtering the McCoy women and children. In 1906 there were no McCoys handy, so he tried to shoot his brother Elias. Unfortunately for Cap, Elias—who, as the second son, had an eye on the family inheritance—was not only on his guard against a possible fratricidal attempt, but even eager for it. So Cap, instead of killing, was almost killed himself.[17]

In the spring of 1883, Martin Frost, who had participated in the bloody battle of 1865, and a brother of Isom Frost, got into an argument with his nephew, 19-year-old Jimmy Frost over some land. In the shoot-out that followed, Jimmy shot Martin through the head. Jimmy was taken to jail on a murder charge, but was later acquitted on the grounds of self-defense. He was later asked, "Did Martin draw first?" With proper respect for his late uncle, Jimmy replied, "I wouldn't be here if he had."[18]

Two years later in April of 1885, Jimmy Frost, with David Frost, W.H. Bedford, Reuben Cave, A. Hamburg, and Tay Howard, came to the annual rodeo at Little Lake Valley. Late in the afternoon on the day of their arrival, the group were engaged in sorting out the stock of the various parties at a corral in the lower end of the valley. Suddenly a rifle shot was heard from the hill above them, and Jimmy Frost slowly fell over dead. But before he hit the ground, he managed to draw his pistol and fire three shots.[19]

The firing between the men in the corral and their unseen assailants on the hill above lasted several minutes. In the shooting A. Hamburg was killed also. David Frost was charged for his murder, but was later acquitted when the jury accepted the views of the defendant's attorneys who claimed that one of Jimmy's shots had hit Hamburg.[20]

The men in ambush who had started the firing were tracked down by Sheriff "Doc" Standley into Trinity County and arrested eight months after the shooting. Standley captured Isom Frost, Jimmy's uncle, and George Gibson. After a long and drawnout legal battle, Isom Frost was convicted of first degree murder, with a recommendation by the jury to the court that he be incarcerated in the State Prison for the term of his natural life. George Gibson was convicted of second degree murder and sentenced to San Quentin Prison for twelve years.[21]

In the feud between the Coates and Frost clans and among the Frosts themselves, Isom Frost was the only one who was punished by the law. For all their killings, only one Hatfield was put to death by the law, although many spent a few months in jail. Ellison Mount Hatfield, who had shot Alphare McCoy, brought everlasting disgrace upon the Hatfield family by being hanged on the scaffold.[22]

During his trial Isom Frost said that he would have been justified in shooting Jimmy if he had done it (for he never admitted the killing) because Jimmy had killed Martin Frost, his brother. And, he argued, "if Jimmy killed Martin, why should he not kill Jimmy?" Isom Frost was pardoned after spending twenty-five years in prison. He returned to Willits where he lived to a ripe old age. A few elderly residents of Mendocino County still remember him as a gentle and kindly old man, his violent past remote and unreal.[23]

Before he died in bed, Isom told a neighbor about the bloody Election Day fight: "I didn't know what was happening, it happened so fast. When I saw Abner Coates draw up his shotgun and fire, and I heard Martin shooting, too, I just drew and fired. It seemed a matter of life and death, and I didn't know what was going on. I didn't want to kill nobody."[24]

"Devil" Anse Hatfield, the father and leader of the Hatfield clan, died in 1921 at the age of 86, and was buried beside his murdered sons. On April 22, 1922, a life-sized statue of Devil Anse, carved by an Italian sculptor out of Carrara marble, was placed on a hill overlooking the cemetery where the old hero lies buried.[25]

No such tribute was ever paid to any members of the Coates or Frost clans in Mendocino County. About a half-mile east of Highway 101, at the extreme southern limits of Willits, is the Little Lake Cemetery. And in the extreme northwest section, under some oak trees, are the graves of the individuals in their respective family plots—side by side in intimate closeness.

FOOTNOTES

1. A.O. Carpenter and E.M. Millberry, *History of Mendocino and Lake Counties* (Los Angeles, 1914), p. 109.
2. R.F. Dibble, "Devil Anse," *American Mercury* (May, 1925), pp. 89-94.
3. Lyman Palmer, *History of Mendocino County, California* (San Francisco, 1880), p. 336.
4. Jill L. Cossley-Batt, *The Last of the California Rangers* (New York, 1928), p. 238.
5. *Ibid.*, p. 239.
6. *Ibid.*, p. 240.
7. *Ibid.*
8. *Ibid.*, p. 242.
9. Palmer, p. 337.
10. Cossley-Batt, p. 244.
11. Palmer, p. 337.
12. Cossley-Batt, p. 244.
13. Palmer, p. 337.
14. *Ibid.*
15. Dibble, p. 90.
16. Palmer, p. 337.
17. Dibble, p. 92.
18. W.B. Held, *The San Francisco Call*, September 15, 1897.
19. *Ibid.*
20. *Ibid.*
21. *Ibid.*
22. Dibble, p. 93.
23. Held, *Call.*
24. Stuart Nixon, *Redwood Empire* (New York, 1966), p. 151.
25. Dibble, p. 94.

FIGURE 9-1. The graves of the members of the Coates and Frost clans in the Little Lake Cemetery near Willits in Mendocino County. Courtesy Donald Carranco.

CHAPTER

10

Anza's Bones in Arizpe

Lynwood Carranco

The western sky had a bright reddish tinge as the sun disappeared over the hill. The cool breeze that was beginning to blow from the east felt good as we stood on a slight rise on the street just above the Sonora River in the town of Arizpe, situated in a picturesque valley in the Sierra Madre Mountains in Sonora, Mexico. The hot ride of six hours from the mining town of Cananea had been over a rocky mountainous trail that went through and along arroyos, through the Baconuchi and Sonora Valleys, and up over a high, steep mountain.

Three large sharply-rugged hills rise abruptly on the eastern side of the river, which in turn are overshadowed by higher mountains. The clouds which had been forming all afternoon seemed to slide down the mountainsides toward Arizpe. The cool breeze soon turned into a strong wind, bending the trees along the river. Lightning illuminated the slopes in the distance, showing sheets of rain racing down the side of the mountains.

In minutes the storm hit the town: rain pelted the tin roofs, the water gushing down the sides of the buildings and along the rocky streets; sheet lightning explosively brightened the area, striking fear into the animals and people; flash lightning spread its jerky fingers horizontally across the sky; and transcending all the elements of nature was the fresh embracing smell of dampness, spreading a coolness over the hot countryside. The storm lasted about an hour and then disappeared as quickly as it had come, moving westward, the chain lightning visible across the western sky.

Arizpe, which has approximately 1,700 people and which is in the center of a cattle-raising and agricultural area, is a typical Mexican country town with narrow, rocky unpaved streets; the houses have flat roofs and barred windows and have interior patios in the Spanish style. The principal landmark rising from the town is the faded pink stone cathedral of Nuestra Señora de Asunción. The church was begun in 1646 by a Jesuit missionary, Gerónimo de la Canal, but was not finished until 1756.[1] The beautiful old church has a high narrow ceiling, and swallows dart in and out of the building to their nests in the roof beams high above the rows of seats.

Church records indicated that Juan Bautista de Anza was buried somewhere in the church, but the location of the grave had long been lost. Anza's grave had developed into a kind of legend among the townspeople through the years. In February, 1963, Father Antonio Magallanes decided to replace the worn wooden floor, and he asked Presidente Gabriel Serano of the city council for help in getting experts to identify bones if any graves were found. Senor Serano asked California Governor Edmund Brown to help, and he answered the presidente of Arizpe by sending Professors Heizer, McCown, and Howell from the University of California.[2]

Persons of rank were customarily buried toward the front of the nave, and here the scientists started to dig. After digging through an earlier tile floor and two wooden floors, the men found three coffins in the burial area. One contained the bones of a young man, one contained the bones of a man at least sixty years old, and the third contained Anza's bones.

Anza had been a lieutenant colonel in the Mexican cavalry, and his skeleton was that of a robust man. The blue coat with a high military collar embroidered with silver thread was easily identified. Beneath the coat was a red vest and the skeleton wore dark trousers that came just below the knees. The shoes were of black leather and were cut low like pumps. The clinching evidence was two insignia of the Third Order of St. Francis, the Franciscan order for laymen to which Anza belonged. Over the chest was the remnant of a scapulary and a rosary. A cord worn by members of the Franciscan Order was around the waist. The coffin was not moved other than to pry off the top plank.[3]

Two hundred six years ago in 1763, the Seven Years' War ended and England seized the French colonies in America, advancing to the Gulf of Mexico, to the Mississippi River, and to the Canadian prairies. This acquisition posed a grave problem to Spain which had acquired Louisiana—just across the Mississippi. Carlos III, Spain's able sovereign, had to defend a continent inhabited by hostile Indians which stretched from the Gulf of Mexico to the Gulf of California. The English threatened the Louisiana border, and the Russians threatened Spanish domination of the Pacific Coast.[4]

To meet these problems, Carlos III sent Rubí and Oconor to arrange a line of presidios to extend from gulf to gulf. He occupied

Louisiana to hold back the English, and he sent Portolá and Serra to ward off the Russians by occupying the harbors of San Diego and Monterey.[5]

Juan Bautista de Anza came out of obscurity to meet the needs of the Pacific Coast frontier. The isolated outposts in New California, supported from a distant sea base, needed overland communications with the settled mainland of Mexico, and the new provinces also needed a stronger colony to hold the threatened land. Captain Anza was a true son of the frontier, his father and grandfather having served the king as frontier captains on the edge of civilization at Fronteras and Janos. For twenty years Anza had seen similar service at Fronteras and Tubac. Although he was only thirty-seven, he was experienced in Indian matters, seasoned through Apache fighting, and he was an expert in campaigning in a semi-desert land.[6]

Anza occupies first place among the men who helped to plant a European civilization on the shores of the Pacific Ocean. He was the first to open a route across the Sierra and the first to lead a colony overland to the North Pacific shores. His monument *is* San Francisco which stands beside the Golden Gate.

Anza was commissioned to perform the difficult feat of finding a way from Sonora to New California, and he accomplished it with consummate skill. At this time the need of defending the recently discovered Bay of San Francisco was realized, and Anza was appointed to raise a colony and to lead it to California over the road that he had opened. This task he performed with even greater brilliancy than the former one.

Anza was an explorer and colony leader. In his first expedition, comparable to that of Lewis and Clark, he made a definite contribution to Western pathfinding. He was a trail-breaker for six hundred miles. The journey to and from Monterey covered more than two thousand miles; his trip to Mexico City to report this work to the viceroy and return to his post involved a horseback journey of an additional three thousand miles!

Anza's achievement was even more notable as a colony leader. On his second expedition with little equipment, he organized and conducted a large company of men, women, and children from the Sinaloa mainland to Monterey, a distance of about sixteen hundred miles. The group left Tubac, its last rendezvous, with two hundred and forty persons. There was only one death, a mother who died in childbirth, during the whole journey, and three infants were born on the way. This remarkable feat was never equalled in the history of the pioneer movement to the Pacific Coast. And the journey was made under varying conditions of drought, cold, snow, and rain. The trip of sixteen hundred miles from Culiacán to Monterey was so difficult that nearly one hundred head of stock died of hardship on the way.[7]

Anza had many competent aids: Fray Francisco Garcés and Fray Juan Díaz, who both later became missionary martyrs, accompanied Anza on the first expedition as diarists; Juan Bautista Caldés, who had been in California earlier with Portolá, rode fifteen hundred miles to carry the viceroy's orders from Anza, and later at San Gabriel, he carried the diaries and dispatches to Mexico, in all a distance of four thousand miles; Father Pedro Font, chaplain, diarist, and astronomer of the second expedition, recorded an accurate and clear account, unsurpassed in the history of exploration in the Western Hemisphere; Father Eixarch, left at Yuma until Anza's return, wrote a detailed story of the beginnings of the Yuma mission; Sebastián Tarabal, "el peregrino," the runaway guide from Mission San Gabriel, served as a guide during Anza's first journey and later accompanied Father Garcés up and down the Colorado River and across the Mojave Desert to California; Lieutenant Joaquín Moraga, second in command, led the settlers from Monterey to San Francisco and later became its chief and mentor.

Anza's two expeditions could not have been made possible without the cooperation of the great Yuma leader, Salvador Palma. The powerful chief influenced his people and neighboring tribes to be friends with Anza, furnished him supplies, and four times he assisted him in crossing the Colorado River. Without his aid Anza could not have accomplished what he did because the Yumas controlled the gateway to California.

Bucareli, the great viceroy of Mexico, is a significant figure in the founding of California. It was he who directed the frontier drama and carried out the policies of Carlos III and Gálvez. Bucareli worked to keep the far-distant California posts from being starved out of existence, and he planned with Anza and furnished him the means for making his expeditions. He eagerly sent the reports of Anza's progress from Mexico City across the Atlantic to the anxious king in Madrid.

Anza had the qualities of a good frontier leader. On the long journeys, he handled his people with tender care and his stock with judgment. His men were devoted to him, and they even volunteered to follow him across the sand dunes on foot to California when there were not enough horses. The men, women, and children followed Anza uncomplaining amid extreme hardships. When the people parted from him at Monterey, they wept to a beloved leader.

The diaries reveal a vivid cross-section view of conditions at the time on the whole Pacific Coast for a stretch of sixteen hundred miles. From Culiacán to Horcasitas, Anza and his colony passed through towns already old. At Horcasitas the travelers entered a wide uninhabited plain. One hundred miles to the north was a string of pueblos in the Magdalena and Santa Cruz valleys. And from Tucson to San Francisco Bay, a distance of more than a thousand miles, the only European settlements along the trail were four slender missions and the presidio of Monterey—with a total of less than one hundred Europeans or half-castes.[8]

On March 23, 1776, Anza set forth from Monterey to explore the port of San Francisco and sites for two missions and the presidio. His party included Father Font, Lieutenant Moraga, and eight soldiers from Tubac. Corporal Robles, who had been to San Francisco Bay with Rivera, and Soberanes went as guides. There were twenty men in all, including six muleteers and servants. On March 27 Anza and his company camped "on the banks of a fine lake or spring of very fine water near the mouth of the port of San Francisco." This was Mountain Lake, now on the southern edge of the Presidio Reservation.

Now followed the historic exploration that finally determined the location of San Francisco, presidio, and mission. Others had paved the way, but Anza and Font did the decisive work. Anza directed the explorations, and Font recorded them in his splendid diary. From the camp on the lake they continued north "to the edge of the white cliff which forms the end of the mouth of the port, and where begins the great estuary." They were at Fort Point, overlooking the inner extremity of the Golden Gate. "The port of San Francisco," said Font, "is a marvel of nature, and might well be called the harbor of harbors."[9]

Nearby and below was the flower-covered tableland which Anza designated as the site for the new settlement and fort which were to be established on the harbor. The next day the group reached "a beautiful arroyo, which because it was Friday of Sorrows, we called the Arroyo de los Dolores," its banks grown with fragrant manzanita. Anza, Font, and Moraga agreed that this would be the best place for the establishment of a mission. And so the sites had been selected for the mission and presidio of San Francisco. Retracing their trail to Monterey, they arrived there on April 8.

Four days later Anza turned over the colony and all its affairs to Lieutenant Moraga. From that moment Moraga was the central figure in the founding of the Presidio of San Francisco. About two hundred, out of the two hundred forty, who had come with Anza became the "Pilgrim Fathers" of San Francisco. The journey to the banks of the lagoon called Dolores by Anza took ten days. Dolores became the cradle of the city erected to the honor of St. Francis. A shelter of branches was made to serve as a temporary chapel. This little bowery, built on June 28, 1776, was San Francisco's first building.[11]

For a month, the little colony remained here at Dolores, camped in field tents or in temporary shelters. Meanwhile Moraga and his men made preparations for building the presidio on the spot chosen by Anza, but he delayed moving the people there, since he awaited the arrival of the *San Carlos.* He could not complete his work without the aid of Quiros and the equipment that he was bringing by water from Monterey.

Learning by way of a returned pack train that the *San Carlos* had left Monterey, Moraga moved most of his colony from Dolores to the presidio site "near the white cliff" (Fort Point). On August 18 the *San Carlos* entered the harbor and anchored on the south shore, near the presidio site, and work was begun on the presidio at once. By the middle of September the soldiers and carpenters had built a little village of log houses with flat roofs, a log residence and office for the commander, and a warehouse. Later a chapel was built. The presidio was dedicated on September 17, the feast day of the Stigmata of St. Francis, and on October 8 the mission chapel was blessed and dedicated.[12] San Francisco, the northwestern outpost of Spain's great empire was finally on the map. This outpost was essentially the work of Bucareli, who had sponsored the entire project, and of Anza, who had opened the trail and conducted the colonists to California. These two men were the real founders.

After Anza turned over the colony and all its affairs to Moraga, he said a last goodbye to his people and was showered with embraces, best wishes, and praises. The return party to Sonora consisted of twenty-nine persons, including Font. On May 11, after a journey of ten days, Anza and his party reached Yuma, where for five months Father Eixarch had labored. Months before, on December 4, Anza had moved down the river with his colony bound for San Francisco. Father Garcés had left one day later and had made a long tour among his friends on the lower Colorado River, leaving Eixarch with servants and interpreters to toil at his half-way post.[13]

While waiting for Garcés, Anza set about crossing the Colorado, which was now a raging flood. In two days, the Indians, led by a medicine man, Pablo, assembled logs for a raft and took the people and baggage across, steered by twenty-two Yuma swimmers. Salvador Palma, the Yuma chief, was as happy as Father Eixarch to see Anza and Font on their return to the Colorado. He was firmly attached to Anza, and he was counting on his promise to take him to Mexico to see the Great Father, Viceroy Bucareli, before whom he wished to plead for baptism for himself and missionaries for his people.[14]

As soon as the crossing was completed, Anza and party, accompanied by Eixarch, Palma, and three Indians, prepared to set forth for Sonora, since they could no longer wait for Garcés. When the party stopped at Caborca, Father Eixarch returned up the Altar Valley to his mission of Tumacácori. Anza continued with the rest of his people to Horcasitas, where after an absence of eight months he arrived on June 1, 1776. Font continued over the mountains to his mission of San José de Pimas.[15]

Garcés had left the Colorado to go directly to the southern edge of the San Joaquín Valley, then eastward across the Tehachapi Range where he reached the border of the desert at the Mojave River. He returned to the Colorado and then explored to the east into New Mexico, being in the wilderness almost eleven months and covering more than two thousand miles. On August 27, he reached Yuma and arrived at his mission of San Xavier on September 17.[16]

After Anza had gotten his affairs into shape, he continued to the capital with Palma, visiting with Font on the way at his mission San José. They arrived at the capital late in October, and Anza informed Bucareli of the proposed missions and a presidio in Yuma land. This was Anza's dream. Palma was honored, and on February 13, 1777, with the approval of His Grace, the Archbishop, he was baptized in the Cathedral of Mexico, the finest temple in all North America.[17]

Anza had hoped to go back to Yuma as commander of a presidio. Instead he was promoted to lieutenant colonel and was made Governor of New Mexico, which then embraced what is now California, Arizona, New Mexico, Texas, and northern Mexico. To protect the northern frontier of New Spain, in August, 1776, the interior provinces were organized into the Commandancy General of the Internal Provinces. Teodoro de Croix became the first Commander-General, and he introduced a policy of offensive warfare against the Apaches and made an alliance with the powerful Comanches for this purpose. However, due to Spain's decision to aid the American colonists revolting against England, funds, material, and troops needed by Croix were diverted for European use, and

José de Gálvez, Spanish Minister of the Indies, ordered him to undertake an inexpensive policy of conciliating the Indian tribes of his jurisdiction.[18]

Governor Juan Bautista de Anza served as governor of New Mexico from 1777 to 1787, and he was charged with carrying out the new peace policy in New Mexico. In 1785 and 1786, he brought about treaties of peace and alliance with the Comanches, Utes, and Navajos, and between the Comanches and Utes. The agreements embraced mutual desires. The Indians consented to maintain peace with the Spaniards and Pueblo Indians and to aid the Spanish in their war against the Apaches. In return Anza granted the Indians peace, trading privileges in New Mexico, and aid against the common enemy the Apaches.[19]

Through the intimate, personal diplomacy conducted by Anza, and with sufficient trade goods and gifts, treaties of peace and alliance were made with New Mexico's frontier Indians, and the province enjoyed a fleeting period of peace and economic prosperity.

Bucareli, having gone to so much trouble to have the Anza route opened, planned to secure it by establishing settlements at the crucial points, chief of which was the Colorado crossing. Palma had returned to Yuma, and the Yumas at this time were equally desirous of a mission.

Preöccupied with his Apache plans, Croix postponed the Yuma missions, and it was not until 1780 that the comandante-general authorized the advance. In order to save money, a mongrel colony resulted, part presidio, part mission, and part settlement. Meanwhile the Yuma zest for conversion had waned. The few settlers and soldiers worked against the friars and disregarded the rights of the Indians. Discontent came to a head in 1781 when Rivera distributed insignificant presents and when his soldiers antagonized the Yumas. On July 17, the Yumas attacked the two missions, killing all the men, including Garcés and Días, and enslaving the women and children. Rivera and his soldiers were all killed on the next day.[20]

This massacre of four friars and more than thirty soldiers ranks with the worst disasters of the Spanish frontier. Croix, the commander-general, blamed Garcés and Anza for the tragedy, and he convinced Gálvez that Anza had minimized the danger at Yuma. And as a consequence Anza lost the governorship of New Mexico—and disappeared from history. Croix was chiefly to blame since he had delayed in establishing the settlements, and his economy in Indian presents and presidial guards was fatal.[21]

After leaving New Mexico, Anza returned to Arizpe, the center of the frontier empire, where he died suddenly on December 19, 1788. He was buried the next day in the church of Nuestra Señora de la Asunción.[22]

One hundred seventy years later in 1965—the early morning air was clear and cool as my wife, two young sons, and I entered the old church to attend mass. As we sat behind the sarcophagus built for Anza's bones and listened to Father Flavio Molina, I could not but feel great admiration for Juan Bautista de Anza. We had driven over the approximate routes that Anza had led his band of colonists through Pimería Alta, routes that the late Dr. Herbert E. Bolton had compiled from original data and personal explorations. Days before I had discussed Anza's exploits with Señor Roberto Torres, one of Cananea's leading citizens and who is much interested in Mexican history. He had summarized Anza by saying that he was "mucho hombre."

And the city of San Francisco did not forget her founder. Near the sarcophagus is a plaque on which the following is written in Spanish:

JUAN BAUTISTA de ANZA
1735-1788
EXPLORER—COLONIZER—SOLDIER—STATESMAN

THIS COMMEMORATIVE SARCOPHAGUS IS A GIFT FROM THE CITY OF SAN FRANCISCO, CALIFORNIA, TO ARIZPE, SONORA, AS A SIGN OF GRATEFULNESS FOR THE HEROIC DEEDS OF THIS NOTABLE PERSON IN THE FOUNDING OF THE CITY OF SAN FRANCISCO.

NOTES

1. Interview with Father Antonio Magallanes, Arizpe, Sonora, Mexico, August, 1964.

2. Interview with Gabriel Serano, Arizpe, Sonora, Mexico, August, 1964. Also *San Francisco Chronicle*, March 4, 1963.
3. Interview with Father Antonio Magallanes. Also *San Francisco Chronicle*, March 5, 1963.
4. Herbert Eugene Bolton, OUTPOST OF EMPIRE (New York: Alfred A. Knopf, 1931), p. vii.
5. *Ibid.*
6. John Walton Caughey, CALIFORNIA (Inglewood Heights: Prentice-Hall, Inc., 1965), p. 120.
7. Bolton, *Outpost*, p. ix.
8. Herbert Eugene Bolton, ANZA'S CALIFORNIA EXPEDITIONS (Berkeley: University of California Press, 1930), Vols. II and III.
9. Bolton, *Outpost*, p. 258. Also Bolton, ANZA'S CALIFORNIA EXPEDITIONS, Vol. III, p. 254.
10. Bolton, *Outpost*, p. 303.
11. *Ibid.* Also "Palou's Account of the Founding of San Francisco, 1776," in Bolton's ANZA'S CALIFORNIA EXPEDITIONS, III, pp. 383-405; "Moraga's Account of the Founding of San Francisco, 1776" (*Ibid.*, pp. 407-420).
12. Bolton, *Outpost*, p. 306
13. *Ibid.*, pp. 284-298.
14. *Ibid.*, p. 316.
15. *Ibid.*, p. 318.
16. *Ibid.*, p. 320.
17. *Ibid.*, p. 330.
18. Ronald J. Benes, "Anza and Concha in New Mexico, 1787-1793: A Study in New Colonial Techniques," JOURNAL *of the* WEST, Vol. IX (January, 1965), p. 63.
19. *Ibid.*
20. *Caughey*, p. 134.
21. *Ibid.*
22. Interview with Father Antonio Magallanes, Arizpe, Sonora, Mexico, August, 1964.

FIGURE 10-1. Front view of Cathedral with Priest's headquarters on left. Photo by Tom Knight.

FIGURE 10-2. Another view of the old Cathedral. Photo by Tom Knight.

FIGURE 10-3. Anza's coffin in the sarcophagus. Note his uniform and the cord of the Franciscan order around his waist. Photo by Tom Knight.

FIGURE 10-4. A closeup of the old Cathedral, begun in 1646. Photo by Tom Knight.

PART
II

LANGUAGE

The Boonville Language of Northern California

Lynwood Carranco *and* Wilma Rawles Simmons

Were you ever a tweed or a weese? Are you an apple-head or a kimmey?

Did you ever have a bucky so you could pike for dulcy? Have you ever been charlied? Did you ever jape to a hob or pike to a locking in a kingster?[1]

These are examples of the Boonville language or "Boont-link" that was spoken in the community of Boonville in Mendocino County of Northern California between 1880 and 1920. Mendocino County is composed of a series of high mountain ranges and small deep valleys. Situated between two mountain ranges, Anderson Valley lies in the southern part of the county, approximately twenty-five miles east of the Pacific Ocean and one hundred and ten miles north of San Francisco. The valley is about fifteen miles northeast to southwest, and it is about two miles in width.

Walter Anderson, who had come west by covered wagon, traveled through Sonoma County, up the Russian River Valley, and finally arrived where Cloverdale now stands. Trailing a herd of elk over the Bald Hills, he discovered the fertile uninhabited Anderson Valley in 1853 or 1854.[2] He and his family settled here, claiming the whole valley by "possessorary" right.[3]

Soon other settlers arrived. Because the valley was becoming too crowded, Anderson sold his property rights to Joseph Rawles and left the valley. Between 1855 and 1860, W.W. Boone established a trading post and post office at the southern end of Anderson Valley and gave the town the name of Boonville. A short time later the town of Philo was established at the other end of the valley.[4]

By 1865 there were approximately nineteen families living in the valley. Many of their descendants who still live in the area are members of the following families: Ball, Clow, Geschwend, Guntley, Ingram, Lawson, McGinsey, Ornbaum, Prather, Rawles, and

Tarwater. The only two pieces of property in Anderson Valley listed on the Mendocino County tax list at the present time in the original family names are properties homesteaded by the Guntley and Rawles families more than a hundred years ago.[5]

Travel in and out of the valley was limited in the early days because of the high mountains and poor roads. In the 1920s a man in his seventies boasted that he had never been outside the valley.[6] Intermarriages among the families of these early settlers were frequent; after a few generations practically all the people were related, and no one had any secrets from his neighbors.

About 1880 the Boonville lingo or Boont-link began as a game among children who, when among their elders, wished to speak freely without being understood. More and more words were added, and soon Boont-link was adopted by all the young people. Gradually the older people also adopted it. The language was used until about 1920, when the advances in transportation and communication brought more people into the valley; it is still spoken as a secondary language among the Boonville old-timers and by people on the outlying ranches.[7]

The first written record of this folk language seems to be by C. Douglas Chrétien, who stated in 1942 that an extended study of "Boontling" would be very desirable.[8] The parts of speech used are nouns, verbs, and a few adjectives. These words are derived from physical, mental, or personal peculiarities or characteristics of well-known residents of the area, or from incidents that occurred. Many of the words are short versions of words or phrases. Boont-link is not a cultural language, being extremely earthy and at times quite vulgar. It is almost completely incomprehensible to outsiders.

In the First and Second World Wars, servicemen from Boonville wrote informative letters to their parents and relatives with no interference from the censors, who were probably as baffled as the enemy would have been.[9]

The following list of Boont-link words and phrases[10] is not complete, since this was a spoken rather than a written language, and many words have been forgotten and lost.

AB [æb], *v.t.* To crowd in and push another person out of line.
ABALONEYITE, *n.* A resident of Albion (Mendocino County).
AIRTIGHT, *n.* A sawmill.
APPLE-HEAD, *n.* A girl; a young woman; a young wife.
ARK, *v.t.* To wreck.
ARKING, *n.* Wrecking.
BAL, *adj.* Good.

BALNESS, *n.* An attractive girl.

BARLOW, *n.* A knife.

BEARMAN, *n.* A storyteller. Allen Cooper, the Boonville innkeeper, was a bear hunter and told many hunting stories.

BE BLUE-BIRDED, *v. phr.* To be bucked off a horse.

BEEMSH, *n.* A good show.

BEESON TREE, *n.* A stock saddle. Mr. Beeson was a saddle maker.

BELLJEEK [bɛl'dʒik], *n.* A rabbit.

BILL NUNN, *n.* Syrup. Bill Nunn liked syrup very much.

BIRD-STORK, *n.* A man with a large family.

BLUE-TAIL, *n.* A rattlesnake.

BO, *n.* A dare or challenge.

BOOKER T., *n.* A Negro.

BOONT, *n.* Boonville.

BOONTER, *n.* A resident of Boonville.

BOOTJACK, *n.* A Coyote.

BORCH, *n.* A Chinaman.

BOREGO, *n.* A sheep.

BORP, *n.* A pig.

BOSH, *n.* A deer.

BOSH HAREEM, *n.* A deerhound.

BRANCH OUT, *v.i.* To step out.

BRANDING IRONS, *n.* Handcuffs.

BRINY, *n.* A coast; an ocean.

BROADY, *n.* A cow.

BUCKEY, *n.* A nickel; named after the Indian on the nickel.

BUCKINJ ['bʌkɪndʒ], *n.* A buck Indian.

BUCK PASTURE, *n.* A man with a pregnant wife.

CHAP PORT, *n.* A cowboy boot.

CHARL, *v.t.* To milk a cow; taken from the sound of milk hitting the bucket.

CHARLIE, *v.t.* To embarrass. Charlie Ball, an Indian, was noted for his bashfulness.

CHARLIE-BALLED, *adj.* Embarrassed; bashful; shy.

CHIGGREL, *n.* Food; a specific meal, such as supper or dinner.

CHIGGREL, *v.t.* To eat.

CHIPMUNK, *v.t.* To hoard.

CLOODY, *n.* Shoe.

COCKED, *adj.* Angry.

COCKED DARLEY, *n.* A man with a gun.

COMOSH ['komaʃ], *n.* A tool to grind sheep shears.

CONDEAL, *n.* A county job.

COWSKULLY, *n.* A desolate area.

CROPPY, *n.* A sheep. The plural is *croppies.*

DEEGER ['didʒ ə˞], *n.* A degenerate person.

DEEJY ['didʒi], *adj.* Not good (referring to a person).

DEEK, *v.t.* To notice; to call attention to.

DEHIGGED, *adj.* Having little or no money; penniless.

DICK, *v.t.* To cheat. A man named Dick, a sheepshearer, counted more sheep than he sheared.

DISH, *v.i.* To rush in.

DISSY, *n.* A shoe with a metal buckle.

DONIKER, *n.* An outdoor toilet.

DREARIES, *n.* The Bald Hills near Anderson Valley.

DREEK, *v.t.* To whip; to beat.

DREEKING, *n.* A whipping.

DUKE, *n.* Fist.

DULCY, *n.* Candy.

EELD'M, *n.* An old woman; an old wife.

EETAH, *n.* An exclamation.

ESOLE ['isol], *n.* An asshole.

FAIR AND RIGHT A PERSON *v. phr.* To lend a person money.

FIDDLERS, *n.* Delirium tremens.

FISTER, *n.* A fight.

FORBES, *n.* A half dollar.

FRATI ['fræti], *n.* Wine. Mr. Frati was the local wine maker.

GANNO ['gæno], *n.* A type of apple. This is a brand name.

GLIMMER, *n.* A kerosene lamp.

GLIMMERS, *n.* Reading glasses.

GLOWWORM, *n.* A lantern.

GORM, *v.i.* To overeat.

GREENY, *n.* A tantrum.

HARDY, *n.* A glove.

HAREEM, *n.* A dog.

HARP, *n.* A person who talks too much.

HARP, *v.t.* To order; to say.

HEDGE, HEERK, *n.* A haircut.

HEELCH, *n.* A greedy person who always takes everything.

HIGGED, *adj.* Well supplied with money.

HIGH-GUN, *v.t.* To beat a person to the draw.

HIGH-HEEL, *n.* The boss; the officer of the law. The constable in Boonville had one short leg and wore a high-heeled boot.

HIGH-HEEL, *v.t.* To arrest.

HIGH-HEELER, *n.* An officer of the law.

HIGH-POCKETS, *n.* A wealthy person. The tallest man in Boonville was considered wealthy.

HIGH-POCKETY, *adj.* Wealthy.

HIGS, *n.* Money.

HOB, *n.* A Saturday night dance.

HOOD, *n.* A peculiar person. A new family moved into the valley, and the children wore hoods to school.

HOOT, *v.i.* To laugh.

HOOTER, *n.* Loud laughter.

HORN, *n.* A drink.

HORN, *v.t.* To drink.

HUGE ARKER, *n.* A great disturbance, such as a storm or an earthquake.

ITCH NEEMER, *n.* A person who has no desire to drink.

ITE [aɪt], *n.* An Italian.

JAPE [dʒep], *v.t.* To drive. Jape was the first name of an early stage driver.

JAPER, *n.* A driver.

JEFFER ['dʒɛfɚ], *n.* A big fire. Jeff Vestal, the hotel owner, was famous for the big fires that he built in the fireplace.

JENNY BECK, *n.* A person who tattles; a stool pigeon. Jenny Beck was the school's greatest tattler.

KEISHBOOK ['kaɪʃ,buk], *n.* A pregnant woman; supposedly an Indian word.

KILLING SNAKES, *adj.* A term to describe a person who is working hard.

KIMMEY, *n.* A young man.

KINGSTER, *n.* A big ornate church.

LENGTHY, *n.* A female deer.

LEVI, *v.t.* To telephone. Walter Levi used the first telephone in Boonville.

LINK, *n.* Lingo.

LOCKING, *n.* A wedding.

LOCKING MATCH, *n.* An engagement.

LOG LIFTER, *n.* A strong winter storm.

MADGE, *n.* A whore. Madge was the madam of a whorehouse in Ukiah (the county seat).

MADGE, *v.t.* To visit a whorehouse.

MASON-DIXON, *n.* The division line between Boonville and Philo. The people of the two towns had constant feuds in the early days.

MINK, *n.* An expensively dressed girl.

MOLDUNE [məl'dun], *n.* An overly large woman. Moldune St. John was considered to be the largest woman in Boonville.

MOSH, *n.* A car.

MUZZ CREEK, *n.* The excessive water running down the mountains.

NETTIED, *adj.* Overdressed. Nettie Wallace was always overdressed.

NONCH, *adj.* Bad; no good.

NONE [nɑn], *v.t.* To refuse.

OLD DAME, *n.* A young man's wife.

OLD DUSTIES, *n.* Hell.

OSTOOK [ɑ'stuk], *n.* A person with one eye; supposedly an Indian word.

OTTO, *v.i.* To work.

PACK'EM-OUT-BILLY, *n.* A dirty sock.

PAPER SKULL, *n.* A small deer.

PEAKED HEAD, *n.* A member of the International Order of Odd Fellows.

PEERL ['pirəl], *v.i.* To rain.

PICK'EM-UP, *n.* A person who starts a fight.

PIKE, *v.i.* To go.

PUSSEEK, *n.* A female cat.

RAGGER, *n.* A dancer.

RAGGIN', *n.* Indecent dancing.

REGION, *n.* A home.

RELF, *n.* A rail fence.

RIDGY, *adj.* Old-fashioned.

ROOGIN ['rudʒən], *v.i.* To be cheated.

ROOPEY, *n.* A drugstore cowboy.

ROOT, *v.i.* To fall; to fail.

RUDGE [rudʒ], *n.* A catastrophe, such as a big storm or an earthquake.

SCHOOLCH, *n.* A schoolteacher.

SEEKER, *n.* A ladies' man.

SEEPY, *adj.* Shiftless.

SHAG, *v.i.* To fall down. Shag Abbott was a very awkward person.

SHARK, *v.i.* To cheat at cards.

SHIKE, *v.t.* To outtrade someone. Shike Wallace was famous for his trades.

SHOVEL-TOOTH, *n.* A medical doctor. The first doctor in town had buck teeth.

SHY, *v.t.* To quit or to leave.

SIRTLE-SEERTLE ['sʌrtəl'sirtəl], *n.* A salmon.

SKEEP, *n.* A preacher.

SOL, *n.* The sun.

SOL'S GRANDMOTHER, *n.* A dead person.

SPAT, *n.* A 22-caliber rifle.

STACK, *n.* A haystack.

STEEDOSS, *n.* A stallion.

STIFF HAT, *n.* A fighter. In the early days the traveling boxers wore high hats.

STRAIGHT NECK, *n.* A German.

SUMERSET, *v.i.* To be overemotional.

SUNNY, *n.* A sunny day.

SYKE, *n.* A horse.

TEEBOWED, *adj.* Deaf; supposedly an Indian word.

TEETLIPPED, *adj.* Angry.

TELEF [tɛ'lif], *v.t.* To call by telephone.

THORPS, *n.* A man's button shoe.

TOB, *n.* Tobacco.

TOOBS, *n.* A quarter.

TRASH MOVER, *n.* A heavy rain.

TRIBBY, *n.* A shoe.

TROJAN, *n.* Dynamite. This is a brand name.

TUDDISH, *adj.* Crazy.

TUFFER, *n.* A sheep that is difficult to shear.

TURKEY NECK, *n.* A person who gawks.

TWEED, *n.* A young person, usually a teen-ager.

UKE, *n.* A native of Ukiah.

WEESE, *n.* A small child.

WES [wɛs], *n.* A white lie.

WHEELER, *n.* A harmless lie.

WILK, *n.* A wild cat.

ZEESE, *n.* Coffee. Zeese Blevens was an excessive coffee drinker.

The following two stories are examples of Boont-link:

THE BOONT HOB[11]

There being a hob in Boont, Pete shied ottoing,
charled the broady, chiggreled, then took his apple-head
and tweeds and piked to Boont for a hedge. He spent
about forbes on a horn or two for himself and gave
the tweeds some buckeys for dulcy.

The hob started with the apple-heads all nettied,
and the seekers active. But the high-heeler got
teetlipped when he deeked that raggin' was going on
and harped to the raggers to either shy or pike.

Then came the midnight chiggrel. Two of the kimmeys,
Punk and Spring Knee,[13] got into a fister and knocked all the chiggrel on the floor. Punk was
high-heeled and kept in branding irons until his apple-head, Em, could get the higs for bail.

The hob started again when the high-heeler said,
"There will be no horning, fistering, or raggin'
while I am the head high-heeler."

Much later, the kimmeys and their apple-heads
gathered up their tweeds and their sykes and piked
to their regions. All harped that it had been a bal hob.

THE BOONVILLE DANCE

There being a dance in Boonville, Fred[12] quit working,
milked the cow, ate, then took his wife
and children and went to Boonville for a haircut. He spent
about four bits on a drink or two for himself, and gave
the children some nickels for candy.

The dance started with the women all fancy-dressed,
and the ladies' men active. But the man in charge got
angry when he noticed that indecent dancing was going on
and ordered the dancers to either quit or leave.

Then came the midnight supper. Two of the men,
Punk and Spring Knee, got into a fight and knocked all the food onto the floor. Punk was
arrested and kept in handcuffs until his wife, Em, could get the money for bail.

The dance started again when the man in charge said,
"There will be no drinking, fighting, or indecent dancing
while I am the head man in charge."

Much later, the men and their wives
gathered up their children and their horses and went
to their homes. All said that it had been a good dance.

THE EELD'M AND THE BORP[14]

An eeld'm found some forbes and buckeys
and felt high-pockety. So she japed to Boont and used
her higs for a borp. On her way region, over the Drearies,
the eeld'm had to pike over a relf. But borp wouldn't pike
and she couldn't jape him region, and she wanted her chiggrel.

Soon a hareem piked by and the eeld'm harped,

THE OLD WOMAN AND THE PIG

An old woman found some half dollars and nickels
and felt wealthy. So she drove to Boonville and used
her money for a pig. On her way home, over the Bald Hills,
the old woman had to go over a fence. But pig wouldn't go
and she couldn't drive him home, and she wanted her dinner.

Soon a dog went by and the old woman said,

"Hareem, hareem, chiggrel borp, borp won't jump relf
and pike region, and I'll get no chiggrel. But hareem noned.
Eeld'm got cocked and harped to a stick, "Stick, stick,
dreek hareem, hareem won't chiggrel borp, borp won't jump relf and pike region, and I'll get
no chiggrel. But stick noned.
        Soon she met a jeffer. Still in a greeny, she harped,
"Jeffer, jeffer, ark stick, stick won't dreek hareem,
hareem won't chiggrel borp, borp won't jump relf
and pike region, and I'll get no chiggrel. But jeffer noned.
        Soon she met a briny, and she harped, "Briny, briny,
quench jeffer, jeffer won't ark stick, stick won't dreek
hareem, hareem won't chiggrel borp, borp won't jump relf
and pike region, and I'll get no chiggrel. But briny noned.
But eeld'm wasn't charlied, and she found a broady
and harped, "Broady, broady, horn briny, briny won't quench
jeffer, jeffer won't ark stick, stick won't dreek hareem,
hareem won't chiggrel borp, borp won't jump relf and pike
region, and I'll get no chiggrel. But broady noned.
        Then eeld'm found a broady kimmey. "Broady kimmey,
broady kimmey, kill broady, broady won't horn briny,
briny won't quench jeffer, jeffer won't ark stick,
stick won't dreek hareem, hareem won't chiggrel borp,
borp won't jump relf and pike region, and I'll get
no chiggrel. But broady kimmey noned. So she piked
to a rope and harped, "Rope, rope, hang kimmey, kimmey
won't kill broady, broady won't horn briny, briny won't quench
jeffer, jeffer won't ark stick, stick won't dreek hareem,

"Dog, dog, eat pig, pig won't jump fence
and go home, and I'll get no dinner. But dog refused.
Old woman got angry and said to a stick, "Stick, stick,
beat dog, dog won't eat pig, pig won't jump fence and go home, and I'll get
no dinner. But stick refused.
        Soon she met a fire. Still in a tantrum, she said,
"Fire, fire, wreck stick, stick won't beat dog,
dog won't eat pig, pig won't jump fence
and go home, and I'll get no dinner. But fire refused.
        Soon she met an ocean, and she said, "Ocean, ocean,
quench fire, fire won't wreck stick, stick won't beat
dog, dog won't eat pig, pig won't jump fence
and go home, and I'll get no dinner. But ocean refused.
But old woman wasn't embarrassed, and she found a cow
and said, "Cow, cow, drink ocean, ocean won't quench
fire, fire won't wreck stick, stick won't beat dog,
dog won't eat pig, pig won't jump fence and go
home, and I'll get no dinner. But cow refused.
        Then old woman found a cow man. "Cow man,
cow man, kill cow, cow won't drink ocean,
ocean won't quench fire, fire won't wreck stick,
stick won't beat dog, dog won't eat pig,
pig won't jump fence and go home, and I'll get
no dinner. But cow man refused. So she went
to a rope and said, "Rope, rope, hang man, man
won't kill cow, cow won't drink ocean, ocean won't quench
fire, fire won't wreck stick, stick won't beat dog,

hareem won't chiggrel borp, borp
won't jump relf and pike
region, and I'll get no chiggrel. But
rope noned.

Then eeld'm found a rat and
harped, "Rat, rat,
chiggrel rope, rope won't hang broady
kimmey,
broady kimmey won't kill broady,
broady won't horn briny,
briny won't quench jeffer, jeffer won't
ark stick,
stick won't dreek hareem, hareem
won't chiggrel borp,
borp won't jump relf and pike region,
and I'll get no
chiggrel. But rat noned.

She piked on to a pusseek,
and pusseek harped, "If you'll pike to
yon broady
and charl her for me, I will chiggrel the
rat." So she
piked to the broady. But broady
harped, "If you will pike
to yon stack and fetch me some chiggrel, I'll charl myself
for pusseek." So eeld'm did. Broady
chiggreled and pusseek
horned. Then the pusseek began to kill
the rat, the rat
began to chiggrel the rope, the rope
began to hang
the broady kimmey, the broady kimmey began to kill the broady,
the broady began to horn briny, briny
began to quench jeffer,
jeffer began to ark stick, stick began to
dreek hareem,
hareem began to chiggrel borp, borp
began to jump relf
and pike region, and eeld'm got her
chiggrel.

dog won't eat pig, pig won't jump
fence and go
home, and I'll get no dinner. But rope
refused.

Then old woman found a rat and
said, "Rat, rat,
eat rope, rope won't hang cow man,

cow man won't kill cow, cow won't
drink ocean,
ocean won't quench fire, fire won't
wreck stick,
stick won't beat dog, dog won't eat
pig,
pig won't jump fence and go home,
and I'll get no
dinner. But rat refused.

She went on to a cat,
and cat said, "If you'll go to yon cow

and milk her for me, I will eat the
rat." So she
went to the cow. But cow said, "If
you will go
to yon haystack and fetch me some
food, I'll milk myself
for cat." So old woman did. Cow ate

and cat drank. Then the cat began to
kill the rat, the rat
began to eat the rope, the rope began
to hang
the cow man, the cow man began to
kill the cow,
the cow began to drink ocean, ocean
began to quench fire,
fire began to wreck stick, stick began
to beat dog,
dog began to eat pig, pig began to
jump fence
and go home, and old woman got her
dinner.

FOOTNOTES

1. Were you ever a teen-ager or a small child? Are you a girl or a young man? Did you ever have a nickel so you could go for candy? Have you ever been embarrassed? Did you ever drive to a dance or go to a wedding in a big ornate church?
2. Lyman L. Palmer, *History of Mendocino County, California* (San Francisco, 1880), pp. 360-61.
3. In the early days a purchaser established "possessorary" rights before a survey by the United States government was made. The price of the land was determined by the current price of the cattle foraging on it.
4. Palmer, p. 363.
5. Interview with Mrs. Austin Rawles.
6. Interview with Mrs. Austin Rawles.
7. Interview with Mrs. Austin Rawles.
8. "Boontling," *California Folklore Quarterly*, I (1942), 96-97.
9. Interview with Mrs. Austin Rawles.
10. Informants: Jack June, Austin Rawles, B.J. Rawles, Joseph Rawles, and Myrtle Rawles. In January of 1964, the Associated Press carried information about Boont-link received from a professor at Chico State College, and most of the larger newspapers throughout the country published a short account of the lingo. Dean Hector Lee of Sonoma State College has an article on "Boont-ling Rides Again!" in the newsletter of the California Folklore Society, *From the Sourdough Crock*, vol. I, no. 10 (1964), 54-57; he includes a short list of terms (p. 57).
11. Interview with Mrs. Austin Rawles.
12. *Pete* was a nickname for Fred Rawles.
13. Most of the natives had nicknames.
14. This story was taught to Wilma Rawles Simmons.

CHAPTER

12

"Boontling"—Esoteric Speech of Boonville, California*

Myrtle Read Rawles

Pike with me up the Navarro to the Briny Highway, from Cloverdal to Boont and deek the Anderson Valley Gannow Beemsh. If you abe a little, you may recognize many kimmeys and appleheads, descendants of the original settlers who are now with Saul's grandmother.

Translation: Come with me up the Navarro to the Sea Highway from Cloverdale to Boonville and see the Anderson Valley Apple Show. If you push your way in, you may recognize many men and women, descendants of the original settlers who are now dead.

If you listened carefully you would be somewhat incredulous and completely confused. You might even be of the opinion that you had wandered into a strange land with a peculiarly different language. However, had you lived in this part of northern California at the turn of the twentieth century, this strange language would be completely comprehensible to you and a part of your everyday vocabulary.

Anderson Valley is now a thriving, well-populated area, and Boonville is its chief shopping and entertainment center. For many years the raising of sheep for wool was the chief industry, and it still flourishes. At the present time apple orchards abound and each year visitors from many parts of the state attend the excellent Mendocino County Apple Fair at Boonville. The lumber industry brought a recent boom to the valley, but at present it is declining. There are schools, churches, a theater, a super market, and a subdivision. The

*Principal informants for the present paper include Jack June, Boonville; Beryl J. Rawles, Santa Rosa; Joseph W. Rawles, Middletown, and my husband, Austin N. Rawles, Ukiah, who has delved deeply into childhood memories. I am indebted to these informants and to numerous other people who contributed bits of information that went into compiling the vocabulary of "Boontling."— M.R.R.

residents own new cars, television sets, transistor radios, automatic dish washers, and laundries; in fact, all the modern conveniences that are to be found in any up-to-date American community today are found here. There is a constant migration into and out of the valley and some of the smartest appearing visitors in all parts of the world might well be and often are from this small community.

It was not always so. At one time there were no strangers in the valley, no modern conveniences, and very little contact with the outside world. It was during this period "Boonters" developed a language of their own, which, after seventy or eighty years, is still in existence among the descendants of the original settlers. Seldom adopted by newcomers into the area, the language is slowly dying out. The mountains are no longer linguistic barriers. Automobiles, airplanes and superhighways have solved the transportation problem. Only a few of the Boonters remember all of the lingo and use it, but at one time Boontling or Boont was the natural idiom of the Boonters.

* * *

Boonville is a small town at the southern end of a long, narrow, winding valley named for Walter Anderson, who settled there in 1851. Located in the heart of beautiful Mendocino County, on the present Navarro to the Sea Highway, between Cloverdale and the Mendocino Coast, this valley must have been an inviting sight to Anderson who saw it first when trailing a herd of elk over the Bald Hills (the Drearies). It is not known whether he ever caught up with the elk, but he did find his new home. Traveling by covered wagon, with his wife and children and all his stock, he settled down, claiming the whole valley by what he called "possessorary" right.

The Andersons did not enjoy their solitude for very long, however. Soon other pioneers found this promising area. Between 1855 and 1860 W.W. Boone established a trading post and post office at the southern end of the valley and gave the village the name of Boonville.

By 1865 there were approximately nineteen families living in the Boonville area. Many of their descendants, still residing there, are the Gschwend, Guntley, Ball, Tarwater, Ingram, Lawson, Rawles, McGimsey, Clow, Ornbaun, and Prather families. Anderson soon decided his land was becoming too crowded, so in 1858 he sold his property rights to Joseph Rawles, who, with his family, had migrated to California from his home state of Iowa. Anderson left the valley, but the Beeson boys, his stepsons, remained, and some of their descendants still reside in the area.

At the present time the only two tracts of land on the Mendocino County tax list in the original family names are properties homesteaded by the Guntley and Rawles families over a hundred years ago. In those days a purchaser established "possessorary" rights before a United States government survey was made. The price of some of the best stock range in Mendocino County was three dollars a head for a cow with calf included. The price of the land was determined by the current price of the cattle foraging on it.

The land was fertile and the settlers raised quantities of wheat, barley, oats, apples, peaches, cherries, cattle, and sheep. Timber was abundant so they had all the lumber they needed. The biggest drawback was the fact that, beyond a limited demand for home consumption, there was no available market for these products. Wool and cattle could be transported to Cloverdale, the nearest railway terminal. One rancher, Joseph Rawles, drove his cattle to Sacramento once a year and sold them there. This trip took about three weeks so the other ranchers were satisfied to sell in Cloverdale or Petaluma.

Travel into and out of Anderson Valley in those early days was limited. All mail came by stagecoach, operated three times weekly between Cloverdale and Boonville, and stopping at the Mountain House where travelers rested and horses were watered. Later, in 1868, the Gschwend Toll Road was built between Boonville and Ukiah. However, travel was difficult and most people preferred to remain at home. In the early 1920's one elderly man in his seventies boasted that he had never been outside of the valley. In spite of this, there was little or no intermarriage among blood relations, but much among neighbors. Many schoolboy and girl infatuations ripened into mature romances and marriage.

* * *

The Boonville or Boont lingo started as a game among the children who wished to talk freely when among their elders without being understood. This has been a common practice among children everywhere, but in most instances has soon gone out of existence from lack of interest and disuse. This was not the case, however, in Boonville. According to an informant, two originators of the language were Ed (Squirrel) Clement and Lank McGimsey, in or about the year 1890, and the two best known sites for its development were Berry's swimming hole and the hop fields at picking time.

Delighted with their success, the children added more and more words to their vocabulary. Soon others became interested; the lingo became very popular among the young adults and even many of the elders. The schoolteacher had to learn it in order to be cognizant of goings-on around her. The language was used quite freely until improvement of transportation and communication brought new people and ideas into the area. High school students hesitated to use it before newcomers for fear of being ridiculed and branded as country bumpkins. It is still known today among the natives, but not so freely used as it was in the early part of the century. To outsiders the language is completely incomprehensible as it has no basis or regular rules. The parts of speech used are nouns, verbs, a few adjectives, and phrases. The words are derived from various sources as follows:

A. Physical, mental, or personal peculiarities and characteristics of certain residents.
    1. *Bearman* meant a storyteller. Allen Cooper, an innkeeper, was a bear hunter and teller of tall tales.
    2. A *Shoveltooth* was a doctor—any doctor. The first resident doctor in the valley had protruding teeth.
    3. *To Charlie* meant to embarrass. An Indian named Charlie Ball was noted for bashfulness.
    4. *Hood*—a peculiar person, different from the ordinary. A new family moved into the valley and the children wore hoods all day long.
    5. To *High-heel*—to arrest. The constable had one leg shorter than the other so wore one high-heeled boot. He was the high heeler and, if arrested, one was high heeled.
    6. *High pockety*—rich. The tallest man in Boonville was wealthy. A high pocket was a wealthy person.
    7. *Jeffer*—a fire, generally a big one. Jeff Vestal, owner of the Boonville Hotel, built big fires in the parlor and elsewhere.

B. Incidents.
    1. *Blue-birded*—to be bucked off a horse. The story goes that one of the boys got bucked off a horse and afterward said, "I got thrown so high that a bluebird could have built a nest on my ass."

C. Apocopes. Compound words and blends.
    1. *toobs*—twenty-five cents, blend of two bits.
    2. *forbes*—fifty cents or four bits.
    3. *haireem*—a dog. A short form of "hairy mouth."
    4. *bell-jeek*—a rabbit, from Belgian hare and jack-rabbit.

D. Occupational expressions.
1. *airtight*—a sawmill.
2. *comōshe*—a machine for grinding sheep shears.
3. *schoolch*—blend of school teacher.
4. *skype*—preacher, from sky pilot.
E. Linguistic imports. A few words have been located in lists from other dialects. Some of these were brought with the settlers from their home states of Virginia, West Virginia, Missouri, Tennessee, and Texas and adopted into the language.
1. The expletive *"Eē-tah"* has been considered a version of the old rebel yell that went into many Civil War battles.
2. *dulcey*—candy. This is an adaptation from "dulce" (Sp.) meaning sweet.
3. *gorm*—to eat, from "gourmandise" (Fr.), gluttony.
4. *gannow*—apple, from Spanish "gano," a type of apple.
F. Onomatopoetic, a few words might be so termed as the word has a meaningful sound.
1. *spat*—a twenty-two caliber bullet.
G. Sobriquets or words derived from special names.
1. *Frati*—wine. Mr. Frati was a vineyardist who made and sold his own wine locally.
2. *Otto*—to work. A German settler, whose given name was Otto, was a very hard worker.
3. *Ite*—an Italian.
4. *Jenny Beck*—a tattle-tale. She was a gossip and tale-bearer.
H. Anagrams or words with a similarity of pronunciation.
1. Abaloneyite—a native of Albion, a favorite coast spot of abalone fishermen.
I. A few expressions may be termed euphemisms or disguised pronunciations. These were words the children were forbidden to use so they hid them in distortions.
1. ēesōle—a questionable character.
2. peeril—to rain.
3. eeld'm—an old woman.

Words have been spelled as sounded, and there are slight variations of pronunciation between old-timers and younger advocates of the lingo as used at the present time. It is interesting, laughable and quite puzzling to listen to one-time residents of Boonville, now engaged in various professions throughout the state, meet and converse, interspersing words and phrases that are completely understandable to them but gibberish to the listener. In the early days when Boonville had a traveling baseball club, the players used the lingo for signaling plays. An informant has told how his son stationed in the South Seas during World War II, sent informative letters home, completely uncensored.

Now that students of folklore are delving into customs, music, and language of different areas of our country, it seems a good time to record this rare and unique bit of folk language before it goes into disuse and is completely abandoned and forgotten. This vocabulary is not complete and probably never will be as new words and expressions are constantly being resurrected from memories of old timers. However, it is complete enough to depict the lingo in all its humor and quaintness. Explanations of the derivations of words or the background stories will be given when known.

In checking through dictionaries of dialects and modern slang, and in the *Shorter Oxford English Dictionary*, only a very limited number of similar words and expressions have been located, and, in practically every case, the meanings are completely dissimilar. For example, in Boontling a hood is a foolish or moronic individual, whereas Wentworth and Flexner's 1960 *Dictionary of American Slang* defines a hood as a hoodlum, a thief or a criminal. The same reference defines a "greenie" as a newcomer or a greenhorn, whereas to a Boonter a "greeny" denoted a loss of temper or a tantrum. So the conclusion may reasonably be drawn that, with the exception of a few isolated instances, Boontling was not an outgrowth of imports from other languages and dialects, but was a spontaneous development by an inventive and imaginative people who thoroughly enjoyed the game of fooling their neighbors.

* * *

Following is an alphabetized vocabulary and explanation of definitions and derivations, furnished by numerous informants.

Abaloneyite—a resident of Albion on the seacoast where abalones abounded.

abe—to butt or crowd in so as to push a person out of line and take his place.

airtight—a sawmill; no waste of power here.

applehead—a young woman or girl, could be a man's wife. Wentworth and Flexner define applehead as a stupid person.

ark—to wreck something, a car for instance, an anagram, probably from "wreck."

barlow—a knife. This was common usage, taken from the trade name, a Barlow knife.

bearman—a storyteller. (See introduction.)

beemsh—good show, a blend of boll (good) and show.

beeson tree—a stock saddle; Beeson was a trade name. The fact that Henry Beeson (step-son of Walter Anderson) also made saddles seems to have been a coincidence.

belljeek—a rabbit, a compound or blend of Belgian hare and jack rabbit.

Bill Nunn—syrup: a sobriquet; Bill put syrup on practically everything he ate.

bird-stork—a man with a large family.

blue-birded—to be bucked off a horse. (See introduction.)

blue-tail—a rattlesnake. This is fairly common usage.

boll—good, very good.

bollness—a good looking girl or woman.

Booker T.—a Negro; from the well-known Booker T. Washington. In common usage.

Boont—Boonville.

Boonter—a native of Boonville.

bootjack—a coyote.

borch—a Chinaman, a blend or possible euphemism for boar Chinese.

borego—a sheep, from the Spanish.

borp—a hog—boar pig.

bōshe—a deer: The *Shorter Oxford-English Dictionary* gives the word "bosch" (bos) as a South African antelope or Bush-buck. The supposition is that the word was introduced here following Teddy Roosevelt's African hunt.

boshe gun—a thirty-thirty-caliber rifle used for deer hunting.

boshe hareem—a deer dog or hound.

bōw—to dare or challenge to a fight.

branching—stepping out for a good time.

branding irons—handcuffs.

briny—the coast, a common expression since 1900, according to Wentworth and Flexner.

broady—a cow.

buckey—a nickel.

buck-inj—an Indian, a blend of buck-Indian.

buck pasture—this expression was used to indicate the predicament of a man with a pregnant wife.

chap ports—chaps, from the Spanish, "chaparajos," meaning leather or fur leggings worn by cowboys to protect the legs from cactus and brush while riding. (Wentworth and Flexner.)

charl—to milk a cow: derivation unknown unless from "chore." A *Dictionary of Slang and Unconventional English*, by Eric Partridge (1961), defines "chare" or "char" as "doing odd jobs."

charlie—to embarrass. (See introduction.)

charlied—embarrassed.

Charlie Balled—bashful. (See introduction.)

cheaters—glasses or spectacles. Common usage. Damon Runyon in "Guys and Dolls" (1932) mentioned "a little guy who wears horn cheaters," Wentworth and Flexner.

chigrel (noun)—food or a meal. As a verb—to eat. This word was a blend of child's gruel.

chipmunk—to hoard or save.

Cloverdal—Cloverdale, the nearest town to the south.

cloddies—heavy shoes, probably from clodhoppers, sturdy or cumbersome shoes, Wentworth and Flexner.

cocked—to become angry, like cocking a gun.

cocked darley—a man with a gun.

comōshe—a tool to grind sheep shears. A mōshe was a machine with a motor.

condeal or canned eel—a county job, blend of "county deal."

cow skully—a desolate area.

crazeek—crazy.

croppies—sheep.

cyke or sike—a horse, from cyclone, a horse hard to ride.

deeger—a degenerate person.

deejy—(adj.) degenerate, generally in reference to a person.

deek—to notice or call attention to, possibly from direct.

dicking—cheating, generally at cards. In underworld parlance a dick is a detective.

dishing—rushing or pushing to be first. *A Dictionary of Slang and Unconventional English* by Eric Partridge (1961), defines dishing (1) having a foot in, (2) getting a footing, (3) having a share or interest in. Ex.—a pig in his trough.

dissies—shoes with metal buckles.

dissie stool—the stool of repentance for a drunk, the state of being on the water wagon. Eric Partridge defines "go dis" to go crazy.

donicker or donagher—a toilet or rest-room. This was common underworld carnival and circus use. (Wentworth and Flexner, p. 155) and H.L. Mencken's *American Language*, 1936.

Drearies—the Bald Hills, a local spot.

dreek—whip.

dreeked—whipped.
dreeking—a whipping.
dulcey—sweet.
dukes—fists. This has been in common usage since about 1880.

eeld'm—an old woman, blend for "old dame." Not complimentary.
Ee-tah—an exclamation. (See introduction). Many Boonters were originally from the South and made no secret of their rebel sympathies.
equalizer—a gun, in fairly common usage in other dialects, underworld and fiction.
ēesōle—an undesirable or questionable character. This is considered a disguised pronunciation or euphemism.

fair and right a person—one who would give or lend money.
fiddlers—delirium tremens.
fister—a fight.
forbes—a half dollar (four bits).
frati—wine. (See introduction.)

gannow—apple: Spanish for a type of apple ("gano").
glimmer—a kerosene lamp. In *A Classical Dictionary of the Vulgar Tongue* by Francis Grose (1963), a glimmer is defined as a candle or dark lantern used in housebreaking. In the slang of American Trampdom and Underworld as a light, an eye or an eyeglass. This was evidently an import with variations.
glow worm—a lantern.
gorm—to eat or overeat. (See introduction.)
greeny—loss of temper, to throw a greeny or temper tantrum.

haireem—a dog, hairy mouth.
hedge—a haircut.
heelch—all or everything. A greedy person when invited to share food or drink would take the heelch. Possibly from "whole cheese."
high gun—to beat to the draw.
high heel—to arrest.
high heeled—to be arrested.
high heeler—an arresting officer.
high pockets—a person of wealth. The wealthiest man in the area was six feet five inches tall. In the *Dictionary of American Slang* this is a nickname for any tall man.
high pockety—rich, having money.
higgs—money.
higged or higgied—having money; to be "dehigged" was to be broke.

hob—a Saturday night dance.

hood—a simple person.

hoot—to laugh.

hooter—a loud laugher.

horn—a drink of liquor. The *Oxford Dictionary* defines horn as a vessel formed or shaped after the horn of a cow or other animal and used to hold liquid or powder.

itch neem'r—without desire to drink. One would say, "I itch neem'r." (Itch no more).

Ite—an Italian.

jape—to drive, generally a car.

japer—a driver of a car.

Jeffer—a big fire. (See introduction.)

Jenny Beck—a tattletale or stool pigeon. (See introduction.)

Jay Esser—a lawsuit, from a well-known lawsuit between J.S. Ornbaun, et al.

keishbook—an Indian word, meaning a pregnant woman. (Spelling problematical.)

killing snakes—a fairly common expression meaning working very hard. One might say, "He's tackling that job as if he were killing snakes."

kimmey—a man.

kingster—an expensive church. George Singley, whose nickname was King George or The King, donated liberally to the church building fund.

lengthy—a doe deer. H.L. Mencken's *American Language* (1936) defines lengthy as an adjective meaning long, extended or prolonged, as a lengthy meeting, states its usage as uncommon.

Levi—to telephone. Walter Levi was the first one to make use of the telephone in Boont.

locking—a wedding.

locking match—an anticipated wedding or engagement to marry.

log lifter—a heavy winter storm.

Madge—any prostitute. Madge was a brothel madame in Ukiah.

madging—visiting a house of prostitution.

Mason-Dixon—division line between Boonville and Philo. In early days a feud (almost) existed between the two communities.

mink—an expensively dressed girl or woman, a wearer of fur.

Moldune—an overly large woman (a sobriquet).

Muzz Creek—excess of water in gutters.

nettied—all dressed up, wearing a super-abundance of lace, ribbons, and finery.

nonch—no good; in fact, bad. A blend of "not much."

old dame—a kimmey's wife.

old dusties—hell.

oshtook—a person with one eye. An Indian word.

Otto—to work hard. (See introduction.)

pack-em-out-billies—dirty socks.

paper skull—a small deer.

Peak'ed Heads—members of Oddfellow's Lodge, usually used by non-members.

peeril—to rain. A euphemism or disguised pronunciation.

pick-em-up—two definitions given for this: (1) a person starting a fight; (2) a method of breaking a horse, by elevating one foot.

pike—to go, to travel. This word is found in several slang dictionaries with similar meanings.

pusseek—a female cat.

region—one's house or home.

relf—a rail fence.

ridgy—old fashioned or back-woodsy. The *Dictionary of American Slang* defines ridgy as a noun meaning a ridge runner, a hill billy or mountaineer, a Southern rustic.

seertil or sirtle—a salmon, sore tail.

skype—a preacher, a sky pilot.

sol—the sun, probably from the Latin.

Sol's grandmother or Saul's grandmother—dead. This was an interesting expression for research. The *Oxford English Dialect Dictionary*, by Joseph Wright, Volume V, defines a *saulie* as a funeral mute or a hired mourner. Grandmother was a naval or military term for any of the big howitzers operated in France by the Royal Marine Artillery in World War I, ca. 1915.

somersetting—being over-emotional or sentimental (head over heels).

spat—a twenty-two caliber rifle.

steedoss—a stallion, stud horse.

stiff hats—professional fighters, from the fact that they wore derbies.

straight necks—Germans, probably from their military bearing.

sunnies—pretty, sunny days.

teebowed—deaf, possibly of Indian derivation.

telēfe—telephone, or to telephone.

thorps—a man's button shoes.

tobe—tobacco.

toobs or tubes—twenty-five cents, two bits.

trash mover—a heavy rain storm.

Trojan—dynamite, a brand name.

trilbies—shoes, probably dress shoes. *American Mercury*, II (Dec., 1917), 554, gives the definition of trilbies to be feet, from the name of the heroine in DuMaurier's novel *Trilby* (1894). She was noted for her beautiful feet.

tuddish—crazy.

tuffer—a sheep hard to sheer, a tough one.

tweed—a child or teen-ager, a sweetie or even tweetie.

Uke—Ukiah, the county seat.

weese—a small child or infant (wee suck).

Wes—a harmless fib. Wes was a local storyteller.

Wheeler—a fit or tantrum.

wilk—a wild cat.

zeese—coffee: Z.C. or Zeese Blevins was a coffee drinker. A horn of zeese would be a drink of coffee.

Ukiah, California

BIBLIOGRAPHY

Books

Adams, Ramon F., *Western Words, a Dictionary of the Range, Cow Camp and Trail*. Norman, Oklahoma: University of Oklahoma Press, 1946.

Carpenter, Aurelius O. and Percy O. Milberry, *Mendocino and Lake County History*. Los Angeles: Historic Record Co., 1915.

Grose, Frances, *A Classical Dictionary of the Vulgar Tongue*, 3rd ed. New York: Barnes and Noble, 1963.

Mencken, Henry L., *The American Language*, Book One. New York: Alfred A. Knopf, 1936.

Murray, J.A.H., *Shorter Oxford-English Dictionary*. New York: Oxford University Press.

Palmer, Lyman L., *A History of Mendocino County*. San Francisco: Alley, Bowen and Co., 1880.

Partridge, Eric, *A Dictionary of Slang and Unconventional English*, 5th ed. New York: Macmillan Co., 1961.

Wentworth, Harold and Stuart B. Flexner, *Dictionary of American Slang*. New York: Crowell, 1960.

Wright, Joseph, *Oxford-English Dialect Dictionary*, Vol. V. New York: Oxford University Press, 1961.

Articles

"Boonville Speaks Boont, its own Peculiar Language," *San Francisco Chronicle*, Leisure Section, about June 25-26, 1950.

Chretien, C. Douglas, "Boontling," *California Folklore Quarterly*, I (January, 1942), 96-97.

June, Jack, "The Strange Lingo of Boonville," *San Francisco Examiner*, Pictorial Living Section, July 19, 1959.

CHAPTER

13

Logging Railroad Language in the Redwood Country

Lynwood Carranco

Logging railroads have played a very important part in the red-wood lumber business. In 1850 the early millowners logged the timber easily around Humboldt Bay because the land sloped toward the bay, which served as a natural log pond to the mills on the shore. When the timber was all cut away from the water's edge, the bull teams and horse teams had to haul the huge logs long distances. This operation became very expensive, and the logging railroads were introduced about 1874. From that time to about 1950, railroads were the important movers of logs in the redwood country.

Trucks have gradually taken over the work done by the logging railroads. The construction of logging railroads is very expensive, and it has been much cheaper to build roads for trucks. At the present time, the Pacific Lumber Company of Scotia is using a main-line haul from its Carlotta Camp to the mill. During the dry season, which is four or five months out of the year, trains are also used from the Larabee Camp to the Scotia mill. The rolling stock belongs to the company, but the crews are contracted by the Northwestern Pacific Railroad Company. The Georgia Pacific Corporation at Samoa discontinued its main-line haul in 1960, and trucks now carry logs from the woods to the log dump at Samoa. The Simpson Logging Company still operates the first railroad of California—the Arcata and Mad River Railroad—using three diesel-electrics on a main-line haul.

Trucks and diesel locomotives have almost pushed the logging railroads into the past, and many of the old-time words and expressions have disappeared with the steam. Steam railroading introduced many new terms. Some of these, such as *bad-order, clean the clock, cut the throttle, have one's head cut in, pull the pin,* and *pull the tit,* became part of the vocabulary of the logging railroad men, as well as of the popular speech of the area.

Many former logging brakemen, firemen, and engineers were consulted to recover the expressions and flavor of this unique vocabulary. Some of the terms may be classified as universal argot of railroad men. But after comparing my list with H.L. Mencken's collection of railroad terms,[1] and one by Cottrell and Montgomery in *American Speech*,[2] I was surprised to find that most of the logging railroad terms were not mentioned in either source.

Mencken calls a locomotive engineer a *hogger* and a *hoghead*, but he does not include *air artist, log hauler, runner,* or *throttle jerker.* He does not refer to *smoke boy* or *smokey* to describe a fireman. The terms *brakie, iron bender,* and *swing brakeman* are also not on his list. Neither list includes the word *mulligan* for 'caboose.'

Lokie is the popular name for a locomotive. Other variations are *locie, lockie,* and *loky.* Names for the locomotives, usually depending on the type, condition, or position in the train run, were many: *climax, corkscrew, deuce, dinkey, galloping goose, Heisler, kettle, mallet, porter, road engine, rod engine,* and *stemwinder.*

Cottrell and Montgomery cite the popular term *caboose hop* for a train comprising only an engine and a caboose. In their list, a *car knocker* is an inspector, but in this area the term designated a man who repaired railroad cars. They refer to a *cherry picker* as a switchman, whereas in the redwood country the term means a light loading machine for picking up logs lost along a railroad.

There were many favorite expressions used in making a fast run: *'ballin' the jack, hang the throttle over the tank, pull the tit, screw the pops down, work in the company's notch,* and *work in the corner.* The air brakes were very important on a logging train, especially on the steep grades. Terms in this category are: *big-hole the air, clean the clock, set 'em up,* and *wipe the gauge.*

Crummy, gill poke, hogger, and *king snipe* appeared in my first word list,[3] and *gandy dancer* was in my second.[4] I have included these terms below because they specifically belong to the vocabulary of the logging railroad and of course are a part of the general logging language of the redwood country. The words that are starred are in the *DAE.*

AIR ARTIST, *n.* A railroad engineer who is skilled in handling air brakes when taking heavy trains down steep grades.

AIR BUNK, *n.* A log bunk with inside air pistons to raise or lower the stakes on the ends of the bunks on railroad cars.

AMERICAN, *n.* A rod engine—either a saddle tank or one with the usual tender.

BAD-ORDER, *adj.* A term originally applied to a railroad car in need of repairs; now used to refer to anything defective.

BAKEHEAD, *n.* A fireman on a steam locomotive.

'BALLIN' THE JACK, *v. phr.* A logging train that is highballing or making a fast run.

BALLOON, *n.* A balloon-shaped track for turning the engines.

BATTERY, DOUBLE HEADIN', *n.* Two or more engines that are spaced for safety and power along a train on a long haul from the woods.

BEAT THE THROTTLE WITH A STICK, *v. phr.* To get more steam out of an engine.

BEND THE IRON, *v. phr.* To throw a switch on the railroad.

BETTER-STEAMER, *n.* On a steam engine, a heavy iron bar which was used illegally by a fireman to tear a hole in the spark arrester screen in order to facilitate the escape of sparks, thus causing the engine to steam better.

BIG-HOLE THE AIR, *v. phr.* To let the air escape from the biggest hole in the valve which applies the brakes sharply in an emergency.

BILLY GOAT, *n.* A small starting motor used on a big diesel engine.

BRAKE, BROKE, *v.i.* Used in reference to past action: 'I used to brake for Hammond's.' 'He braked for P.L. [the Pacific Lumber Company]'; 'He broke for P.L.'

*BRAKIE, *n.* A brakeman.

BULGINE ['bʌldʒɪn], *n.* A locomotive.

*CABIN CAR. *See* CABOOSE.

CABOOSE, *CABIN CAR, HACK, *n.* The car for the train crew to ride in. On logging roads the caboose was used to haul freight or equipment. *See also* MULLIGAN.

*CABOOSE HOP, *n.* A train that consisted only of an engine and a caboose.

CAR KNOCKER, *n.* A man who repaired railroad cars.

CAR LINE, *n.* A light line used to pull railroad cars into position so that the logs could be loaded.

CHERRY PICKER, *n.* A light loading machine for picking up logs lost along a railroad.

CHINA BOY, *n.* A Chinese. Chinese laborers were employed in the woods as swampers and fire tenders, and as early as 1875 they were brought to the county to construct roads and railroads. On February 6, 1885, a Eureka councilman was killed by a stray bullet fired from the gun of one of two quarreling Chinese.

Because of this incident all of the Chinese in the county were forced to leave by April of 1886.

CLEAN THE CLOCK; WIPE THE CLOCK; WIPE THE GAUGE, *v. phr.* To apply the emergency air brakes on a locomotive. This draws all the air out of the line and causes the indicator needle on the gauge ('clock') to drop to zero; thus, the 'clock' is empty or cleaned.

CORKSCREW, *n.* A geared engine on a logging railroad, usually a Shay.

CRACK THE THROTTLE, *v. phr.* To start a steam engine slowly.

CRUMMY, *n.* Originally a transportation car on a railroad (usually a caboose), so called because of its usual condition. Now the term is applied to a station wagon or bus that transports men to and from work in the woods.

CUPOLA, *n.* The lookout hatch on a caboose.

CUT THE THROTTLE, *v. phr.* To coast, to take it easy.

DERAIL, *n.* A device on a railroad switch used to prevent cars from running out on the main track.

DEUCE, TWO-SPOT, *n.* The number two locomotive on a train run.

DIAMOND STACK, *n.* A big diamond-shaped spark arrester on the stack of a locomotive.

DINKEY, *n.* A small locomotive.

DIRECT-GEARED, *adj.* A term to describe a rod locomotive.

DOG'ER, *v.i.* To put chalks under the wheels to stop a locomotive.

DOUBLE HEADIN'. *See* BATTERY.

DOUGHNUT, *n.* A smoke ring from a locomotive.

DYNAMITER, *n.* A bad-order car which has something wrong with the air.

*EMPTIES, *n.* Flatcars or any kind of empty logging cars going back to the woods for more loads.

FILL OUT, *v.i.* To add cars to a train.

FIRE BOY, *n.* A fireman.

FIRE UP, *v.t.* To get steam ready in a locomotive before the crew arrives.

FISH-PLATE, *n.* A heavy plate between two ties on which the ends of rails were fastened to make a rail joint.

FLAGGIN', *part.* Protecting the rear end of a train by using a red flag, fusee, or torpedoes.

FOGGIN', *part.* Making a fast run on a logging railroad.

FOREST ENGINEER, *n.* Usually a logging engineer from the company office.

FOUL, *v.t.* To stop a car on a siding near the main line so that a passing train will hit it.

FREE STEAMER, *n.* A locomotive which is easily fired.

FREEZE THE PIN, *v. phr.* To stretch the slack on a train so that the brakeman cannot pull the uncoupling pin.

FROG, *n.* The crossing piece of a railroad switch.

FUSEE, *n.* A red flare used for emergencies on a railroad.

GALLOPING GOOSE, *n.* Any steam or diesel locomotive which does not run properly.

GANDY DANCER, *n.* A section hand on a railroad. The dance was the movement made in tamping ties.

GEARED ENGINE, *n.* A Climax, Heisler, or Shay locomotive (*see also* HEISLER and SHAY). The power from the cylinders was transferred to the driving wheels through different gearing arrangements. These engines with a short wheel base were used on steep, crooked logging roads where extra power was needed.

GILL POKE, JILL POKE, *n.* A horizontal lever used to dump logs from flatcars into a pond.

GRADE, *n.* A railroad route.

GUARD RAIL, *n.* An extra rail laid on the inside of the running rail on sharp curves on a logging railroad line to prevent derailment.

GUIDE ROLL, *n.* A roller which was used to guide a cable on an incline railroad.

HACK. *See* CABOOSE.

HANG THE THROTTLE OVER THE TANK. *See* PULL THE TIT.

HAVE ONE'S HEAD CUT IN, *v. phr.* To think clearly and not make mistakes. Originally, this widely used expression meant to cut in the air brakes on a train in order to have control of the train. A man with his brains disconnected is as helpless as a train with no brakes.

HAVE ITS VALVES SQUARE, *v. phr.* To be a locomotive in good working order: 'The engine has its valves square.'

HEAD TRAIN LOADER, *n.* In the former days of railroad logging, the top man in a loading crew.

HEISLER, *n.* A geared locomotive that was used on the logging railroads. The cylinders were slanted at 45 degrees and set at right angles to the engine frame. The drive was accomplished through the connecting rods to the geared axles, with side rods on all three trucks under the engine and the tank.

HIDE GRAVEL, *v. phr.* To force gravel under the ties in raising the track.

HIT THE STEEL, *v. phr.* To be fired or quit a job. In the early days of railroad logging, this meant 'to walk the track away from camp.'

HOG, *n.* A locomotive.

HOGGER, HOGHEAD, *n.* A locomotive engineer.

HOGHEAD. *See* HOGGER.

HORSE 'ER OVER, *v. phr.* To reverse an engine on a steam locomotive.

HOSTLER, *n.* A roundhouse man.

IDLER, *n.* An empty car which is coupled to another car having a load of logs longer than the car, thus permitting the load to be coupled into a train.

*INCLINE, *n.* Under the old system of lowering logs down a very steep railroad grade, the cars were lowered on a dead incline by cable from a stationary engine. On a live incline, the power plant itself was pulled up and down the hill, either by carrying logs on cars or by skidding them on the ties.

INDEPENDENT AIR, *n.* The separate air brakes on a locomotive, not connected to the train line brakes.

IRON BENDER, *n.* A railroad brakeman.

*JACK SCREW, LOG JACK, *n.* A lever-operated jack used in the early days to jack large logs on and off railroad cars.

JILL POKE. *See* GILL POKE.

JOHNNY DYER, *n.* An airhose connection that was cut into the train line in the middle of a log train. If the swing brakeman rode here, he could apply the air brakes in an emergency.

JOHNSON BAR, *n.* A long, heavy lever that was pinned on a notched steel arc and connected to the valve motion on a steam locomotive. It was used to reverse the direction of the engine, as well as to change the timing and amount of steam admitted to the cylinders through ports in the steam chest.

KETTLE, *n.* A locomotive which leaked steam.

KING SNIPE, *n.* The foreman in charge of logging-railroad maintenance.

KITCHEN CAR, *n.* The cook car in a railroad camp.

KNUCKLE, *n.* That part of a coupler on railroad rolling stock which engages the coupler on another car or engine.

LINK AND PIN, *n. phr.* The early type of coupler used on logging trains. These couplers were used on the Arcata and Mad River Railroad as late as 1941.

LOCIE. *See* LOKIE.

LOCKIE. *See* LOKIE.

*LOCATION, *n.* The rough line which is first laid out for a logging railroad.

LOCOMOTIVE CORD, *n.* The wood for locomotive fuel cut in two-foot lengths and piled 2 x 4 x 8 feet to make a cord.

*LOG DUMP, *n.* In the old days this was the end of a railroad where the logs were dumped into the water.

LOGGING CAR, *n.* Any logging car used on a railroad.

LOG HAULER, *n.* An engineer on a logging train.

LOG JACK. *See* JACK SCREW.

LOKIE, LOCIE, LOCKIE, LOKY, *n.* A locomotive.

LOKY. *See* LOKIE.

LONG CAR, *n.* A long flatcar for handling long logs.

*MAIN LINE, *n.* The main railroad used in logging.

MALLET, *n.* A locomotive with two sets of engines fed from one boiler. Mallets were used on logging roads where big loads were hauled on steep grades.

MULLIGAN, *n.* Another name for a caboose. In the early days of logging, the noon meals were taken out to the men in the woods in a special car called the mulligan. The term referred to the mulligan soup which was served. Later the term was applied to the caboose or to any car that transported men from the woods to the cookhouse.

*NARROW GAUGE, *n.* A railroad less than 4 feet 8 1/2 inches wide. The Arcata and Mad River Railroad was famous for its odd 45 1/4 inch gauge.

ONE-SPOT, *n.* Locomotive number one. Engine number two would be the two-spot.

ON THE SPOT, *prep. phr.* To take it easy. The logging crew on a railroad would arrive at a log dump or landing early with nothing to do until it was time for their next trip. The crew would be on the spot—taking it easy.

PORTER, *n.* A small locomotive used in logging operations.

POT, *n.* A locomotive.

POWER, *n.* All the locomotives owned by a company. The expression is heard, 'The company has lots of power.'

PULL THE PIN, *v. phr.* To quit: 'He pulled the pin yesterday.' On the railroad this meant to pull the pin to release a car.

PULL THE TIT, HANG THE THROTTLE OVER THE TANK, *v. phr.* To pull the throttle of a locomotive all the way out, thus making a fast run: 'Pull the tit—let's go.'

RACK CAR, *n.* A railroad car equipped with stakes or racks to handle wood.

ROAD ENGINE, *n.* A main-line engine on a logging railroad.

ROD ENGINE, *n.* A standard main-line steam engine, directly connected by piston rods from the cylinders to the driving wheels.

ROLL LANDING, *n.* A landing with big logs down both sides of the track which was level with the car bunks—used to roll logs onto the train cars.

ROUNDHOUSE, *n.* A building, generally circular or semicircular, with a turntable in the center, utilized for storing, repairing, and switching locomotives.

RUN, *n.* A full or complete trip from the woods to the log dump.

RUNNER, *n.* A locomotive engineer.

RUN-TRAIN, *n.* Usually the head brakeman on a logging railroad which had no conductor.

SADDLE TANK, *n.* A small locomotive with the water tank over the boiler to increase the weight on the driving wheels.

SAFE SIDE, *n.* The side away from the dump in unloading cars.

SAW, *v.i.* To shunt or to work one train past another in the opposite direction when the siding is too small to hold all of either train.

SCRATCH, *v.t.* To remove a car from a train and to put it on a siding.

SCREW THE POPS DOWN, *v. phr.* To screw down the pop valves on a steam engine so that it will carry a higher head of steam than it is supposed to.

SET 'EM UP, *v. phr.* To turn up the retaining valve handles on a train air brake system, before going down a hill with a heavy load of logs, which causes partial braking on the wheels so that the engineer can build up more pressure in the brake cylinders.

SHACK, *n.* A brakeman.

SHAY, *n.* The most popular of the geared locomotives used in the woods. The several cylinders are upright on the engineer's side of the frame, and the boiler is offset to balance them. A propeller shaft driven by cranks runs along one side of the engine and is geared to the axles.

SKELETON CAR, *n.* A log hauling car on a railroad which has no floor on the car.

SKIDDER CAR, *n.* A heavy railroad car used as a permanent base for a skidder, that is, a big donkey which powers a skidder system, a method of logging used in rough country.

SKID FLAT, *n.* A flat spot on a railroad car wheel caused by sliding.

SLACK, *n.* The play between couplers on cars which takes up the shock in starting and stopping.

SLACK ON THE PIN, *v. phr.* To back up in order to relieve tension on couplers so that a car can be coupled.

SMOKE BOY, SMOKEY, *n.* A fireman.

SMOKE SIGNALS, *n.* Sometimes trains were taken on a logging railroad without authority. The men had to keep a sharp lookout for smoke from other trains in order to get onto a side track or to back up quickly: 'We had to watch for smoke signals.'

SMOKEY. *See* SMOKE BOY.

SNUBBING LINE, *vbl. n.* A car line used to spot empty cars for loading at a landing.

*SPARK ARRESTER, *n.* Usually a screen fitted over the smokestack of a locomotive to prevent the sparks from escaping.

SPEEDER, *n.* A rail motor car employed to repair the railroad, to bring supplies to camp, or to haul men.

SPIRAL, *n.* A twisted road intended to ease out of a curve on a railroad.

STACK, *n.* Abbreviation for *smokestack*.

STAKE-MAKER, *n.* The man who cuts car stakes or blocks to hold logs on the railroad cars.

STEAM JAM, *n.* A steam-powered brake on a locomotive.

STEAM UP, *v.t.* To fire up a locomotive.

STEEL, *n.* Railroad rails.

STEMWINDER, *n.* A Shay engine.

STRING OF FLATS, *n. phr.* A train of empty flatcars.

SWING BRAKEMAN, *n.* The third person or brakeman on a railroad crew. If there were over forty-eight cars, there were a conductor and two brakemen. At times the swing brakeman rode in the middle of a logging train.

SWITCHBACK, *n.* A series of levels on a railroad so that logging trains could saw back and forth over a steep hill or ridge.

TAKE THE SLACK, *v. phr.* To bunch up the cars in a train before starting.

TALLOWPOT, *n.* A fireman on a locomotive. In the early days he used to put the tallow in the pots.

*TANK, *n.* (1) A locomotive; (2) the water of a locomotive; (3) a water tank along the line.

TEAKETTLE, *n.* A small or a leaky locomotive.

THROTTLE JERKER, *n.* The engineer on a locomotive.

TIE 'EM DOWN, *v. phr.* To set the hand brakes on a log car.

TORPEDO, *n.* An explosive that was put on a track to warn an approaching locomotive of danger.

TRACK, *n.* In railroad logging, the railroad which served the camp was known as the track.

TRAILER, *n.* A flatcar pushed ahead of an engine to couple on to cars standing on the track which were too light to couple on to the engine.

*TRAIN, *n.* A string of flatcars loaded with logs and ready to be pulled out of the woods.

TRAM, *n.* A wooden railway on which log cars were pulled by oxen, horses, or donkeys. These were the first railways in the Humboldt County (the center of the redwood industry).

TWO-SPOT. *See* DEUCE.

UNIT, *n.* In railroad logging, a unit consisted of both the yarding and the loading engine set up on one car.

WAY CAR, *n.* A railroad car used for many purposes: caboose, supply car, and so on.

WEAR A WHITE FEATHER, *v. phr.* To be a steaming locomotive with the safety valve blowing off steam.

WIDEN ON 'ER, *v. phr.* To open up the throttle.

WIPE THE CLOCK. *See* CLEAN THE CLOCK.

WIPE THE GAUGE. *See* CLEAN THE CLOCK.

WOOD BURNER, *n.* Originally, a locomotive fired by burning wood.

WOODEN RAILROAD, *n.* A logging railroad with wooden rails. Oxen or horses provided the motive power.

WOOD UP, *v.t.* To load the wood car on a locomotive tender with wood.

WORK IN THE BROTHERHOOD NOTCH, *v. phr.* To coast along easily—when the engine has plenty of steam and the fireman is relaxing.

WORK IN THE COMPANY'S NOTCH, WORK IN THE CORNER, *v. phr.* To put the throttle in the last notch (wide open) on a steam engine when pulling a big load in order to supply the greatest pulling power.

WORK IN THE CORNER. *See* WORK IN THE COMPANY'S NOTCH.

Y, *n.* A track laid out in the contour of the letter *Y* for turning a locomotive.

*YARD, *n.* The tracks at the end of a railroad line.

YARD GOAT, *n.* A switch engine.

FOOTNOTES

1. H.L. Mencken, *The American Language* (New York, 1948), II, 713-16.
2. W.F. Cottrell and H.C. Montgomery, 'A Glossary of Railroad Terms,' *American Speech*, XVIII (1943), 161-70.
3. 'Logger Lingo in the Redwood Region,' *American Speech*, XXXI (1956), 149-52.
4. 'More Logger Lingo in the Redwood Region,' *American Speech*, XXXIV (1959), 76-80.

FIGURE 13.1. A logging train of the Excelsior Redwood Company in the 1880's. The logging trains hauled the logs to Humboldt Bay where they were rafted to the mill on Gunther Island. Ericson Photograph.

CHAPTER

14

Americanisms in the Redwood Country

Lynwood Carranco

Americanisms, as defined by Mitford M. Mathews, editor of *A Dictionary of Americanisms (DA)*, are words or expressions that have originated in the United States.[1] The *DA* supplements the *Dictionary of American English (DAE)*, which gives the histories of words as they have been used in the United States.

The argot of the lumber industry in the Redwood Country, specifically Humboldt County, California, has influenced the popular speech of the area. Humboldt County, California, since 1850, has been one of the largest lumber-producing counties in the United States. In the ten-year period through 1960, Humboldt County lumber production averaged 1,500,000,000 feet of lumber cut annually, with an average yearly return of $150,000,000. In Humboldt County timber is 70.7 per cent of the basic industry.[2]

When the white pine grew scarce in Maine, the first migration of men was to Michigan, Wisconsin, and Minnesota. The second migration was to the Pacific Northwest and to the Redwood Country. Many of the words and expressions were brought by the migrating midwesterners and the New England woodsmen. But the newcomers had to develop new ways of logging the big redwoods and had to invent new words to describe the new tools and the new logging methods. In the fir and redwood region, where there is a heavy rainfall, the loggers (not lumberjacks in the western woods) had to learn to get around in "tin pants." The job of chopping down trees and sawing them into logs is "falling and bucking"; that the man in charge of such work is the "bull buck"; that "gyppo" or "by the mile" or "by the inch" or "by the bushel" means piece or contract work; that the "candy side" is one of two or more logging crews in the same camp which is best equipped, and so on.

The early bull team days provided one of the most popular expressions—the SKIDROAD. Bulls or horses skidded the logs across

cross skids laid across the road. The skidroad was the heart of the early logging show, and this term was transferred to First and later Second Street in Eureka, a wide-open town before World War II. This area was near the waterfront, not far from the railroad depot, and catered to all types of characters. The loggers were the most numerous. There were many saloons, restaurants, and lodging houses, and many of them had names with a timber flavor. Names like "High Lead," "Logger Club-Rest," and "Lumber Jack" can still be seen. Whorehouses flourished everywhere. These brothels were labeled "Rooms," and old-timers tell many humorous stories of trying to obtain lodging at these places when they first arrived in town. For years the girls operated within a block of the police station.

The first-dated quotation for the logging SKIDROAD in the *DAE* is 1880. SKIDROAD, as a lower section of a city, is traced to 1928 in the *DA*. SKIDROW, which developed from SKIDROAD, is dated in the *DA* for 1944. This term, popularized by reporters ignorant of the logging business, has spread to the East, much to the disgust of the northwesterners in the fir country of Oregon and Washington who claim emphatically that there never was and never will be such a term as SKIDROW (also spelled SKID ROW).

The loggers transferred other logging terms to Eureka's skidroad, which were very popular in the Redwood County before the war. HOOKER, the name for the foreman of a yarding crew, was a whore. Amazingly enough the *DAE* lists HOOKER as whore or resident of the Hook (1859) because of the number of "houses of ill-fame" frequented by sailors at the Hook (Corlear's Hook) in New York City. In the Redwood Country a whorehouse was a HOOK SHOP or a HOOK JOINT. There were many varieties of hooks used in logging to make quick couplings, especially in yarding logs. And of course the loggers always got HOOKED—a poor exchange for the price.

The hard-working lonely loggers in the lumber camps invented or borrowed new words for objects that fitted their needs. A SCHOOLMARM in the woods has always been a tree with an inverted crotch or two trees growing from a single trunk. The loggers wear corks or shoes with short, heavy spikes in their soles to give sure footing on logs. Any smooth surface on which a logger's corks will not hold is the popular "slicker than a schoolmarm's leg."

Two expressions that have a long history in the lumber business have always been popular in the redwood country. A RAFT OF, meaning a quantity of persons or things, is recorded in the *DAE* for 1833. Rafts were important in the early days of logging. The logging trains brought the logs from the woods to Humboldt Bay where they were dumped and made into rafts to be transported by a stern-wheeler steamer to the lumber mills on the bay. EASY AS FALLING OFF A LOG, said of something easy, is recorded in the *DAE* for 1889. This popular expression is kept alive by the men on the log ponds.

The expression, ON THE SKIDS, taken from the logging skid-road, is often used to describe a person who is slipping and not doing a good job any more, or to describe one who has not the moral character that he once had. SWAMP OUT is another current logging term used in popular speech. The verb SWAMP means to clean out brush by chopping and clearing, as to prepare a road in logging. SWAMP OUT means to clean out a place, such as to "swamp out a room." The expression NOW YOU'RE LOGGIN' is a common one throughout the area. High school students and adults all use it. This expression is similar to "Now you're okay" or "You're doing fine."

LOWER THE BOOM is another expression which means to take severe action of some kind against a person as in "lower the boom on him." A BOOM is a pole or metal arm that sticks out of a loading rig that loads logs onto trucks or railroad cars.

SIDEWINDER and WIDOW MAKER are widely used expressions for anything that may fall from above, causing injury to a person. The earliest dated quotation for SIDEWINDER in the *DAE* is 1840, and the meaning is a heavy swinging blow of the fist. In the Redwood Country the term refers to a falling limb or snag that may fall from above in falling trees or in yarding. A WIDOW MAKER is also a limb from a fallen tree which belatedly falls after being snagged in the boughs of another tree. SIDEWINDERS and WIDOW MAKERS have been the cause of many deaths and injuries in logging.

Logging railroads have played a very important part in the redwood lumber business. In 1850 the early mill owners logged the timber around Humboldt Bay because the land sloped toward the bay, which served as a natural log pond to the mills on the shore. When the timber was all cut away from the water's edge, the bull teams had to haul the huge logs long distances. This operation became very expensive, and the logging railroads were introduced about 1874. From that time on to about 1950, railroads were the important movers of logs in the Redwood Country.

Trucks and diesel locomotives have almost pushed the logging railroads into the past, and many of the old-time words and expressions have almost disappeared with the steam. Steam railroading introduced many new expressions. Some of these, such as BAD-ORDER, CUT THE THROTTLE, HAVE ONE'S HEAD CUT IN,

PULL THE PIN, and PULL THE TIT, became part of the vocabulary of the logging railroad men, as well as the popular speech of the region.

BAD-ORDER, which originally referred to a railroad car in need of repairs, is now used to describe anything defective. CUT THE THROTTLE means to take it easy. To HAVE ONE'S HEAD CUT IN is to think clearly and not to make mistakes. Originally this expression meant to cut in the air brakes on a train in order to have control of the train. A man with his brains disconnected is as helpless as a train with no brakes. The popular PULL THE PIN means to quit: "He pulled the pin yesterday." On the railroad this meant to pull the pin to release a car. To PULL THE TIT originally was to pull the throttle of a locomotive all the way out, thus making a fast run. This fast-disappearing expression now means to shut anything down, usually a mill: "Wish they would pull the tit."

The *DA* traces HIGHBALL to 1913 as a signal order on the railroad. In the Redwood Country woods, HIGHBALL is a signal from the woods to the donkey operator that means "go ahead." From HIGHBALL has originated the term HIGHBALLIN', meaning to go fast. A HIGHBALLIN' OUTFIT is any company that makes its men hustle—no loitering on the job.

The much-used verb JILL-POKED is from the logging railroads. The original JILL POKE originated in the building of the skidroads. A notch was cut on the opposite ends of a log or skid. A slight post or JILL POKE was driven down alongside the notch with a wooden maul to keep the logs or skids from moving. A JILL POKE is now a horizontal pole or lever used to dump logs from flat cars into a log pond. To be JILL-POKED is to be hit or to be shoved off any object. It is also used in popular speech to be treated unfairly: "The mill owners have been jill-poking him."

The first-dated quotation in the *DAE* for HAVE THE DEAD-WOOD ON HIM is 1851. The next quotation (1867) mentions that the expression came from a game of "ten-pins," and "that a fallen pin sometimes lies in front of the standing ones so that the first ball striking it will sweep the alley." This expression, meaning to have unquestioned advantage or superiority over someone, is a common one, kept alive by the lumber industry.

LOW MAN ON THE TOTEM POLE, a popular expression along the entire West Coast, has been used in the Redwood Country for many years. The loggers who came from the fir country in the Northwest where there were many totem poles brought the expression south to the big trees. The term usually refers to the man with the lowest or poorest job, who cannot pass the buck to anyone else.

A swivel is an important joint used everywhere in rigging in the woods to prevent lines from twisting. SWIVEL HEAD had developed from the term and of course refers to anyone who spends his time staring stupidly around him, especially a green logger or the many tourists who come to see a woods operation.

DINGBAT has an interesting history dating back to 1861 (DAE). The term was first used for money, but was later used for any one of various things, such as wood, money, bullet, and so on. In popular speech as in the lumber business the term is used for any unknown object: "What is that dingbat?"; "What is the little dingbat in the carburetor called?"

The ARMSTRONG METHOD, work done by hand and not by machine, originated in the sawmills. Before the introduction of the modern setworks (a machine with gears on a carriage that the sawmill setter operates from a signal from the sawyer to determine the desired thickness to be cut from a log or cant), a log was advanced for cutting by a pawl and ratchet system. The sawyer signaled the ratchet setter and he pumped the ratchet to get the required thickness. This was a difficult and tiring job—using a strong arm or the ARMSTRONG METHOD.

The DA traces HANG UP to 1854, and the meaning is to stop or suspend one's efforts. This term has long been an important one in logging. The first-dated quotation associated with logging in 1878 and is used to discontinue a drive: "The logs were hung up for want of water to float them." At the present time HANG-UP, used as a noun, has the following meanings: (1) logs caught behind trees or stumps in a logging operation; (2) tangled rigging; (3) any operation that has failed. The verb HANG UP has the following meanings: (1) to get logs caught behind trees or stumps; (2) to get the rigging stuck to prevent logging; (3) to get a tree stuck against another in falling; and (4) to get fouled up in any operation. In popular speech HANG UP as a rule is used to describe a thwarting of one's efforts to do something.

Two rather new expressions from logging that have become part of the local speech are BOARDIN' WITH AUNT POLLY and ROCKIN' CHAIR MONEY. BOARDIN' WITH AUNT POLLY means to draw insurance as in the following statement: "He's boardin' with Aunt Polly." The popular ROCKIN' CHAIR MONEY is used when a person draws unemployment compensation when he is out of a job: "He's gettin' his rockin' chair money."

A common excuse for being late to work, which has worked into the local speech, is the localism, THE OLD WOMAN SLEPT ON MY NIGHTSHIRT. Another localism, which has followed the same pattern, is to SPLIT THE BLANKETS, which refers to a divorce: "They are splittin' the blankets"; "They split the blankets."

Thus, throughout the years the redwood lumber industry has been an influential element in the vocabulary and has continued to contribute materially to the speech of the Redwood Country.

FOOTNOTES

1. (Chicago, Illinois, 1951), p. v.
2. *In the Heart of the Redwoods Resource-Rich Humboldt County California* (pamphlet), prepared by the Humboldt County Board of Trade (Eureka, California, 1961).

FIGURE 14-1. Oxen bringing in logs to the skidroad in the 1890's. The skidroad, logs laid at right angles to the center-line of the road, was the most difficult, expensive, and serious part of the logging operations in the Redwood Country. A.W. Ericson Photograph.

PART
III

FOLKLORE

CHAPTER

15

Three Legends
of Northwestern California

Lynwood Carranco

Northwestern California—specifically the Humboldt Bay region—was long one of the most isolated in the West, and even today it is by no means the best known. Its exploration was curiously delayed. This region did not become known to the world in any detail until long after more accessible regions, north and south, had been crossed and recrossed, hunted and trapped over, surveyed and mapped and settled. Extremely rough country, dense forests, deep rivers racing through precipitous canyons, a lack of natural passes, and a warlike Indian population—all combined to turn back the cautious and to defeat the effort of any but the most persistent and bold frontiersmen. The exploration of this region was the familiar drama of the conquest of the wilderness, but played under conditions of great difficulty.

This rugged country was among the last regions in the United States to be explored. Humboldt Bay was not explored until the end of 1848—when San Francisco, less than 300 miles to the south, was already a city of 20,000. Three popular legends that originated in this area and are popularly believed to have a historical base are the following: (1) The Kings Peak Legend, (2) The Lost Cabin Legend, and (3) The Bigfoot Legend.

According to the Kings Peak legend, there is supposed to be a hidden treasure of gold and other valuables in a cave (N512) on Kings Peak in southwestern Humboldt County. Kings Peak is approximately ten miles above Shelter Cove and about thirty miles below Cape Mendocino on the coast. It is a rugged mountain with steep ridges which extend to a height of more than 4,500 feet, and is almost unknown since many attempts to survey it have failed. The mountain is a mass of slides. The high points which are of shale rock are continuously sliding off into the canyon below.[1]

231

There are variations of the Kings Peak legend. One popular version states that a galleon was wrecked on the coast near Kings Peak, and that all those who were aboard were drowned. Another version states that the Indians killed the survivors. The Indians salvaged the valuable cargo of gold, gems, spices, and other goods and carried their loot to a cave in Kings Peak. Years later there was an earthquake which sealed the opening of the cave forever. The Mattole Indians have repeated the story through generations, and it is now part of the folklore of the area.[2]

The first of the Manila galleons crossed the Pacific in 1565, and the last galleon put into port in 1815.[3] Yearly for the two and a half centuries that lay between the two dates, the galleons made the long and lonely voyage of five to seven months between Manila in the Philippines and Acapulco in Mexico. As the richest ships in all the oceans, they were the most coveted prize of pirate and privateer. Piracy on the Pacific side of America never reached the proportions that it assumed in the Caribbean, but it did exist. English privateers took four of the galleons.[4]

The Philippines were added to New Spain in 1565, and this acquisition brought about a renewed interest in California. It was not until 1763 that a direct contact with Manila began. The Manila-bound galleons, carrying huge quantities of silver coin, headed straight out to sea from Acapulco and turned westward in the latitude of 12 degrees or 13 degrees.[5] Leaving the Philippines, the galleons followed the great circle route, northeast toward Japan, east toward the California coast on the Japanese current, and south following the California coast to Acapulco.

Silks, wax, chinaware, spices, and other eastern staples were the principal items involved. The trade assumed such great proportions that merchants in Spain protested to the court that they were losing the market of New Spain. The king obliged the merchants by restricting the Mexican-Philippine trade to a single 500-ton vessel each year, with a cargo not to exceed 250,000 pesos in value.[6]

Annually, until almost the very end of the Spanish colonial period, the Manila galleon in making its coastward trip, closely followed the California coast from Cape Mendocino, usually the first landmark, to the tip of Baja California. Landings were infrequent, but for almost two centuries the California coast was the one regular contact that the Spaniards had with the California region. Some of the galleons were used for exploration of the California coast, notably the one of 1595, commanded by Cermeño.

On the east-bound trip there were two courses open to the galleons when signs of land were discovered. These signs, the fungous growth on the ocean, were usually sighted about 300 miles from shore. The first course was to continue directly ahead until land was sighted before changing direction; the other course was to turn to the southeast and to reach land in the area of Lower California. The former was the usual procedure in the early history of the line, and the other route was generally followed in the eighteenth century. A convenient and customary point for demarcation in the early times was the headland of Cape Mendocino.[7]

As a rule the galleons did not venture too close to the rugged California coast for fear of being shipwrecked. A further deterrent to familiarity with the northern coast was the dense fog that often hung over the land, concealing possible reefs and headlands. The galleons *Espíritu Santo* and *Jesús María* narrowly escaped being shipwrecked near Cape Mendocino in 1604.[8]

During the history of the line, more than thirty galleons were lost, thousands of lives were lost, and over sixty million pesos of money and merchandise disappeared with the galleons.[9] There is no evidence that a galleon was wrecked on or near Cape Mendocino, but it certainly could have happened. Urns of doubtful origin have been found at sea by commercial fishermen off shore, and large pieces of wax have also been found along the coast north of Cape Mendocino. Could these items have come from a wrecked galleon? This evidence has kept the legend alive through the years.

The two versions of the Lost Cabin legend have been colorful and exciting—even though there have been no clues in the last hundred years. This romantic legend is centered in Del Norte County and the county seat of Crescent City. In 1849 and 1850, a story was circulated throughout the Pacific Coast and as far away as the East Coast—a story that even rivaled the legend of Captain Kidd's treasure.

According to one version of the story, a miner, in the early days of the mining excitement in California, crossed the Coast Range Mountains and prospected the gulches and ravines of the foothills near the ocean. One day he struck it rich and found much gold (N596). He then built a cabin in the wilderness so that he could accumulate a fortune and then return East to his home and friends.

The lonely miner worked day after day for many months, adding to his hoard of gold until there was a small fortune. One day he was suddenly attacked by Indians. They left him unconscious, thinking that he was dead. The Indians could not find the well-hidden treasure, so they set fire to his cabin, burning it to ashes. When they had gone, the miner recovered consciousness, but his reasoning powers were gone. He wandered out of the forest to civilization. He later succeeded in reaching his home in the East where he died. It is not known how he finally reached the East, but before his death, his mind became normal and he called his friends to him. He told them the story of the hidden treasure and described the area in which the cabin was located. The Lost Cabin was supposed to be somewhere on the northern coast of California, specifically in the French Hill area of Del Norte County.[10]

In 1891 the local Humboldt County newspapers carried the news that a Judge Loveland of Eureka and the Peugh Brothers of Table Bluff had located the famous "diggins" of the Lost Cabin. In answer to the newspaper accounts, J.E. Eldredge, the editor of the *Del Norte Record*, replied that they had not discovered the Lost Cabin mine. The following is his version of the legend.[11]

The first person who went in search of gold, according to Eldredge, happened to be Colonel C. Hall, a close friend of the Eldredge family. In the year 1849, Colonel Hall crossed the plains from Missouri to California in search of gold. He came to Trinidad in 1852. While he was there, three men came down from the mountains. One of the men, Vermile Thompson, was an old acquaintance of his from Missouri. After the usual greetings, Thompson produced a large quantity of gold dust and nuggets and told him where the gold had been found, and that there was plenty left at the place of mining. The men had three pack mules loaded with gold dust. Thompson said that they had built a cabin in which they had left their tools. Papers were in the cabin with full instructions where the mine was located. Colonel Hall became interested. He believed his friend, and he obtained from him a sketch of the country and the location of the cabin, from which could be heard the ocean's roar. The three men left immediately for the East.

Hall organized a party and started in search of the rich "diggins." The party followed the coast and spent a summer in fruitless search. The story spread, and soon there were many parties from all parts of the country in search of the Lost Cabin mine.

Hall became discouraged and returned to his native state in 1854. In 1855 he returned with his family and settled in Crescent City where he remained for some years. Later he moved to Lakeport where he met Thompson who had also come west to settle. Thompson refused to talk again about the Lost Cabin mine.

The search for the Lost Cabin mine brought about the founding of Crescent City. In the spring of 1851, a party under Captain McDermott was searching for the Lost Cabin in the vicinity of what is now known as French Hill.[12] From the top they saw the curve in the coastline and they thought that it was a large bay. Because of this discovery, another party in 1852 proceeded in search of the harbor. The party, headed by Captain Bell, arrived at the beach and named the harbor Paragon Bay. A messenger was sent to San Francisco, and an expedition was soon organized which later resulted in the founding of the town of Crescent City.[13]

No trace has ever been found of the Lost Cabin mine—if there is such a mine—but many people have searched for the gold since 1848. And the treasure is still waiting for the lucky person.

The Bigfoot legend (F517.1; F551) literally exploded recently into one of international interest. This legend, which can be traced back to 1850 by the local Indians, became popular again in 1958 when Mr. Andrew Genzoli, columnist and historian for the Eureka *Humboldt Times*, published a letter in his column about the presence of a big-footed individual in the uninhabited Bluff Creek area of the mountainous inland country of Humboldt County.

Mrs. Jesse Bemis, wife of one of the road crew working on a timber access road in the uninhabited area, wrote to Mr. Genzoli in September of 1948 about the existence of a wild man. This creature was given the name of Bigfoot, since he had left his huge tracks in the area. Jerry Crew, a tractor driver on the road job, brought in to Eureka a plaster-of-Paris cast that he had made of the big track. Mr. Genzoli published the story on the front page with a photograph of Jerry Crew holding a huge plaster foot sixteen inches in length and seven inches in width.[14]

The story was put on the wires of the Associated Press and almost every paper in the country printed the story, while inquiries came in from abroad. Since then numerous expeditions have ventured into the Bigfoot country, and at least two have been conducted on a scientific basis.

Ivan Sanderson, famous zoologist and writer, accompanied by two other scientists, traveled into the mountainous country, looking for Bigfoot. Sanderson used the information about Bigfoot for a magazine article and for part of a book. The magazine article, "The Strange Story of America's Abominable Snowman," which was printed in the December, 1959, issue of *True* magazine, was told in a sensational manner with many inaccuracies. Mr. Sanderson wired Mr. Genzoli the following day when he saw the prepublication copy:

"Have just seen prepublication copies of my article . . . am utterly disgusted . . . distortion and unauthorized insertions that I did not write."[15]

Sanderson did a better job of telling the story of Bigfoot in his book, *Abominable Snowmen: Legend Come to Life*, although there were still inaccuracies. There is a false story of a pack of dogs being killed by what was believed to have been Bigfoot. Much credit is given to Ray Wallace, who since appears to know even less about the Bigfoot story than other people concerned in the incidents. Most of Sanderson's material was taken from Mr. Genzoli's writings on Bigfoot in the *Humboldt Times*.

Another scientific expedition was conducted by Tom Slick of San Antonio, Texas, who heads research organizations. Slick and Kirk Johnson had sponsored two expeditions to the Himalayas in search of the Abominable Snowman. A suspected relationship between Bigfoot of Bluff Creek and the Abominable Snowman of the Himalayas was thought to exist.[16] This expedition under Peter Byrne has been secretive to discourage outsiders from coming into the area.

On a camping trip in 1960, Dr. Charles Johnson, an orthopedic surgeon, accompanied by his family and a friend, reported that they had discovered tracks sixteen to eighteen inches in length in their camp. Dr. Johnson reported that the prints were human feet with huge toes, and that the step measured from three and a half to four feet.[17]

Later in the same year Bigfoot broke into the headlines of the San Jose newspapers. Dr. Maurice Tripp, geologist and geophysicist, took photographs of a seventeen-inch footprint that he found in the Bluff Creek area. He indicated the weight of the "huge puppy" to have been more than 800 pounds.[18]

Other stories of persons finding huge tracks have been published since 1960. Over the past three years Mr. Genzoli has received about a thousand letters concerning Bigfoot. These letters have come from children, adults, hunters, scientists, writers, explorers, and the curious. Bigfoot still roams the inland country eluding those who try to capture him, although he has been kind enough to leave his oversized tracks.

Bigfoot, the legendary creature, has been observed over a greater part of the Humboldt and Del Norte and Siskiyou areas. The legend is an old one in the culture of the local Indians. They say that the large, hairy half-human creatures have roamed the hills since the beginning of time.

In 1896 L.W. Musick published a book in verse form from the office of the *Crescent City News* called *The Hermit of Siskiyou* to "aid in the perpetration of some of the quaint legends that have become in a degree historical of the region represented. . . ."[19]

In his poem he describes the Hermit or someone who appears to resemble Bigfoot:

> You may have heard the story, too
> Of how upon Mount Siskiyou,
> Was seen an ape, or spook, or tramp,
> In region near to Happy Camp—
>
> Some years gone by—
> That was of stature taller than
> The ordinary height of man—
> Who fed on berries, roots and brouse,
> Nor, of abode, had tent or house,
>
> And from whose eye
> There gleamed the fierceness of the beast
> That, thwarted of voracious feast,
> With sulleness, feigns to retire
> Far in the jungle, to his lair;
> Though loiters near his wanted prey
> Till enemy hath gone away.[20]

In an appendix note Mr. Musick explained that this part of his poem was based on a story which appeared in the *Del Norte Record* of January 2, 1886. The story was written by a correspondent from Happy Camp in Siskiyou County:

I do not remember to have seen any reference to the 'Wild Man' which haunts this part of the country, so I shall allude to him briefly. Not a great while since, Mr. Jack Dover, one of our most trustworthy citizens, while hunting saw an object standing one hundred and fifty yards from him picking berries or tender shoots from the bushes. The thing was of gigantic size—about seven feet high— with a bull-dog head, short ears and long hair; it was also furnished with a beard, and was free from hair on such parts of its body as is common among men. Its voice was shrill, or soprano, and very human, like that of a woman in great fear. Mr. Dover could not see its footprints as it walked on hard soil. He aimed his gun at the animal, or whatever it is, several times, but because it was so human would not shoot. The range of the curiosity is between Marble Mountain and the vicinity of Happy Camp. A number of people have seen it and all agree in their descriptions except that some make it taller than others. It is apparently herbivorous and makes winter quarters in some of the caves of Marble Mountains.[21]

Thus the legend of Bigfoot has become a symbol of the vast primitive wilderness of Northwestern California where Nature reigns supreme, and he has also become part of the history of Humboldt

County and perhaps the world. Bigfoot has remained hidden for thousands of years, and let us hope that he remains hidden for thousands of years to come.

FOOTNOTES

1. Andrew Genzoli, Eureka *Humboldt Times*, October 5, 1958.
2. Andrew Genzoli, columnist of the *Humboldt Times* and a foremost authority on Humboldt County history, said that Johnny Jack, a Mattole and Wiyot Indian who lived at the mouth of the Mattole River, told him the story when he was a youngster.
3. William L. Schurz, *The Manila Galleon*, p. 15.
4. *Ibid.*
5. Peter Gerhard, *Pirates on the West Coast of New Spain*, p. 54.
6. John W. Caughey, *California*, p. 56.
7. Schurz, p. 239.
8. *Ibid.*, p. 240.
9. *Ibid.*, p. 256.
10. This version of the story is found in the *Shasta Courier* for June, 1858. A.J. Bledsoe in *Indian Wars of the Northwest* (1885, pp. 137-138) tells the same story with some slight variations.
11. J.E. Eldredge, Crescent City *Del Norte Record*, January 18, 1883. L.W. Musick in his book, *The Hermit of Siskiyou* (1896), also quotes the J.E. Eldredge story.
12. Bledsoe, p. 138.
13. *Ibid.*, p. 139.
14. Andrew Genzoli, *Humboldt Times*, October 5, 1958.
15. *Humboldt Times*, November 22, 1959.
16. *Ibid.*, January 10, 1960.
17. Eureka *Humboldt Standard*, June 23, 1960.
18. *Humboldt Times*, October 11, 1960.
19. Musick, p. i.
20. Musick, pp. 37-38.
21. Musick, pp. 79-80. This book was loaned to the writer by Mrs. Lee English of Brookings, Oregon.

A Miscellany of Folk Beliefs
from the Redwood Country

Lynwood Carranco

This collection of popular folk beliefs and superstitions is the first from Humboldt County, otherwise known as the Redwood Country. My first concern was to collect the folk beliefs of loggers. Although Humboldt County has been one of the largest lumber-producing counties in the United States since 1850, collecting logger folk beliefs proved a difficult task, even though I had worked in the lumber mills and woods and even though the lumber industry of this area has its own argot. Loggers have always been practical men, and many of them that I consulted did not know or had heard few folk beliefs. Examples of expressions used are "steep as a cow's face," when describing the working country, or "logging uphill," when working hard at a specific task and getting nowhere.[1] Other expressions common at the present time are "He runs around like a blind dog in a meat house" and "He's busier than a one-armed paper hanger with crabs." But these expressions cannot be included under the category of folk beliefs or superstitions.

Three old-timers, all over 79 years of age, donated four superstitions, perhaps indicating that there might have been more in the "good old days" before changes occurred in the lumber industry. Most loggers now live in town with their families and commute to their jobs. Comforts, marriage, machine logging, and highways have completely changed the old "typical" logger of the past to a good respectable citizen.

The following logger folk beliefs were the only ones that I could find:[2]

1. It was bad luck to start a new job of hauling in logs on a Friday (N128). After a winter layoff of three or four months, loggers would get the landing, skidroad, and lines ready. In order not to begin on Friday, a few logs would be brought to the skidroad on Thursday. (Frank Frazer)
2. Some loggers would quit if a fat man came to work in the woods because three successive accidents would happen (N134.1). (Frank Frazer)

3. Many loggers would not report to work on Friday the thirteenth (N128; N135.1). (Walter Light)
4. If a logger got killed in the woods, two more would soon die after in the same way (D1273.1.1.3). (Walter Light) This superstition is popular at the present time among woodsmen and mill workers.
5. Many loggers used to wear copper bands around their wrists or ankles to keep from getting rheumatism. (Harry Ryan)
6. The best cure for a hangover is to have sexual intercourse in the morning before going to work. (Harry Ryan) This folk belief is popular at the present time.
7. A good blow-job will clean out your tubes. (Harry Ryan) This superstition is popular at the present time.
8. If you want to change your luck, have sexual intercourse with a colored woman (N131.1). (Harry Ryan, Frank Frazer, Walter Light) A popular superstition at the present time.
9. One eye on the treetops will save two. (Widow-makers, limbs from fallen trees which belatedly fall after being snagged in the boughs of another tree, are the cause of many deaths and injuries in logging.) Popular expression at present time.

Commercial fishing has become Humboldt County's third leading industry. The following folk beliefs were collected from commercial fishermen:

10. Never leave your hatch covers upside down because you will not get any fish in your hold.
11. If you can hear the ocean roar in the early morning, do not leave the harbor to fish in the ocean because the sea will be too rough.
12. It is bad luck to rename a boat (N131.4).
13. Do not whistle on board or you will whistle up a storm (C480.1).
14. Never leave port on a Friday or you will have bad luck (N128).
15. Red at night, sailor's delight/Red in the morning, sailor's warning.

Most of the following examples of popular folk beliefs and superstitions have been collected since 1962 from the contributions of students in my upper-division language classes and from high school students of the Humboldt Bay area. Members of the Humboldt County Historical Society, the largest in the state, also contributed many items.

BIRTH, INFANCY, CHILDHOOD

16. To tell the sex of an unborn baby, hold the mother's wedding ring over her head on a string (H528). If it swings back and forth, the baby will be a girl; if it swings in a circle, the baby will be a boy.
17. Redheaded children were conceived at noon on a Sunday.
18. If a pregnant woman eats pickles, the baby will be a boy.
19. If a woman craves meat when she is pregnant, she will have a baby boy.
20. A pregnant woman should not watch a fire because her child will be born with a scar.

21. If a pregnant woman looks at pictures of boys, she will have a boy (same for girls).
22. If a pregnant woman worries, her child will be deformed.
23. If a pregnant woman sees a rabbit, her child will have a harelip.

BODY, FOLK MEDICINE

24. A woman should put her feet in a bucket of ice water to keep from getting pregnant.
25. If a man wears wool socks when he goes to a whorehouse, he will not get the clap.
26. If a woman eats crabmeat, she will increase her sexual potency.
27. Suck on a dime to stop a bloody nose.
28. If your toes next to your big toe is longer than your big toe, you will have a high intelligence.
29. If you scratch your left ear twice every day, you will live to be 100 years old.
30. If the palm of your hand itches, you are going to lose your job.
31. If you throw your tooth on the ground and a dog steps on it, a tooth resembling a dog's tooth will grow back in your mouth.
32. When your right ear burns, someone is talking good about you; when your left ear burns, someone is talking bad about you.
33. If you jerk a bottle out of a baby's mouth, his soft spot will fall out. To counteract this, quickly pick the baby up and turn him upside-down and slap the bottom of his feet.
34. People who have red ear lobes have hot tempers.
35. If you eat burnt food, your hair will become curly.
36. If you have a bald spot, it is because someone wished it on you. The bald spot will disappear when that certain someone dies.
37. Cut a bean in half; place half of it on a pimple and bury the other half. The pimple will be gone in the morning.
38. Rub garlic on your mustache to keep away germs.
39. Thin-lipped people are mean and cruel.
40. Keep your feet in manure for twelve hours to get rid of the gout.
41. "Ding it." In oil-drilling smashed fingers are common. Green hands are told to "ding it"—to soak the affected part in a woman's vagina overnight. (Sacramento Valley)
42. Put a dead cat under a porch during a full moon, and it will remove warts from your hand.
43. Touching frogs will produce warts.
44. Cut your wart in half and bury one-half of it at a fork in the road at midnight. The buried half of the wart will keep sucking blood out of the other half, and the wart will die.
45. To get rid of a wart, tie a knot around the wart, and say a prayer in the Bible. The wart will disappear within three days.
46. If you rub a piece of bacon on a wart and then bury the bacon, your wart will go away.
47. Garlic worn around the throat will scare away vampires.
48. Keep a spider in your house to ward off evil spirits.
49. Some Filipino people sleep with a handkerchief over their face to keep the spirit inside the body and to ward off evil spirits at the same time.

50. If a person is wild, he is possessed by the devil and should be sent to someone to be blessed or to have the devil driven out.

DEATH, FUNERAL PRACTICES

51. There will be a death in the family if a dish breaks in the cupboard for no apparent reason (D1812.5).
52. You can tell when a person is going to die by looking at his fingernails because that is where death first shows itself.
53. If a crow flies over your house, there is going to be a death in the family (B147.2.2.1).
54. In a card game, a hand of aces and eights will cause death.
55. If water falls on an open grave, someone in the funeral will die within the year (D1812.5).
56. If you dream of muddy water, someone in your family will die. If you dream of snakes in muddy water, someone close to you is going to die (D1812.5).
57. If you celebrate your birthday early, you will never live to see another one.
58. If there are ripples in the middle of a lake, someone will drown soon.
59. If you are named after someone who is dead, you will die young.
60. Wild lilies will grow over the grave of a baby who is born dead and buried on a flat area in the hills.
61. If a rooster comes inside your door and crows, there will be a death in your family (B147.2.2).

ANIMALS, ANIMAL HUSBANDRY

62. To determine how high a river will rise, watch to see how high a squirrel will put his nuts in a tree.
63. Baby calves are dug from rotten logs. (Told to children)
64. A farting horse never tires.
65. Your cow will give bloody milk if you kill a frog.
66. A horse with three stockings (i.e., three white hoofs) is no good.
67. It is bad luck for bear and cat hunters to tree an animal twice in the same tree.
68. If a horse has one white foot, buy him; two white feet, try him; three white feet and a white nose, take off his hide and give it to the crows.
69. A horse with a "rainbow" or "roman" nose will be hot-tempered.
70. A horse with four white feet and a white nose is crow's feed.

SPORTS, FISHING, HUNTING

71. Before going deer hunting, do not sleep with your wife if she is menstruating. Sleep in another room because the deer will pick up the odor and run away.
72. Do not sleep with your wife for three nights before going deer hunting. A woman has a strong genital odor which clings to a man, and a deer will quickly pick up the odor.
73. Deer will be attracted to you if you carry a cut-up apple in a bag on your belt.

74. Fishing is better when there is a full moon.
75. It is good luck to spit in the water when the fish are not biting.
76. Spit on your fishing hook to catch a big fish (N131).
77. You will have good luck catching fish if you spit in the water before dropping your bait in the water (N131).
78. The number of whores seen before a ball game will determine the number of hits you will get in the game. (A common expression among ball players in San Francisco in the early 1900's.)

WISHES, DREAMS

79. After her children leave home, if a mother dreams of seeing one of her children in rags, the person is in some sort of trouble.
80. If the corner of your skirt is turned up and you make a wish, then turn the corner of your skirt back down, your wish will come true.
81. If you see a redheaded girl on a white horse, lick your index finger, place it on the opposite palm, then make a wish as you strike your palm with your fist. Better luck will occur if there is a hay wagon near the redheaded girl on the white horse.
82. If two people say the same sentence at the same time, make a wish, and put their little fingers together, the wish will come true.
83. If an eyelash falls out, put it on your finger, make a wish and blow it away. Your wish will come true.
84. Each time you see a white horse, lick your right thumb, press into your left palm, stamp the same spot with your right fist, and then make a wish.
85. If you dream of a wedding, you will hear of a death; if you dream of a death, you will hear of a wedding (D1812.3.3.10).
86. If you wait until after breakfast to tell a dream, it will come true.
87. If you dream the same dream three times consecutively, the dream will come true.

MARRIAGE, FUTURE HUSBAND

88. If you marry a plumber, you will have leaky faucets for life.
89. On the first day of May, hold a hand mirror over your left shoulder so that the water in the well is reflected and you will see your future husband there. (Brought to Humboldt County from Kentucky)
90. With another person, pull the wishbone of a chicken under a table. The one who gets the shortest end will marry first.
91. If you sweep under someone's feet, the person will get married.
92. If you walk around a pear tree several times (seven times according to another folk belief) backward and then look at the moon, you will see the face of your future husband.
93. On Halloween, go into a dark room with your back to a mirror; look over your left shoulder with a handmirror and your future husband will be reflected in the mirror.

COSMIC PHENOMENA

94. A crescent moon standing up means good weather; a crescent moon lying down means rain (D1812.5.0.15). (German expression in Trinidad in the early 1900's)

95. Always hide the scissors during a lightning storm or lightning will strike your house.
96. Do not dehorn a cow by a full moon or it will bleed to death.
97. If you find a ring around the moon, it will storm. The number of stars within the ring will indicate the days (D1812.5.1.5.1).
98. Do not kill pigs or cows during an old moon because the meat will spoil.
99. Corn and beans must be planted during a new moon, while potatoes are planted in the last quarter.
100. Beans grow taller if they are planted by the dark of the moon.

WEATHER, SEASONS

101. There is a storm at sea if there are many sea gulls circling about the shore.
102. If the wind is from the north, do not venture forth;
    If the wind is from the south, throw bait in the fishes' mouth.
    And if the wind is from the west, fishing is best;
    And if from the east fishing is least (D1812.5.0.15.1). (From Colorado)
103. If the smoke hangs low on the ground, it is going to rain.
104. If you leave your clothes out in the rain, the rain will turn the clothes whiter.
105. When you see a storm cloud coming, take a double-bladed ax and put it in a stick of wood, strike a match under one blade, point the match toward the cloud and the cloud will break apart and go on each side of you.
106. If the weather is sultry, there is a good chance for an earthquake.
107. If there is a wide black stripe near a caterpillar's head and a narrow stripe at the tail, there will be an early winter.
108. When the wind blows hard, a sacred Catholic candle is chipped into the stove, causing the wind to part and blow around the house.
109. If the acorns blast early in the fall, there will be a hard winter.

BAD LUCK, GOOD LUCK

110. A chopping ax in the house is bad luck (N135).
111. If a baby is born on Christmas, he will have good luck.
112. If you cross your fingers while you are dancing with a boy, you will have good luck. (N131).
113. If you put your slip (apron, etc.) on wrong side out unintentionally, it will be good luck for you if you don't change it.
114. Pick up a pin with the point toward you, and you will have good luck all day.
115. If you sing before breakfast, you will have bad luck. (From Iowa)
116. If a man visits you on New Year's Eve, you will have good luck the following year. If a woman visits you on New Year's Eve, you will have bad luck the following year (N134). (A belief from New York City)
117. Do not work between Christmas and New Year's or you will have bad luck.
118. You will have bad luck if you cut your fingernails on Friday (C726).
119. It is bad luck to walk on a grave.
120. It is bad luck to drive a green car or green motorcycle.

The following items, which originated among the local Indians, have become part of the folk beliefs of the area.

121. Frogs will predict whether a river will flood. If they head for high ground or climb up trees, the river will flood.
122. If a person is drowned in a river, the Indians do not eat fish or swim until the body is found.
123. If you see an image of a person somewhere in nature, something bad will happen to him.
124. If cones are heavy on a fir tree, it will be a hard winter.
125. If you see a bat flying in your house, you will have a good hunting season.
126. If a woman fishes at Luffenholz Beach, the surf-fish will not run for 14 years.

MISCELLANEOUS FOLK BELIEFS

127. The dust from a rattlesnake's rattles can make you blind.
128. If someone bumps into you in the hall at school, chances are you will become good friends. (Common among high school students)
129. If you hide behind a door and eat a wishbone, you will become pretty. (Originally from Missouri)
130. Old pots make the best stew. (From France)
131. If you wear yellow on Thursday, you are a queer. (Common among high school students)
132. If you smell a dandelion in the day, you will wet the bed at night. (From Nova Scotia)
133. To break the jinx of leaving things at a place, spit on the top step and count to thirteen.
134. While driving in a car, if you don't lift your feet when you are going over a railroad track, you will lose your boyfriend. (Common among high school students)

The following are Hawaiian folk beliefs, collected by Hawaiian students.

135. Take some green leaf onions with you to a funeral to ward off the evil spirits of the dead person.
136. Never point at a cemetery. If you do, bite that finger as hard as possible or a relative will die.
137. If you are not good to your parents and grandparents, they will come back after death to haunt you.
138. If you drop your chopsticks, it means that you are naughty and will get a spanking soon.
139. If a woman touches raw dough during her menstrual period, the dough will not rise (**C145**).
140. Portuguese people have bad tempers.
141. If you carry pork over the Pali (a mountain pass on the island of Oahu), the menehunes will come out. This means that you will usually have an accident.

142. If you pick the lehua flower, it will rain.
143. If a tea leaf stands upright in your tea cup, make a wish and it will come true.
144. After attending a funeral service, wash your face and hands before entering your home. This prevents your bringing evil spirits of the dead person into your home.
145. If you give knives for gifts, you are showing that you do not like the person unless you include a penny with the gift.
146. Hanging a white doll on your porch will stop the rain.

FOOTNOTES

1. See Lynwood Carranco, "Americanisms in the Redwood Country," *WF*, XXII (1963), 263-267.
2. Informants: The late Harry Ryan, age 89; Walter Light, age 82; and Frank Frazer, age 80.